TROPICAL CHILDHOOD

Cultural Transmission and Learning in a Rural Puerto Rican Village

DAVID LANDY

Professor and Chairman,
Department of Anthropology,
and
Professor of Anthropology,
Graduate School of Public Health,
University of Pittsburgh

HARPER TORCHBOOKS ❧ *The Academy Library*
Harper & Row, Publishers, New York

TO

THE CHILDREN AND PARENTS OF VALLE CAÑA

—whose cooperation made this study
a reality and whose warm friendship
and lust for life made the work
a rare pleasure and bright challenge.

TROPICAL CHILDHOOD

Preface to the Torchbook edition copyright © 1965 by
David Landy

Copyright, 1959, by The University of North Carolina Press

Printed in the United States of America.

This book was originally published in 1959 by The
University of North Carolina Press and is here reprinted by
arrangement.

First HARPER TORCHBOOK edition published 1965 by
Harper & Row, Publishers, Incorporated
49 East 33rd Street
New York, N. Y. 10016.

Preface to the Torchbook edition

About fifteen years have passed since the fieldwork for this study was done and about seven since its first publication. What have I learned in the interim? How would I do it differently? In Chapters 1 and 12 many of the limitations of the study were spelled out as well as several specifications by which future studies might use this one as a base and point of departure. There is little need to reiterate them here. Generally the book received quite favorable reviews but at least one criticism I have taken seriously, namely, that more attention should have been channelled into the specific relations between the processes and elements of socialization and the social structure. Additionally, though no critic mentioned it, I would have—given more field time—investigated possibilities more thoroughly for obtaining ethnohistorical data, not only from older informants but also by detailed study of documents. The value of ethnohistorical research in anthropology has been clearly demonstrated in recent years and Oscar Lewis, especially, in his restudy of the Mexican community of Tepoztlán, has indicated how such data lend a time depth to the perception of present-day culture that may completely alter its significance to the contemporary observer. Certain preliminary work with such documents, however, compels me to note that they contain generally few direct references to socialization, though this will vary with the particular community history.

As a general framework I followed the principles of transactional theory as applied to human behavioral systems. Concepts and hypotheses were borrowed not only from cultural anthropology but were also based on psychoanalytic and stimulus-response learning theories. While one reviewer suggested that I was perhaps in thrall to too many theoretical masters, it remains difficult for me to evolve a model of the socialization process not dependent to some extent upon all of the above schools of thought, except perhaps that a "conditioning" approach might replace the "s-r" notions of human education. A cultural approach to socialization without a theory of teaching and learning is inconceivable, use of psychological theories of learning without the cultural dimension seems purely animal and nonhuman, and both seem to require certain premises and concepts from psychoanalysis if human growth and interaction are to be understood in vibrant and dynamic terms, rather than in the, to me, more pallid consequences of "pure" ethnographic description of culture or "pure" learning theory description of behavior and development.

I have been even less impressed with certain other critical claims, for example, those that would place, usually without supporting evidence, a different interpretation upon the findings; or those that take the author to task for not writing the kind of volume that the critic would have written; or those that criticize the work as being "statistical" and therefore of no use to their profession. Since the rationale for the statistical approach has been explained in Chapter 1, the latter charge is annoying; my only regret is that I could not have made it even more systematic by utilizing a larger sample and a more sensitive set of mathematical measures and tests. Surely the day is rapidly fading when anthropologists recoil in horror from data that have been even minimally quantified; I anticipate the time as not far distant when we shall have mastered statistical methods sufficiently to force us to become more systematic collectors and interpreters of sociocultural data, not to displace, but to supplement and strengthen traditional anthropological methodology.

Another set of variables on which I could have wished for more data is that of actual consquences of change on the island insofar as child training and behavior learning are concerned. In the spring of 1964 I chanced to be in Puerto Rico for a few days and was able to spend a day in the village of Valle Caña, my first revisit since 1952. I did not recognize large portions of San Juan and its environs. Perhaps most dramatic of the alterations apparent to the sudden observer were the mushrooming industries, swank hotels and places of entertainment. Socioeconomic repercussions of industrialization and tourism will certainly have to be taken into account in future research. The village of Valle Caña itself was also drastically modified. The predominating cane fields that seemed at times to engulf the community had given way to large tracts of pasture land; almost all land was now given over to cattle-raising. To my questions of why this came about the most frequent response was that obviously it paid better than cane. Undoubtedly it does, but for whom I do not know. The outward appearance of the community had changed in other ways also. Now there was a paved road to the top of La Hoja where earlier I could reach the area only along a footpath, and there was talk of opening up the beautifully scenic countryside to hotels and other tourist attractions. Along El Camino were many more houses made of concrete and a furniture store (where none existed during my stay) in front of which a small truck full of stoves, refrigerators, and other appliances was being unloaded. A relatively more prosperous look greeted the eye. Many persons I had known had left the community, often in whole families, to live either in San Juan or elsewhere on the island, or in the States. Presumably the new economic base had displaced some Vallecañeses. Such changes raised many exciting questions, especially in connection with points originally discussed in Chapter 12 and throughout the book. The possibility—and necessity—of a restudy was stimulating.

Another phenomenon of recent interest and importance has been the swelling backwash of migrants returning from the continent, often after an absence of many years. At the time of this study outmigration was far in excess of inmigration and was conceded to be a critical safety valve for the demographic and economic pressures of one of the world's highest rates of population increase. Government and privately-sponsored programs for birth control have not significantly lowered the birth rate. Studies now underway of the growing numbers of returning migrants, apparently after unsuccessful adaptation to life in the States, indicate that in- and out-migration are nearly equal. Despite rapid industrialization, it is not likely that the economic system can support such proliferating numbers of people What this will do not only to the current relative prosperity but also to such sociocultural processes as those studied herein can at present lie only in the realm of speculation.

One student of the problem told me that frequently such returnees will invest meagre savings in small businesses in the city, almost certain to fail within a few months, and shortly are thrown with their families upon public relief. On the other hand, quite by chance I came upon Enrique, happily working as a waiter in a well-known Spanish-style restaurant in San Juan. I had known Enrique fifteen years ago when, also as a waiter, he worked in the Faculty Club of the University of Puerto Rico. Then he was anxious, worried, plagued with economic and personal insecurity, trying to support a family on about fifteen dollars a week. Enrique invited me to his home in Santurce, a small, well-built, neatly kept structure that he had purchased.

He sat contentedly with his family and with some friends who happened in, and over a beer told of a painful odyssey to New York and other places shortly after I left the island, of a succession of frustrating jobs and unemployment, technical training under the G. I. Bill which he could not put to use, and finally a period of several months in a Veterans Administration Hospital while he recovered from a psychological breakdown. Now he had worked for several years back in San Juan, making one hundred dollars or more a week with tips, one of his daughters was in business school, and Enrique was, of course, delighted to be back again in a climate and culture he loved. So here, at least, was a returned migrant who was better off than ever, though it is doubtful that he is representative of the group as a whole.

In a number of ways this research study continues to be unique. Insofar as I am presently familiar with the relevant literature, it remains the only full-scale study of socialization in Puerto Rico, and one of only a handful in the entire Caribbean area, or, for that matter, in all of Latin America. It is a pity that except for such studies as those of Jules Henry dealing with the Pilagá in South America, practically no investigations exist in Middle or South America that attempt systematically to study socialization process. (I am not, of course, referring to chapters or part-chapters of ethnographic monographs that treat briefly and almost incidentally of child training and learning.) In fact, the present study is one of only a few in anthropology generally that focus on socialization in as systematic a fashion, with a specified universe and sample, with systematic and semi-structured interviews and projective techniques that have been validated at least in the United States, with built-in and post facto checks on reliability and validity, with specified central tendencies and ranges of variation for almost all critical variables, and with the deliberate objective of comparing the results with data also systematically gathered on two social class groups in a Northamerican community.

It is my fervent wish that, as anthropology continues in all its branches to come of scientific age, the uniqueness of this research will disappear, and methods and techniques for the study of cultural transmission and learning will be continually sharpened and applied to the world's cultures.

July 1965   D. L.
Zacapoaxtla, Puebla, Mexico

Acknowledgments

THE ERA HAS passed when the anthropologist could pitch his tent and work alone. Especially in the areas which—though geographically peripheral—have linkages with the large civilizations of the world, many sources of aid present themselves, and some at least should be acknowledged.

The primary acknowledgment must be rendered the Social Science Research Center of the University of Puerto Rico and its director, Millard Hansen, for foresight in launching the Family Life Project, of which this study is a part. Special thanks also are due Reuben Hill, of the University of Minnesota and director of the Family Life Project, for his forbearance and understanding in helping the writer see his portion of that project through to completion. His careful and detailed criticisms were indispensable in achieving greater clarity and utility for the data. Gratitude is also expressed to J. Mayone Stycos of Cornell University for many helpful suggestions.

A good portion of the field work, the mother interviews, doll play, and school tests was carried out by Doris Diaz de Gregory. Her fluency in both languages, her hard work in the often grinding day-to-day routine, and her many insights into Puerto Rican culture and behavior put me in her debt beyond measure.

Thanks are due Raimundo Suárez Lazú, who interviewed the fathers. His first-hand knowledge of Puerto Rico's people and his genuine love for them made him an immensely popular figure in Valle Caña, and his deep knowledge of the land and its people made him an invaluable staff member.

I am also indebted to Emilio Santiago, Sylvia Costa de Martí, and América Boneta de Saavedra, all of whom worked competently and unstintingly on tabulating and analyzing the preliminary data. And it will be impossible to repay the many kindnesses and assistance of the staff of the Social Science Research Center, particularly Angela Gonzalez de Bobonis, Maria Socorro Ortíz de Martinez, and Carmen H. Lopez de Serrano.

It would be impractical to list all the individuals in the University of Puerto Rico and its various departments, as well as in government and private agencies, who gave me much moral and material assistance. In particular I should want to single out the College of Social Sciences and its Dean, Pedro Muñoz Amato; the College of Law and the libraries of the University; and the Departments of Public Health, Agriculture, and Education of the Government of Puerto Rico. Their advice and encouragement did much to insure whatever success attends the study, and they will all know of my boundless gratitude for their goodwill and help.

Without the cooperation and courtesies extended by the Laboratory of Human Development, Harvard University, it would not have been possible to utilize either the methodological scheme or the techniques (doll play, parent interviews, IBM data on their New England study). In particular the aid of Eleanor Hollenberg, Harry Levin, Eleanor Maccoby, and John W. M. Whiting must be mentioned with deep thanks. Drs. Whiting, Maccoby, and Levin unselfishly devoted much time to preparing me initially and their correspondence in reply to my often frantic queries in the field was always helpful. I also wish to thank Professors Clyde Kluckhohn, Evon Vogt, and William Caudill for helpfully reading and criticizing an early draft.

I find it difficult to express my appreciation to, and great dependence on, my wife, Louise Fleming Landy, and our daughter, Laura. A true study of rural Puerto Rican family life would have been out of the question had my wife and daughter not led the way in establishing the kind of rapport with Vallecañeses that all anthropologists seek. Working with me on every phase of the work, as well as managing the household, Mrs. Landy's capabilities and devotion were indispensable. And Laura received an important part of her socialization as a child of Valle Caña; indeed she learned Spanish while English was still an alien tongue spoken by those queer people, her parents!

                                                                    D. L.

Contents

Figure

Tables

TROPICAL CHILDHOOD

Mankind can never have lived as a mere struggling crowd, each for himself. Society is always made up of families or households bound together by kindly ties, controlled by rules of marriage and the duties of parent and child. Yet the forms of these rules and duties have been very various.

—EDWARD B. TYLOR, *Anthropology* (1899)

Tell ye your children of it, and let your children tell their children, and their children another generation.

—JOEL 1.3

CHAPTER 1

Rationale and Method

Introduction

"THE Child is father of the Man," said Wordsworth and in a sense epitomized the theme of this book. Folk wisdom and poetry, dogma and chant, echo down the ages of man's existence the relation of his behavior to the cultural antecedents of that behavior. "As the twig is bent" is of course no mere botanical allusion. Naturally other components are implied in such clichés, including the continuity of biological inheritance. As an anthropological-psychological study, we are not directly concerned here with genetic inheritance, but it should be clear to the reader that we fully accept its importance. However, in the present state of scientific knowledge, only a handful of empirically verified facts about human genetics is known. While just as complex as biology, the patterns of a culture, the other crucial determinant of human behavior, seem more readily observed, though perhaps no more readily verified. Since man seems to need to live in societies, the most human fact about "human nature" is culture. This is a study of the *social* inheritance of the culture of a tropical island community.

In 1951 the Social Science Research Center of the University of Puerto Rico originated the Family Life Project, the principal objective of which was to investigate factors in Puerto Rican culture which affect the traditionally heavy reproduction rate on the island (M. Hansen 1952). Reuben Hill, then of the University of North Carolina, directed the project and J. Mayone Stycos, then of Columbia

3

University, was assistant director in charge of the research on fertility patterns. The writer was assistant director in charge of a field study of family patterns and child rearing in a rural community.

The goals of the research reported in this volume were: (1) an exploratory-descriptive ethnographic study of socialization, or cultural transmission and learning, in a rural Puerto Rican village within the context of its culture and social structure; (2) systematic comparisons of child training and child behavior between these village families and those of an urban New England community then also under investigation by the Laboratory of Human Development at Harvard University. Using such comparative data would not only aid in attaining comparability of method and material, but comparing the Puerto Rican village's way of transmitting and learning its culture with that of a community in the United States—a nation with which the island has been in culture contact for six decades—would afford some indices of culture change and acculturation in one region and one social segment of the dependent society.

From the action point of view, it was felt that such an intensive study of family, childhood, and cultural transmission in a single community would throw light on the cultural factors affecting fertility sought in the demographic researches of the Family Life Project (Hill, Stycos, and Back 1959). Further, it was hoped the study would prove helpful to professional persons and laymen concerned with problems of child training and development in a rapidly changing culture.

From the theoretical point of view it was hoped that this might be the kind of comparative study using comparable material that social scientists like Inkeles (1953) and Whiting (1954) have called for, and it could thus probe not only cultural but incidentally social class similarities and differences. It was also felt the research might be fruitful of hypotheses for cross-cultural testing and might even through such a systematic approach throw light on the process of socialization itself.

Earlier an anthropological team from Columbia University had attempted to document ethnographically a variety of communities on the island in terms of their particular subcultural adaptations to environment and historical circumstance (Steward, et al. 1956). Previous and concurrent studies explored culturological and sociological aspects of reproductive behavior (Hatt 1952; Hill, Stycos, and Back 1959; Stycos 1955). But little had been done to explore systematically the process of Puerto Rican socialization. Furthermore students of family life had long recognized that "there exists a dearth of knowledge concerning the lower class family" (Komarovsky and Waller 1945) and these form almost 90 percent of the island's people. As Cottrell (1948:24) put it, "We need comparative descriptive studies of family patterns in the different urban, rural, class, and ethnic settings, together with analyses of the personality structures which emerge from these different family patterns." Anthropologists had also begun to see the need for family studies in order "to arrive at a more reliable and objective statement of the culture of a given society and obtain a better understanding of the relationship between culture and the individual" (Lewis 1950:469).

An Ethnohistorical Note [1]

The prehistory of Puerto Rico indicates that it was occupied mostly by a gentle, agriculturally based Indian tribe, the Arawak, who probably came there from South America. Recent archeological evidence discloses that preceding the Arawak were a nonagricultural gathering people whose way of life has been tentatively called "Coroso" (Alegría, Nicholson, and Willey 1955; Rouse 1952a, b), but at present very little is known of this group. Later the Arawak were followed by the predatory Carib, who by the time of Columbus' discovery of the island in 1493 were beginning to place the Arawak on the defensive. Arawak culture may be described as Circum-Caribbean (Rouse 1953; Steward 1948), with certain local differences. Into this hierarchical society (not, however, as rigidly stratified as Andean cultures, for example) the Spanish came seeking gold and, having almost exhausted the island's mineral and human resources within one century, finally decided to exploit its agricultural possibilities. By this time the Arawak culture had largely disappeared as an entity, though parts of it had been absorbed into the *mestizo*-dominated culture which emerged.

For four centuries the island was a loyal, dependent, and usually impoverished Spanish stepchild, but as internal strivings for independence were beginning to grow, the Spanish-American war resulted in a transfer of rule to the United States. While living conditions have

1. An ethnohistorical review of Puerto Rico with a detailed reference bibliography will be found in Landy 1959b. See also Steward, *et al.* 1956, especially chapters 1-5 and 11-13, for an excellent documentation of the ways in which the island's culture history has helped to shape the outlines of its contemporary lifeways.

improved somewhat under American rule and the island has gained a
large amount of autonomy, including a democratic constitution, the
pressing problems of overpopulation and scarce natural resources
plague the people and stifle social progress to a large degree (Annals
1953; E. Hansen 1955; Hill, Stycos, and Back 1959; Perloff 1950;
Stycos 1955). American interests have concentrated their capital in
the sugar industry and this has come in the past half-century to dominate the economics of the island. To a community largely dependent
on cane we turned for our ethnographic study of cultural transmission.

Theoretical Orientation

Since anthropologists are interested in arriving at principles enabling
some measure of understanding and prediction of cultural process, it
will be presumed that they will attempt to understand the primary
process of how a society learns, teaches, and maintains its characteristic
behaviors. More than a quarter-century ago Kroeber (quoted in White
1949:48) felt that "... perhaps the thing which essentially makes culture is precisely those transmissive and preservative elements, those
relational or binding factors, which social scientists have indeed occupied themselves with, but have been inclined to regard as after all of
secondary importance in comparison with the dynamic phenomena
of invention."

Shortly thereafter Sapir (1934:595-597) condemned anthropology's
neglect of "the intimate genetic problems of the acquirement of culture by the child," and forecast that when such research was undertaken, "the concept of culture which will then emerge, fragmentary
and confused as it will undoubtedly be, will turn out to have a tougher,
more vital importance for social thinking than the tidy tables of contents attached to this or that group which we have been in the habit
of calling 'cultures.'"

These barbs stung many anthropologists into activity, as evidenced
in the critical survey by Kluckhohn (1944) and Mead's (1946) ex-
haustive review of "Research on Primitive Children." The study of
the acquirement of culture by the person logically has been part of
the larger area of "culture and personality" studies, and for each of its
adherents there must be at least one angry critic (e.g., Hsu 1952;
Inkeles 1953; Lindsmith and Strauss 1950; Orlansky 1949). Despite
such criticism, which often has offered valuable insights within a

shroud of pessimism, the writer concludes with Bateson (1944:733) that it remains "Our task, as anthropologists or psychologists . . . to recognize and define the regularities in this complex tangle of phenomena."

Socialization is the process by which the child acquires the traditions, values, and practices of the man and in turn transmits them, modified, to his own offspring. Because this process characterizes the first, and at times most crucial, experiences between the individual and his social and natural environment, it is the primary cultural process, the pivot to which are attached, in one aspect or another, all the systems and processes of a culture. If generational transmission is weakened or broken, the whole cultural configuration is ultimately impaired or demolished, and the society must adopt a new culture or disintegrate. If it is rigidly maintained along traditional lines when the pressures of acculturation, for example, push and pull in other directions, personal and social conflicts are inevitable.

But the person-society equation is never static. With growth the individual must continually relearn and redefine his roles with their requisite action patterns, and continually restabilize his behavior in the light of internal and external changes. With Parsons (1951:207-208), we use socialization here ". . . in a broader sense than the current one to designate the learning of *any* orientations of functional significance to the operation of a system of complementary role expectations. In this sense, socialization, like learning, goes on throughout life. The case of the development of the child is only the most dramatic because he has so far to go."

Socialization may be viewed as the implementation, enforcement, and modification of a culture through time by its transmission from one generation to another. The process has two major aspects. The *learning* aspect consists of modifications in the individual's behavior potential through being inculcated with, or simply copying, the values (or expectations) and practices of his family and society. The *teaching* or transmissive aspect includes the inculcating procedures known as child training or child rearing and the conscious or unintended teaching of the child by persons and agencies (games, books, myths, movies, etc.) not directly responsible for the child's upbringing.

Each person plays the dual role of learner and teacher from birth to death. The relative magnitude of each role, in terms of reciprocal responsibilities and expectations, is conceptualized in Figure 1.

In viewing socialization as a total cultural process, it is helpful as a general orientation to assume a transactional frame of reference (Cantril and others 1949; Dewey and Bentley 1949; Frank 1951; Grinker 1953). This view assumes that all relevant systems and processes—biological, physical, psychological, sociological, cultural—in a given human system or process are in transaction with each other, constantly changing and being changed by the continual alterations going on in all parts of the system or process. This reasoning is abstracted from the same source as all knowledge of human behavior, the human organism, which "functions by continually altering its structure, as an ever changing but persistent configuration, through which the environment is continually ebbing and flowing" (Frank 1951: 511).

FIGURE 1

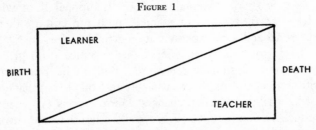

Relative Magnitude of Socialization Roles for the Life Cycle of an Individual

I do not propose in the present research to test even part of this complex theory, but prefer rather to use it as a broad frame of reference and a constant reminder that the "reverberating effects" (Spiegel, quoted in Grinker 1953:158-161) of any change in any part of such a system or process limit "the validity of observations being made" (*ibid.*).

Transactional theory does not displace but supplements and aids in better identifying selfactional and interactional theory. All three "levels are human behaviors in and with respect to the world, and they are all presentations of the world itself as men report it" (Dewey and Bentley 1949). The present research deals primarily with behavior at the interactional and selfactional levels. But at any level of abstraction the structural categories we use are attempts to picture a dynamic system or process; as Parsons (1951:21) has shown, "As dynamic knowledge is extended, the *independent* explanatory significance of structural categories evaporates."

A basic foundation of transactional theory is the differentiation between closed systems, which are in equilibrium, and open systems, which must never be in complete equilibrium to remain viable (Bertalanffy 1950). Socialization may be understood dynamically only as an open cultural-psychological system. The writer has explored this assumption elsewhere (Landy 1957).

Whiting (1954) believes that in cross-cultural analysis of behavior variables it is feasible, and in fact necessary, that we assume that a society, in terms of an abstracted "typical" member, can be thought of as acting like an individual. Thus it becomes possible to apply principles of psychological theory to cultural variables. To make this transfer, Whiting feels it is necessary to utilize the cultural concept of custom as being analogous with habit in the individual. The writer prefers to utilize the term "practice" in preference to either "habit" or "custom." It will be clear in context when this refers to an individual and when to a group. Whiting (1953:32-33) defines a custom as consisting of three essential attributes: (1) agent (subject or performer of an action); (2) circumstances (conditions or occasion for the action); and (3) action (overt or symbolic behavior which is performed). This is a direct transformation to the cultural level of a habit on the psychological level. Thus a custom would be: "Vallecañese mothers, when their children ask them questions regarding sexual behavior, respond with evasion, misinterpretation, and/or punishment." A habit would be: "Cruz' wife Anita, when her son Juanito asks questions about how babies are made, tells him they are sent by the Virgin, and if he persists, punishes him as being *presentado* (fresh)." Our use of practice, at either level of analysis, will include the same elements and mean the same thing. But we are attempting to avoid some of the various interpretations now extant in anthropology and psychology regarding the meaning of custom and habit.

We use the term "value" as Kluckhohn (1951:395) defines it: "A conception, explicit or implicit, distinctive of an individual or characteristic of a group, of the desirable, which influences the selection of available modes, means and ends of action." A "tradition" is a value, practice, or complex of linked values and/or practices, transmitted in a society by social learning and imitation from generation to generation. This is similar to Spiro's (1951) "cultural heritage" and Linton's (1936) "social heredity," but is preferred so as to eliminate even terminological implications of a genetic nature. A tradition must be of at least two-generational duration. For example, values and practices involved in smearing bitter substances on the mother's nipples to hasten weaning comprise a tradition when this has been done, according to informants and other data, for several past generations. When one or more mothers substitute patent drugs for native herbs, then involved here are a newly acquired value of reliance on "store-bought" medication and the practice of implementing this value. If they extend beyond a generation, they become a tradition.

A "pattern" is a regularity of collective behavior considered in terms of frequency, intensity, and spatial-temporal distribution. A "culture" is the interrelated [2] configurations of all patterns characteristic of a society. A "society" is a specified group of persons practicing the same culture and related through a network of common understandings which define the culture.

It has seemed desirable to eschew the concept of "personality" here, since there is a welter of ambiguity and uncertainty surrounding its use. This very ambiguity may have limited the usefulness of the tremendous quantity of effort which has gone into "culture and personality" research (see, for example, Opler 1956, for a cogent summary of this problem). One of several notable exceptions, and an important methodological contribution to the field, is the careful statistical analysis and definition of a kindred term, "modal personality," by Wallace's (1952) research on Tuscarora Indian personality. He defines the "modal personality structure" of the Tuscarora by permitting the definition to evolve from statistical analysis of Rorschach test results, instead of vice-versa. While this has many advantages, I prefer to deal with concrete behaviors as they are derived from the sources of research data which are spelled out in the next section.

Since anthropologists have made few notable advances in applicable psychocultural theory since Kluckhohn's (1944a) trenchant admonitions, our theoretical concepts and assumptions, aside from those enumerated above, come principally from three major sources: (1)

2. One is tempted to say "functionally" interrelated, as this has become commonplace in anthropological and sociological terminology. But this concept so used may be deceptive. Before this assumption can be made it is necessary to specify *all* the patterns, the specific modes of linkage, and whether these are functional for *all* members of the society in terms of their values and goals. Before this step is reached it would seem necessary to modify the concept to include the idea of disfunction as well, as Merton (1957) has done so brilliantly. At any rate, this study makes no pretense of including, or even of knowing of the existence of, *all* the patterns comprising the culture of the social unit with which it is concerned.

classical psychoanalysis as used by Freud and his followers; (2) neo-Freudian theories, particularly the work of Horney, Fromm, and Sullivan; and (3) the dynamic behavior theory of the "stimulus-response" or "learning theory" school, as adumbrated by Clark Hull and contemporary psychologists who have built on it. Some strong impressions on my own thinking have been made in the attempts to test analytic concepts experimentally in a learning theory framework, as in the case of Dollard and Miller (1950) and the case of Whiting and Child (1953).

This study is not designed to test psychoanalytic or learning theory. It calls upon these theories to help conceptualize and provide a framework for the ordering of data on socialization. Either of the theories may be used to explain consistent or contradictory behavior. Thus if one finds that abrupt and severe weaning produces high aggression and dependency in children, it could be explained that this is because the sucking drive has been punished or harshly inhibited. This would also presume aggression and dependency as secondary drives or needs growing out of drives or needs for sucking, for prolonged contact with the mother or mother-substitute (the bottle), for maintaining comfortable and undemanding—though regressive—levels of behavior. If one finds that gradual and mild weaning produces high aggression and dependency in children, one could conclude that the dependency is due to the prolonged rewarding, i.e., reinforcement, of fixated dependent behaviors, and the aggression is due to frustration of the child who might otherwise be maturationally ready, and even impelled by the behavior modeling of older siblings, to want to advance to a less infantile behavior mode.

Of course, this is an oversimplification of learning theory or of psychoanalysis (which invokes other labels for behavior like oral and anal frustration). Aid in explaining some apparent contradictions is found in additions to these theories, such as Whiting's concept of conflict-produced drive strength (a strong drive derives not only from consistent reward but also punishment or frustration of a form of behavior), or Whiting and Child's division of the psychoanalytic construct of fixation into positive and negative types. However, for purposes of the present study, we would like to explain differences which may arise in comparing the primary cultural process of Valle Caña and the United States, or within the socialization process of the Puerto Rican village, as due primarily to cultural and social (class) factors.

Similarities might then be presumed to be due to cross-cultural and, by implication, possibly universal socialization phenomena.

Sears, Whiting, Nowlis, and Sears (1953) raise the possibility that apparent inconsistencies between clinical data and ethnological and psychological data as seen in interviews, observation, and other media, may signify that the clinician and experimental psychologist are really working on the basis of the same referents, but as they are differentially perceived by their subjects and differentially reported. The mother on the analyst's couch gives a report of child-rearing practices which is different from what she gives the nontherapeutic interviewer. "As sources of direct data, neither is more 'valid' than the other. They are simply different" (*ibid.*:229). Both, however, depend on recall, whereas direct observation of child behavior and child rearing is not data of the same order.

These writers feel that two theories are needed, one based on recall and one based on observation. They point out that "direct observation has the advantage of being uninfluenced by memory distortion, but the grave disadvantage of providing an almost inevitably small sample of behavior" (*ibid.*:228). One might inquire whether, with this reasoning, we should not also have a separate theory for behavior as recalled in "depth psychotherapy" as compared with the probably more casual approach of the mother to the research interviewer.

Observation has been the traditional tool of the ethnologist, though unlike the small groups experimenter (who also, in a sense, supplies a small sample), data are not broken down into molecular detail. The ethnological approach has been necessarily molar and therefore cruder and less susceptible of precise measurement. With all their disadvantages, we have used a semistructured interview and a projective technique (direct observation and recording of presumed fantasy behavior). We shall utilize the data yielded by these techniques mainly toward our own ends, rather than the psychologists'.

Many of our socialization data are presented within the framework of three major systems of behavior development: dependency, aggression, and identification and superego. These are the systems around which behavior theory of socialization has mainly been built, and in a broad sense they could subsume part of psychoanalytic theory as well. Since dependence also involves independence, at least by implication, since aggression implies passivity as a complement, and since identification and superego development imply the degree of transmission and absorption of cultural and familial standards as well as the preparation of the child for independent functioning apart from his nurturing agents, much human behavior may be seen within the scope of these systems. Nevertheless, one could logically question the restriction of behavioristic thinking to these systems. Sears (1950a) points out, for example, that "Whereas the word 'injure' can be used to describe the arousing of pain motivation, there is no word in English to specify the act that describes the arousal of nurturance motivation." There probably is some association between certain aspects of our own culture and the great amount of energy expended by American social scientists in the study of aggression.

Since the above theories are well-known, I shall not discuss them further in this introduction. Helpful summaries of classical and modern psychoanalytic theory will be found in Blum (1953), Healy, Bronner, and Bowers (1930), and Mullahy (1955). Stimulus-response learning theory will be found in Dollard and Miller (1950), Miller and Dollard (1941), Dollard, Miller, and others (1939), Mowrer and Kluckhohn (1944), and in the several papers by Miller, Dollard, Sears, Levy, Maslow, and Bateson in Newcomb and Hartley (1947). Attempts to apply the theory to anthropological problems will be found in Gillin (1948), Holmberg (1950), Whiting (1941), and Whiting and Child (1953).

Methodology and Scope

After two months of preliminary planning and conferences at the University of Puerto Rico with the staff of the Family Life Project, the anthropologist and his field assistant reconnoitered the island by automobile for several days. It had been decided to seek a small, relatively isolated sugar-producing community, since cane is the island's chief crop and source of income. Two localities near the geographical center and one on the southern coast had to be abandoned because of inability to obtain housing facilities. Finally the village of Valle Caña (pseudonym), a few miles inland on the eastern side of the island, was selected and housing was found in the small summer cottage of a nonresident landowner. This was about a mile from the village. In a few months when a house in the center of the main settlement became available we moved there. The assistant, my family, and I spent eight months in the village.

Our first contact happened to be a small *cafetín* (confectionery and bar) owner, a former caneworker who went to work in the *municipio* (town) as a fireman before we left the village. Through our landowner we made contacts with middle- and upper-class individuals and gradually, as is the practice in ethnological procedure, extended our circle of acquaintances. However, contrary to ethnographic tradition, we found it helpful at the outset to take a census of the community, or universe, which we chose to define as all those living within a two-kilometer radius of the main settlement of El Camino (113 families). This seemed to coincide with the effective community boundaries as perceived by the people. The census (Appendix A) covered many categories of demographic, sociological, and psychological data. It also proved highly useful as a means of initiating contacts with every family.

From the census, eighteen lower-class families were selected according to the following criteria, which seemed to meet our requirements for representativeness of the lower-class, cane-dependent population (about 80 percent):

1. About half (eight) are from the road settlement and half (ten) from the open country.

2. All are intact nuclear families: spouses plus one or more offspring.

3. *Hijos de crianza* (see Chapter 2) are included in about half the families, as in the universe, and every family also contains at least one biological child between the ages of four and seven. (These were singled out for special study. See below.)

4. About half these children are girls (eight) and half boys (ten).

5. Maximum annual family income is not above $800 yearly top income for three-fourths of the island's families (see Chapter 3).

6. Selected children are preschool or not above the first grade.

7. The father works in cane, or derives his livelihood from cane now or did in the very recent past, and the family lives among caneworkers and shares their culture.

8. Families are divisible into two groups: "small" families of one to five children, "large" families of six or more (as it turned out, eight small, ten large), using as the average the 5.7 mean number of children per family of the universe.

9. While number of children could include biological and adopted children, for our purposes we count only those presently living or surviving to five years. It is arbitrarily assumed that those below this age were not important determinants of current values and practices in socialization.

10. All families come from Valle Caña and use the same school, post-office, stores, and other facilities.

11. A fairly representative number (see Table 2, p. 70) of marriage forms were chosen: three Catholic, one Evangelical, eight civil, six consensual.

12. The sample is fairly representative of the religious distribution of the community: eight Catholic, three Evangelical, three Catholic/Evangelical, two Catholic/Spiritist, one Catholic/Spiritist/Evangelical, one Catholic/Evangelical/Nonbeliever (see Table 1, p. 42).

13. Race is not a criterion (see pp. 33-35).

After a few months we began to administer free doll play to each of the eighteen selected children, using a rented cabin for the mountain children and our house for those who lived on or near the road. This proved to be premature for these shy and sometimes negativistic children and was temporarily postponed. We then began with much greater success to interview the sample mothers very extensively, focusing on the selected child for child training and development and wife-husband relationships. This interview (Appendix B) took about four to six hours, accomplished mostly while the busy mother continued her domestic tasks. It was carried out by the field assistant, Señorita Diaz. Previously the interview had been pretested with three mothers who were comparable in most respects to the panel mothers but had been excluded from the sample. As a result of the pretest certain changes were made. (Some problems of interviewing in Valle Caña are discussed in Appendix C.)

Given the strict separation of sexes in the village, it would not have been possible for a male successfully to have interviewed these women, but Señorita Diaz, who had excellent rapport, obtained very satisfactory results. Notes were taken in Spanish and each evening all interviews and field notes were translated and typed by her and myself. Nearly all prolonged contacts with women and young girls were handled by Señorita Diaz and by my wife. Most male contacts were handled by me. Late in our residence, a part-time field assistant, Raimundo Suárez Lazú, was introduced by the ethnologist to the father of each sample family and other males. He later returned to interview them. The father interviews were only about one-third as long and detailed as the mother interviews and took about two to three hours to administer. Since most questions were taken from the mother interview, the father interview is not reproduced in the appendices.

I have no doubt that the general handling of the sexes by a same-sex researcher made for a much fuller and more rounded picture than if the ethnologist had attempted to cover both sexes, as so often happens in anthropological field studies. Señorita Diaz and Señor Suárez had had previous interviewing experience and each was also trained specifically by myself to administer our techniques. I had had about two months of experience in coding and scoring the mother interview and in administering and scoring free doll play at the Laboratory of Human Development. Señorita Diaz administered the doll play while I scored the actions. Doll play, too, had been pretested on five non-panel children in the field. Some methodological kinks were never straightened out, due to factors possibly inherent in the situation or technique. These problems are discussed in detail in Landy 1959a. We finally completed doll play with the panel children, though four had to be classed as nonparticipators and given extra observational attention.

As is usual in ethnographic studies, extensive contacts were made and information obtained from key figures in the community such as teachers, the principal, town mayor, town priest, druggist, municipal doctor, village minister, social workers, landowners, storeowners, and certain other formal and informal leaders and principal personnel. Demographic and vital statistics for a ten-year period were extracted from the files of the municipal office of vital statistics with the co-operation of the mayor and his aides. One life history of a male Valle-cañese was obtained.

Additionally, three types of objective and projective tests were given to about four hundred preadolescents and adolescents in the local secondary school which served Valle Caña and nearby *barrios*. However, reliability and validity have not yet been established for these data. Furthermore, it was only recently that we obtained information on the dropout rates in these grades. This is necessary for ascertaining the degree of representativeness of the group. So for these reasons and those of space, data on these older children will not be included in the present study; but it is hoped they will later become a supplementary monograph to complete our picture of the growth cycle and socialization process in Valle Caña.

We have tried in this research to utilize to the fullest the ethnographic technique of participant observation. However, we have also felt the need, expressed by many critics of ethnographic studies in the past, to try to describe our data as precisely as we could, to define norms generally only when we had some idea of the range and the variation. So we have attempted not only to impart to the study the anthropological "cultural feel," but also demographic and sociological perspective. We have attempted an approximation to scientific precision by using measures of child training and child behavior which are cross-culturally comparable. We have also insisted that in a literate culture, a derivative and adjunct to great civilized societies in the Old and New Worlds, any available evidence as a result of record-keeping which would be useful should be utilized (see Lewis 1951).

To some extent this may occasionally give parts of the book a "sociological" flavor. But when this will help us to be more precise, as in determining income, or more accurate, as in determining the frequencies and extent of certain practices, disease patterns, and so on, such information may prove more useful than the often indeterminate "pictures" presented by some ethnographic "purely descriptive" monographs. I am not proposing that we substitute statistical analysis for ethnographic "descriptive integration," but rather that the two modes of analysis supplement and enrich one another. As soon as the anthropologist generalizes, he implies frequencies, distributions, central tendencies, variations. The validity of what he may say can only be enhanced by attempts at more precise statements. And comparability of cross-cultural data, a stated aim of nearly all ethnography, is also increased thereby.

Reliability and Validity

Reliability refers to the faithfulness with which an instrument will repeat a measurement under conditions similar to those surrounding the original measurement, or to the amount of agreement reached by independent judgments of the same variables. Validity is the extent to which an instrument or measurement measures what it purports to measure.

The primary ethnographic instrument is the ethnologist. It should be a relatively easy matter for him to obtain similar measures of a set of variables under similar conditions time after time. What is not simple to determine is the degree to which changes in the circumstances have been unconsciously compensated and balanced by changes in the ethnologist's perception and point of view.

To some extent he can correct for errors of judgment in the field as well as informant bias by checking and cross-checking his information with more than one informant and then rechecking discrepancies with the original informant. This leads not only to control of inform-ant bias, but to clarification of meanings and symbolic significances. It may also produce new insights regarding the content and signifi-cance of the particular datum as well as new views of the informants themselves, as representatives of their culture, regarding such variables as accuracy, precision, time perspective (an incident changes with time and the number of mouths that report it), and other aspects of local behavior.

The anthropologist may also try to check information by utilizing other instruments like structured or unstructured interviews which have been somewhat standardized by previous use in other cultures (as happens in this research), projective techniques, documents, and other means of data collection. Since no instrument which he has yet borrowed from other sciences, or occasionally invented, has proved to have universal reliability and validity, such extra tools may weigh more than they are worth in the anthropological field kit and consume unnecessary time and expense. If, for example, a projective test agrees with his ethnographic data, he may conclude that the test "confirms" his findings, but since he knows little of the actual validity of the instrument under varying cultural and situational conditions, this is cold comfort and may in the end be an added source of perplexity, irritation, and uncertainty, instead of a methodological boon (Mensh and Henry 1953). On the other hand, suppose his field data and test results disagree? Which does he rely upon—and why? The answer very often is a rationalization of his method and a protestation of scien-tific and personal integrity ("after all, everything ultimately depends on the honesty of the researcher").

In the present research we have utilized the kinds of cross-checking and rechecking of field information referred to above whenever it was feasible.

To some degree reliability of the free doll play technique had been established by earlier work at the Laboratory of Human Development and at the Child Welfare Research Station at the State University of Iowa by Sears, Whiting, and others (Nowlis 1952). However, validity was, and remains, an open question. Additionally, the doll play mate-rials are standardized only as to content, not form. That is, each "house" is an open-roofed replica of a presumably "typical" house of the cultural group under investigation. But in an attempt to achieve cultural compatibility, I constructed the materials for Valle Caña after being in the field for several months with the goal of having them resemble a "typical" lower-class Vallecañese dwelling and family. Some possible experimental effects of this, including certain limitations on validity, are discussed in a separate publication by this writer (Landy 1959a). Since the child's behavior is scored on the spot, it would not have been possible to obtain a reliability rating except by having employed another scorer in the doll play situation directly. This would have been not only expensive but impractical in terms of the doll play situation as it existed in this island village.

Reliability checks on the mother interview were more feasible. In Puerto Rico I judged the eighteen interviews. My wife then judged the interviews. When we compared judgments we obtained an agreement of 71 percent on all variables, counting agreement as either full accord or agreement within one point of a scaled point. After comparing our answers and discussing each case in which there was a disagreement of two or more points, my wife and I again judged independently all the interviews and obtained an 88 percent agreement. All cases of disagreement between the two sets of scores were then averaged, so that we finally had a set of composite scores which were more reliable than either of us could have achieved individually.

Later in the United States, Miriam Lewin Papanek of the Laboratory of Human Development, who had no previous knowledge of Puerto Rican culture but was an experienced judge of the mother interview, rated the eighteen interviews independently after we had checked her judgments on the first two to establish some common criteria of judgment. On our first check of all eighteen sets of her judgments with the composite judgments of my wife and myself, we obtained an agreement of 90.3 percent. The breakdown is as follows for 2520 judgments (18 × 140 scales):

Amount of Disagreement	No. of Judgments	Percent	Amount of Agreement
None	1632	64.8	
1 point	642	25.5	90.3
2 points	118	4.7	
More	35	1.3	
Indeterminate, or Insufficient Data	93	3.7	
Total	2520	100.0	

As a result of checking all scorings that differed by two or more points, and those where points indicating indeterminacy of a score or insufficient data were used by one rater and a scale point by the other, it was found that 18 of the 140 scales should be eliminated from the reliability comparisons because: (1) They were "multiple-coded" or otherwise not true scales and had been inadvertently included. (2) The indeterminate or insufficient data scoring was not mutually exclusive with one or more scale points, creating some ambiguity. Had ground rules been more clearly set in advance of Dr. Papanek's judgments, it was clear that we would not have disagreed as widely on such scales. Since these scores were then made equivalent to some of the scale points in question, these might have been used to inflate our agreement percentages. Nevertheless, they were eliminated from the test for reliability.

Dr. Papanek then reviewed her judgments and we obtained an agreement of 92.1 percent, as follows, for 2196 judgments (18 × 122 scales):

Amount of Disagreement	No. of Judgments	Percent	Amount of Agreement
None	1418	64.6	
1 point	603	27.5	92.1
2 points	113	5.1	
More	26	1.2	
Indeterminate, or Insufficient Data	36	1.6	
Total	2196	100.0	

Father interviews were judged solely by my wife, but not tested for reliability, and are used only occasionally throughout the study. The principal emphasis, aside from ethnographic material, is on the mother interview as a source of antecedent variables in child training, with doll play used as a secondary adjunct to consequent measures of child behavior, also derived from the mother interview.

The ancient question of validity plagues us, however, even with our reliable mother interview, but we may suggest some partial extenuators. First, the pretest of the mother interview was used to make the interview clearer and more meaningful. Furthermore, there were daily checks as a result of our examining each portion of the interview for communicability and intelligibility as we translated and transcribed it, and any apparent misunderstandings were then taken up with the mother at the next session by requestioning her, usually in a somewhat different way, about her unclear response. Other ambiguities discovered after we left the field were then noted and Señorita Diaz made a revisit to Valle Caña for one week to recheck these as well as ask certain additional questions about sex education and adopted children which were not originally included but which we had since come to feel were essential. As a final safeguard, whenever there is a wide discrepancy between an interview scale and our observational data, this is stated at the appropriate place in the study and we either reach a decision as to which seems more acceptable to us or leave this to the reader's judgment.

The reader may still ask: How do you know the mother was telling the truth? How do you know she was not telling you what you wanted to know, or what she felt was proper, rather than what she actually believed or practiced? To some extent we feel such a possibility has been cancelled out by the precautions taken above, though we point in parts of the study to some cases where they might indeed have told us what was proper. This is also considered in the discussion near the end of Chapter 9. It is patent, of course, that where distortions like these occur, they are in terms of the values of the distorter and therefore still provide useful information.

Additional Limitations

I feel reasonably certain that many of the findings here are generalizable to similar lower-class communities in Puerto Rico. However Wolf (1952) has shown that there are important class and occupational differences with regard to behavior and socialization in three class and occupational groups on the island, and Mintz (1951), Wolf (1951), Manners (1950), and Padilla (1951) have shown that differential ecological conditions also play a part in determining culture and behavior in four island communities (see also Manners and Steward 1953 and Steward, et al. 1956).[3] Therefore, except where stated, this research will be limited in generalizability to Valle Caña lower-class society.

In retrospect we would have preferred more information on traditional, past generation socialization. Data on this are limited to a few

3. Our original analysis of field findings used the doctoral theses of Mintz, Wolf, Manners, and Padilla, and our references throughout are to these documents. Subsequently their data were reworked and placed in a single volume as illustrations of certain theoretical propositions (*The People of Puerto Rico* [Steward, et al. 1956]).

informants and to a few questions in the mother interview. Ethnohistorical documents (Landy 1959b) scarcely mention this important area of culture.

Other limitations and desiderata could be included here, but such a recital would be tedious. Rare indeed is the researcher in human behavior who, gifted with the revelations of hindsight, would not have performed his task somewhat differently, with more or less of this or that ingredient. Rare also is the reader who will not perceive such shortcomings. The data and our inferences and interpretations from them will have to stand on their own merits. The reader has been partially prepared in this introductory statement and will receive further instruction along the way. Let us squeeze into the bursting confines of our *público*, one of those remarkable public jitneys that carry *Puertorriqueños* at breakneck and exciting pace to all parts of their island. We shall speed eastward from Río Piedras, the university suburb of San Juan, to Caguas, change to another *público* going further inland, and thence to still another, bound even further east for the *municipio* we call Agua Lluvia. But we shall disembark before then at the rural community of Valle Caña.

CHAPTER 2

Culture and Society in Valle Caña—1

The Community

A FEW miles inland from the east coast of Puerto Rico, in a broad, fertile, sugar cane belt, lies a low, rainy valley, flanked on either side by formidable rocky mountains near the eastern end of the Cordillera Central. In one part of this valley and on the nearby mountain slopes is the community which we call Valle Caña.

Although only part of a *barrio*, Valle Caña bears the same name, just as the town, Agua Lluvia, has the name of the entire *municipio*.[1] The whole *barrio* encompasses about 5.5 square miles, but a cluster of houses and stores that huddle along the main hard-surfaced road that runs through the *barrio* to the *municipio* is also known as Valle Caña and more intimately as El Camino (the Road). The people who live here and the others who live in the open country on either side of El Camino, along winding terraces and rough hills, call their own small groupings by affectionate or derisive names.

Along a high, tortuous mountain that stretches out behind the stream that meanders through Valle Caña is a subcommunity of shacks perched precariously along the mountain's knife-like edge. This is La Hoja (the Blade), and its people form an important segment of Valle Caña. Economically they are among the poorest, but some are

1. In Puerto Rico, the *municipio* is both a town and the several *barrios* surrounding the town. Roughly equivalent to the Anglo-Saxon concept of village or neighborhood, *barrios* have the function of political wards, or sections, of the *municipio*, which is roughly analogous to our county. The most important economic, social, and political part of a *barrio* usually bears the same name as the whole. Similarities in physical layout are found with other Latin-American countries (Gillin 1947, 1949).

permitted to plant root crops on those sides of the mountain which are too steep to be useful to the landowners for cane cultivation.

The bottomland soil is admirably suited for cane and is the most valuable type of land on the island. During the time of growing, when practically nothing has to be done to care for the cane, the whole valley and lower slopes of the mountains are covered with the plush, verdant green of the thickly massed cane. During *la zafra* (the harvest) the green recedes before the onslaught of the cane cutters, until finally the whole land looks as though it had been shaved by a giant razor. The cane stumps quickly turn brown, but the new cane grows so fast that within a month the patches of shoots begin to appear again and soon the whole countryside has resumed its customary green covering.

The climate, which fluctuates within a relatively narrow range, is nearly always pleasant, although the spring and summer months sometimes become fairly hot. During the "winter" there are times when the air becomes chilled, but the temperature seldom drops below 65 degrees. While there is much sunshine in Valle Caña, it is situated in the heaviest rain belt on the island. It rains hard and often, especially during the winter.[2] Abundant rain and sun are the bases of the cane crop, and often one has the sense almost of "seeing" the cane spring up, the growth cycle is so rapid.

At any time of the year Valle Caña, like most of the rural communities of Puerto Rico, appears to the passerby to be a quiet, sleepy little settlement. This is particularly so during *el tiempo muerto* (the dead season), the time between harvests when for six to nine months of the year there is chronic unemployment. For Valle Caña is a community that lives, and dies, by sugar cane. If the crop is good the men can expect several months' work, during which they try to pay the debts accumulated during the dead season and perhaps buy something new to wear. If bad, the work may last no more than two or three months. Even during the *zafra* the village may not seem unusually alive to the casual observer. But for most of the people it is a time of rejoicing. The eye is brighter, the laughter lighter, the gait a bit quickened, the stomach fuller. Here and there a pretty new store dress is seen or a stiff new pair of trousers. The people ride the bus into Agua Lluvia

2. For 1950 there were 177.65 inches of rainfall in Agua Lluvia *municipio*, ranging from 7.31 inches in March to 25.27 in February (*Anuario Estadistico* 1952: 20-24, Table 9).

or Cañaveral more often. The children get more pennies and buy more *lindberghs* (flavored ice cubes sold for a cent by grocers). For a little while one can forget the dead season just past or the one looming ahead.

The Population

Our research universe comprised all the families living within about a two-kilometer radius of El Camino. These were 113 families, 62 percent of which lived in El Camino and the rest in the open country, mostly along La Hoja.

The average household may be computed at 5.5 persons [3] but this figure is somewhat misleading. More than 80 percent of the families were intact nuclear units, comprising spouses and children. There were twenty broken families, six headed by husbands, fourteen by wives. Thirty families included adults in addition to the spouses.

The term "family" is further complicated by the presence in Valle Caña of *hijos de crianza* (literally, children of rearing), who form a broad category of children additional to biological offspring of present unions. In Valle Caña 111 *hijos de crianza* were being cared for by fifty-one families; thus half the families had at least one. Fifty-four percent were *hijastros* (stepchildren and offspring of former matings, legal and nonlegal); 29 percent were *nietos* (grandchildren); and the rest were a miscellany of nephews, nieces, children of distant relatives, and "foster" children (legal and nonlegal). [4]

3. Close to the mean of 5.9 per rural household in the survey of Roberts and Stefani (1949:6, and Chart 1, p. 5). Unlike the composition of their sample, our poorer households averaged more children than the wealthier ones.

4. The law recognizes only one type of child in addition to children of a marriage, the *hijo adoptivo*, adopted through legal procedures which became more complicated and rigorous in the 1948 Civil Code. The law tends to regard rather liberally cases in which the paternity of a child is involved, especially if the child is a minor. Unless there are serious complications, the courts accept the *padres de familia* or *padres de crianza* as custodians of the child.

The proportion in Valle Caña was higher than expected. Seventeen lower-class families were reinterviewed and nearly all independently named the categories included here. I have good reasons to suspect that the middle-class family does not usually define stepchildren and grandchildren in this way, though I know of one Vallecañese case where this is so. I believe that the poorer families are more concerned with absolute numbers of mouths to feed and less concerned with labeling household members more closely in accord with legal definitions.

I am indebted to Dean Manuel Rodriguez and Dr. Denis Martinez Irizarry of the University of Puerto Rico College of Law for information about the legal aspects of *hijos de crianza*.

Conditions of marriage and family life generally in Valle Caña tend to produce relatively large numbers of children who, for various reasons, are transferred to parents other than their own and oftentimes, after several years, transferred back again. The widespread consensuality, premarital or extramarital "natural" children (for whom the father is now legally responsible, though this is not yet widely accepted among the people), and philandering, especially on the part of the male, all produce several classes of children which are thus incorporated into a household. In the cities many of these children are left to shift for themselves and become vagrants, but in the country someone usually takes them in. In Valle Caña they are found in all social classes, but their status and treatment vary. A child taken from a lower- into a middle-class family is often used pretty much as a servant or laborer. His treatment is not as indulgent as that of the family's own children but is better than that of a hired servant.

A child taken into a lower-class family is always from another lower-class family. Once accepted by the family heads, after a period reported by them as varying between six months and ten years, he is considered in the same terms as the family's own children and accorded more or less the same treatment. Very often, though he may go out to work on his own when he grows up, he maintains close ties with the family, even after his own marriage. Here are some typical comments and practices concerning child exchange:

I had an *hija de crianza*. I took her when she was four years old. She was a cousin of mine. I had her for eleven years and then her mother took her away. My aunt gave her to me because she did not have any money to keep her.

I had a niece of my husband's for three years. When I took her she was three years old. . . . Her father asked me for her and I had to give her to him because he was alone. Her mother died, when she had another child, in childbirth. An *hijo de crianza* is a child that one brings up and trains. One serves as a mother and loves them as if they were one's own.

I have had six *hijos de crianza*, the children of my husband. He has had my two, also. A child that one brings up and has to treat as a mother and respect as such . . . a child that one brings up and gives him everything, that is an *hijo de crianza*. Any boy or girl that one brings up, it does not matter if he is related or not, is an *hijo de crianza*. If I have had him for five years I would then consider him an *hijo de crianza* because you come to love him. It depends on when one starts to love him.

I took charge of a niece of mine almost as soon as she was born because her mother was my sister, but she "went crazy". I had her for four years and then my mother took her because I went away with my present husband and I could not attend to her very well. Her mother wanted her, but I gave her to her grandmother. For a time I also had a child of my husband's. But then she went with her aunt. He has not had *hijos de crianza*—well, mine—except that I gave those to my mother . . . and now they are *hijos de crianza* to her.

. . . Since I did not have any children and my sister had three, I asked her for one, so she could keep me company. Such is life. You love them more than your own since their parents are absent; you love them with pity and consideration and treat them better. . . . Afterwards, since her mother needed her to help, she took her away. I cried when she left . . . as if she had been my own daughter. Later she would come to visit me. Since she was taken away, maybe I cannot say that she was an *hija de crianza*, strictly speaking.

The total number of children, living and dead, is 649, and averages 4.2 per household, excluding *hijos de crianza*. But for many of these wives and husbands, the present mating was not the only reproductive opportunity. From former marriages and premarital and extramarital liaisons, these wives also had an average of 0.5 children additional to current offspring. The husbands had even more, an average for the community of 1.13 children in previous matings. Thus a total of 180 children (52 by wives, 128 by husbands) was produced by present marriage partners before and/or besides their contemporary children.

As in most countries the flow of migration is mainly rural to urban. Thus Valle Caña is an "old" community, since the mean age of all wives is 47.7 years and of all husbands 55.4 years. But the mean age of wives of *intact* families is 39 years and husbands 47 years (a difference which is to be expected), while the surviving single family heads were much older. It is not at all unusual for a woman to be bearing a child at the same time her daughter is also pregnant. Being a grandmother in Valle Caña does not put an end to one's child bearing, and a woman often raises her own children and grandchildren at the same time, a situation also characteristic of other Caribbean societies like Jamaica (Cohen 1956).

Geographic Mobility

It was not possible to get reliable information on migration from the village, but those who were in the community at the time of the study did not seem to care very much about departing, except to the United States, and so the community as it stands is composed mostly of geographically nonmobile people. While many Vallecañeses have relatives and friends living on the mainland, it remains a dream for most except the new generation, among whom some have set New York or some other continental area as a definite goal. During the author's residence the harvest was disappointing, and a few older men were seriously considering the call of farm corporations in the United States for temporary laborers.

Ninety-eight percent of the wives and 96 percent of the husbands were born in Valle Caña or neighboring *barrios* and *municipios*, and only 2 percent of the wives and 6 percent of the husbands have ever been off the island.

Occasionally a man tries to make a break from the village and establish himself in an economically more fortunate community. Two went to San Juan during my stay in the village. One finally returned without luck, but another managed to get a steady job in a factory and was saving enough to send for his wife and several children. In the city there is more money to be made if one finds a job and life there is more exciting than in the village, but living costs are higher. Living conditions, except in the new government housing projects, are often at an even lower standard than in the country and certainly unhealthier. The Puerto Rican urban slums have impressed visitors from other lands with their tremendous overcrowding and lack of sanitation.

Often, too, when one of the younger men or women finds enough money to get to the United States (two left during my stay) he becomes confused and saddened by the drastic change and, when nostalgia will not release its grip, returns to the village, even though there is scant hope of employment. According to one study (Mills, Senior, and Goldsen 1950) the Puerto Ricans who do get to the United States are usually the most enterprising, and the effect ultimately may be to drain off much useful talent.

Living Conditions [5]

Living conditions of lower-class Vallecañeses are based upon climate, poverty, and tradition (in which we include ignorance as well as knowledge).[6] The relative temperateness of the year-round climate means that flimsy cover will serve as shelter against the wind, rain, and sun. A few logs, cut and trimmed with machetes, are stuck into the ground, slats of planks or branches are made, and upon this frame anything is thrown that will keep out the water—old scraps of tarpaper or corrugated zinc, boards salvaged from torn-down houses, old signs, palm fibres, and grasses. Buying any kind of building material is economically impossible for most of the lower class; lumber, for example, is mostly imported and very costly. If a leak occurs it may be mended or one may simply move one's hammock or cot a few inches away so that the drops splatter to the floor. One lives in these shacks until they fall down. Then the family either builds another, if material can be had, or tries to move in with neighbors or friends. During sudden winter chills children and adults frequently sniffle with running colds.

The average working-class dwelling consists of two rooms: the *sala*, or living room, used for eating, social affairs, and sleeping as many as can crowd into hammocks and cots; and sometimes a bedroom which can accommodate one or two beds or cots, a hammock and a *coy* (baby's hammock) across or near the beds. One-room houses are not unusual, especially in the case of small families, bachelors, or widows. At the rear of the houses is usually the *cocina* (kitchen), which is made either of palm branches or scraps of tin too old and worn for anything else. The stove (*fogón*) is a tin-covered board, or rock slabs, upon which are placed a few small stones as a grate. A pot is set over the stones with a fire below on the earth. Fuel consists of branches and twigs which fall off trees (firewood is seldom cut) or charcoal for those who can afford the fifty cents per sack. The housewife spends

5. For an excellent detailed and objective study of Puerto Rican living conditions see Roberts and Stefani 1949. See also Manners 1950, Mintz 1951, Padilla 1951, Siegel 1948, Wolf 1951.

6. Moore and Tumin (1949) have noted that ignorance in a Guatemalan community functioned to retain the status quo, and they have concluded that functions of ignorance as well as education must be accounted for by anthropologists. I would carry this further and postulate that ignorance may function either to cement (by not knowing of change) or to change (by not knowing of the advantages that already exist) the status quo. Knowledge, it follows, also might have either function.

most of her time in the kitchen and, since there is no chimney, the place fills with smoke so that a visitor is choking and gasping in a few minutes. But the wives who work in these kitchens seem immune to the smoke and stand for hours over a steaming pot, their eyes smarting.

Other than sleeping accommodations, furniture and furnishings are scant and crude. A few families afford the popular commercial "set" of wood and wicker or hemp, but for most the only seat is a bench and often not even this. Few have regular tables but rather boards which are nailed to one or two legs and stuck against the wall. Usually only the father eats, alone or with other adult males, at the table, the children and mother standing or sitting anywhere they can, generally on the floor. Aside from a kitchen knife there are few utensils. Nearly everyone eats with a spoon and/or his fingers. Vessels consist of old, chipped, china plates, tin pie-plates, gourds, or old pots. Except on special occasions, drinking containers are tin cans, which most say they prefer because "they keep the water cool and the coffee hot."

Breadfruit (*panapen*) is wild and rather plentiful, but few Valle-cañeses like its taste and it is used mostly as an emergency food. When available, the local roots are preferred, particularly *ñame, yautía, yuca*, as well as *guineos* (green bananas) and *plátanos* (plantains). When there is money the national dish, rice and beans, is preferred. It is usually cooked with a pungent sauce of canned tomatoes, garlic, and *alcaparras* (capers), and sometimes green olives may be included. *Bacalao*, dried codfish imported from Newfoundland, is much desired and can be kept without refrigeration.

Most families on La Hoja and a few in El Camino have small patches where they raise root vegetables and have a few chickens and perhaps a hog or two. The latter are slaughtered most frequently at *Navidades* (the Christmas season) and *Tres Reyes* (Three Kings Day). This day is traditional and celebrated around the sixth of January with more energy than is the American practice. A family will often sacrifice during the year to keep a lean, razorback hog alive, so that at *Navidades* and *Tres Reyes* they may have relatives and friends over to share the festive board. Pork which has been hung until it is very dry and gamey is considered fine eating. Pork skins are fried (*chicharrones*) and nearly every other part of the animal is eaten, the intestines being stuffed with blood, liver, etc., to make blood sausage.

Only two lower-class families in Valle Caña had running water. In El Camino there is a public spigot (*pluma de agua*) which is piped in from a distant mountain reservoir of the *municipio*. The mountain people have to go as far as half a mile to isolated mountain wells for drinking water or catch rain water in barrels for drinking and dish-washing. Baths are taken in a mountain pool. Though it is distant from most houses, the young people at least find it a pleasurable hike, for they can play and splash around in the icy water. Clothes are washed in the nearest part of the small stream which wanders out of the distant mountains and roughly parallels the edge of La Hoja.

As difficult as it is to get water, most adults manage to keep fairly clean, though during the day the children, especially in the more iso-lated homes, get quite dirty. But most children are washed at least once daily and clean clothes put on them. The people take great pride in their bodily cleanliness and in their dress, and it is a matter of honor to have clean and, if possible, new clothes. Clothes which are the least bit torn or patched are abhorred, but of course they are worn when noth-ing else can be bought. Just before my family and I left the community we decided to give away some of our old clothes. Knowing the attitude of the people, it was difficult for us to decide what to give them, since our own clothing was worn long after it had become old and shabby. I was ashamed to give away some things which, for ordinary wear, I might still have used in the United States, but when we were ap-proached by two especially indigent families who swallowed their pride and asked us for clothing, we gave them these things, making sure not to include anything which appeared very tattered. This pride in appearances means that a presentable facade must be maintained at all costs, making for an ill-afforded conspicuous consumption which has been noted by many observers.

However, this pride in dress is not accompanied by pride in home conditions. First one's body is clothed and fed, then other things are taken care of. The house comes last and little time is spent making it neat or ornamental. Most homes, even those with a little more income, are quite bare. Decorations are largely absent or restricted to a gaudy store-bought ornament, a religious picture or image, or perhaps a pic-ture from an old magazine or catalog. An upper-class informant sug-gested that this lack of aesthetic surroundings can be traced to the attitude of the Spanish landowners who felt it best to keep their slaves and serfs in a state of ignorance with the fewest possible worldly possessions, holding the premise that the more they had and knew of, the more they would feel they needed. They even destroyed the serfs' attempts at decoration, and being themselves interested primarily in making money in Puerto Rico and taking or sending it back to Spain, they reduced their own aesthetic needs to the minimum. Whether this statement is accurate, the general picture of living conditions has changed relatively little since early times. From Oviedo, Las Casas, Abbad y Lasierra, Ubeda y Delgado, Fernandez Juncos, Brau, Coll y Toste, Melendez, Cruz Monclova, Colonel Flinter, Van Middeldyk, Dinwiddie, and the first special United States commissioner to the island, Carroll—from all these we derive a configuration of the state of Puerto Rican life that throughout the centuries is amazingly constant, even static, or, as some writers have termed it, "stable" (Landy 1959b).

In any event there are certain factors in the contemporary situation which unintentionally perpetuate this tradition: (1) the poverty, which, as we shall see later in this chapter, is extreme, in absolute or relative terms; (2) the dependence on cheap and out-moded imports from the United States; (3) a traditional lack of initiative in utilizing local materials to any degree beyond bare necessity, which is recognized by the government and which it is attempting to modify through educational pamphlets, moving pictures, and work teams sent into rural areas to show the people how to work as groups and make use of existing resources; and (4) possibly a feeling—though this is my inference and only indirectly expressed to me by Vallecañeses—that with so little money no effort would ever bring their homes up to the aesthetic level of their own middle class, much less to the glittering fantasy world of American magazines and movies.

Of more immediate importance than aesthetics, however, is the problem of crowding. Since there are few clothes or other possessions, they are placed in a box, old suitcase, or trunk or hung on a nail and do not present a problem. But it is different with sleeping arrangements. It is not unusual for three to five children of varying ages and both sexes to sleep in the same bed, often not a full-sized bed. Frequently the mother and father sleep together with the smallest child, sometimes with two children, but just as frequently the father occupies the hammock and the mother sleeps in the bed or cot with from one to four children. Men and women say that, under these circumstances, they wait until the children are asleep before they have intercourse, so the children will not know what is going on. As one father said to me, "We do this so the children will not know. But sometimes we wonder if they do not know anyway. If they wake up at night, but do not make a noise, maybe they can hear us." Confirmation of this problem comes from a psychiatric social worker in San Juan who has worked for many years among lower-class Puerto Ricans and believes that many children grow up with aggressive and fearful fantasies about sex because they may hear the sounds in the night but do not see the act and thus store up all manner of distortions.

Racial Consciousness

Race is not a major social problem in Valle Caña. Nevertheless there is a good deal of racial consciousness or color consciousness.[7] For example, one woman's ". . . in-laws are prejudiced against me because of my color. [She has Negroid features but is not an extreme type.] They won't speak to me, not even my sister-in-law who lives in that house there next door. They even fought with my husband because of me." Yet, in a strict anthropological sense, race becomes almost undefinable in Valle Caña. The intermixture of European white, African Negro, and Arawak Indian has proceeded to such a degree that only the very extreme types may be labeled at all. Consequently the investigator must depend, as the Vallecañese himself depends, upon his subjective judgments to decide which individual belongs to which category. In common use are such terms as *"negro," "blanco"* (white), *"indio"* (Indian), *"trigueño"* (wheat-colored), *"mestizo"* (mixed; recently adopted by local government agencies), and some others.

While all classes are very aware of skin color, eye color, and hair, nose, and lip form, discrimination of the kind noted in the preceding paragraph is not widespread within the lower class. Even if it were attempted, the outstanding fact that each family, almost without exception, is itself quite mixed (with light *and* dark siblings the rule) makes such an effort almost impossible. There is a general ideal of lightness, or whiteness, and of smooth or wavy as opposed to kinky hair, but, at least in lower-class society, the individual of any phenotypical combination is more or less accepted socially and those who happen to have less desirable characteristics feel only envy if the topic

7. The first term is used by Mintz (1951:XII/3); the second by Siegel (1947:187). These contain the most useful and lucid discussions of race in Puerto Rico of anything with which I am acquainted. Other discussions will be found in Gordon 1950; Reuter 1946; Rogler 1944, 1946; Sereno 1948; Williams 1945. All these assume a "race problem," apparent or diagnosed, as the point of departure for a variety of essays.

is discussed in their presence. The following bit from my field notes is
illuminating:

The woman of the house was telling of a family who had moved and were
leaving their house to another family from La Hoja. . . . The woman of
the house was obviously Negroid and her visitor seemed white to me, but
she remarked in the former's presence that the new family had such pretty
children because they all had blue eyes, blond hair, and very white skins.
The visitor said she wished her children had been as pretty as these, but
unfortunately they had been "ugly and dark" as she was. To me, the
woman was far from dark and could easily have "passed" in any white
community. The Negroid hostess agreed emphatically with her visitor.

We could detect few signs of open discrimination at the employment level. *Mayordomos* (farm and cane foremen), storekeepers,
school teachers, caneworkers, were all hues from the lightest to the
darkest. The predecessor of the present *alcalde* (mayor) of Agua
Lluvia, whom we met on our initial reconnaisance of the area, was a
very dark Negro and his son held an appointed position in the government of Cañaveral, a neighboring *municipio*.

In subtle ways the feeling of race does come to the surface but
usually in joking, often affectionate terms. Thus the term *negrita* is
used as a mark of endearment to describe a girl or woman, as we
learned when our child was thus addressed. On the other hand it is
quite common for mothers, often themselves of a very dark color, to
frighten their children into obedience with threats of kidnaping by
"an ugly old black man" or the *cuco* or *coco* (Puerto Rican equivalent
of bogey-man), to whom is ascribed various traits like "black" and
"animal." During a showing in the village of a film by the Department
of Education, there was much laughter whenever the camera focused
on a Negro in the film, much of this derision coming from Negroid-
appearing individuals themselves. This over-consciousness of one's
own darkness, or the possibility of being so classified if one does not
demonstrate ridicule on some occasions toward the darkness of others,
has been termed "cryptomelanism" by a psychiatrist (Sereno 1948:10).
Few individuals want to be classified as Negroes and almost no one
classified himself that way. The term *trigueño* is used to classify anyone from a very light to a definite Negroid type. For example, the
registrar of births in Agua Lluvia classifies parents as she personally
sizes them up. She used to ask them, but there was so much anger and

reluctance at the question, she now simply glances at them and decides whether they are Negro, white, *trigueño*, or *mestizo*. She classifies herself as *trigueño*, although she is quite dark, but will classify others of about her same color as Indian or Negro.

Children are quite aware of the differences, yet it seems to make little difference in their social attitudes. While white children may be more popular, only once did I observe a child left out of play because he was Negro. But at school dances it is a fact that Negro girls usually will be chosen last as partners, even by boys of the same general phenotype.

There is a strong consciousness of race in Valle Caña, but it is not a crucial deterrent, it seems to me, in most lower-class social relationships. Every child knows that, other things equal, his opportunities for social and economic mobility may, to some undeterminable extent, be influenced by his color or hair form. On the other hand, the darkest of children will not feel that he is of such a different species that he cannot mingle with children of lighter complexion and straighter hair and share the security and warmth of such associations.

The factor of race, therefore, has not been included as a research criterion or subject for analysis in this study. But the similarities and differences in social attitudes and behavior regarding race in Puerto Rico as compared with the United States on the one hand, and other places in Latin America on the other, deserve prompt scientific investigation.[8]

Health and Disease

Vallecañeses proudly describe the improvement of the people's health in recent years, speaking with wonder of the fine new facilities in town and the miracle drugs. While there are better opportunities to treat disease than formerly, preventive medical education and meas-

8. A careful study by a physical anthropologist (Thieme:1952) of a representative sampling of all 77 *municipios* of blood types, PTC tasters, and anthropometric, dental, and physiological characteristics (data on the last three as yet unpublished) concludes: "The frequency of ABO and Rh blood types in Puerto Rico, as well as non-tasters of PTC, is as would be expected in a mixed Negro-white-American Indian population. However, variability within this population is significant" (*ibid.*:109). The Indian component in the total population is larger than one would surmise from most literature on the subject. This confirms a feeling I have had on the basis of observation alone. Most important of all, Thieme recognizes the need for such studies to use censal data for true representativeness and to take cultural attitudes into primary consideration in weighing phenotypic factors.

ures have only lightly touched the community, except the water supply from the government-controlled aqueduct at Agua Lluvia.

There is a local health unit whose activities seem confined largely to dispensing cough syrups and purgatives for the various parasites (particularly hookworms and tapeworms) that attack the community, especially the children. Two or three days a week a nurse comes in from the *municipio* and administers purgatives. She makes no home visits but sees the mothers who come to the milk station in the mornings for government-supplied dried milk. She is powerless to do anything without a doctor and one has not visited the unit for over a year. When the former doctor was there once a week he gave a prenatal clinic, a clinic for children up to six, and yearly blood tests and X-rays.

A few mothers come in once or twice a month for contraceptives, jelly, and condoms. These are the only materials they are permitted to have without prescription by the hospital doctor. A small room filled with medicines gathers dust since they cannot be dispensed. The nurse says she could give lectures and perhaps help mothers with advice, but they do not come around except to get an injection prescribed by the doctor or druggist in Agua Lluvia.

Teachers distribute containers and get children to bring in specimens which are sent to the district hospital for analysis. Of sixteen children who had parasites recently, only nine returned for prescribed purges. The nurse felt the children did not come because they disliked the purgatives and their mothers did not force them. Emergencies are sent to the municipal hospital and from there, if needed, to the district hospital, about fifteen miles further north. If one can get to the phone at the policeman's house, an ambulance can be summoned. Otherwise the people must reach the hospital by *público* or bus, and if they do not have the ten-cent fare they must walk.

There is hardly a home where one or more children are not running around with suppurating sores, constantly scratching and dirtying them with no maternal interference. Parents seem vaguely aware of some connection between dirt and disease but most are too occupied or casual to do much about it.

Bení, age seven, scratched his legs on thorns and was feverish. We suggested taking him to the hospital in town but the mother said there was no doctor there (temporarily true). We then suggested the free American mission clinic in Cañaveral. The parents said they would bring the child but never did, though we gave them an introductory letter to the doctors, whom we knew. Bení's smallest brother, one-and-a-half years old, had a bad fever, too. After several days, the child in a coma, the parents took him to town—not to the hospital, but to Don Santo, a local druggist who freely prescribes medicine and is much respected.

The two-year-old son of Isabel was very sick. We suggested the hospital or clinic again. Isabel demurred. "Today I must do my washing." "What about tomorrow?" "Tomorrow," she said, matter-of-factly, "I must iron."

In nearly all cases the mother must take the child to the doctor. The father does not usually consider this his responsibility, even when not working. This apparently casual attitude toward children's illnesses seems somewhat contradictory since many adults are hypochondriacal about real or imagined illnesses. Perhaps there is a compensatory relation between their adult hypochondria and the casualness or indifference with which their own childhood illnesses may have been handled. We have observed that the middle-class doctor at the hospital tends to treat lower-class patients with what appears to be an indifferent and at times contemptuous attitude; this may also influence parents toward reluctance to have dealings with doctors.

The belief system of Vallecañeses regarding health and disease is a compound of traditional or "folk" theories and hazy knowledge of modern medicine. The classifying of many substances as "hot" or "cold" and the prohibitions against mixing hot and cold things are still widespread, even among many more educated persons. Hot and cold, as throughout much of Latin America, are applied to foods and nonfoods, and a person's sickness may well be diagnosed as due to the wrong combination of these substances. If a woman has roasted coffee (hot) and immediately goes to bathe in the stream (cold) or passes under a type of tree which may be cold, she will get a spasm and may later "swell up."

There is also widespread belief in the efficacy of native herbs, and nearly every mother reported giving them to her babies when they were a few days old, in the form of "teas." They are considered especially efficacious for stomach ailments although the doctor says most of them do more harm than good. But, as we have seen, a mother does not usually rush her child to the doctor.

. . . [My child] started walking very late. I don't know the reason because I never took him to the doctor. I only treated him with home remedies.

I bought a medicine from a Spiritist that cost me twenty-five cents but that did not cure him. I also would rub his legs and knees with cooking oil mixed with worms but that didn't cure him either. Finally with crabs from the sea—I would open them alive and rub the insides on his legs and this cured him. This remedy was given to me by my mother-in-law.

Although the people do not usually reject modern medical care, the doctor often has difficulty getting their cooperation. They have a predilection for any kind of injection. Often when they have been given free pills or capsules they will throw them away and go to Don Santo, the town druggist, for *una inyección*, which costs a few dollars. So strong is this feeling that they often report cathartic relief almost before the needle is withdrawn.

Unless they become violent, mentally retarded or mentally ill persons usually are kept in the family and community, although sometimes efforts may be made to place them in government institutions. Several persons considered *loco* are not socially rejected, though they are often objects of contempt. Individuals with physical deformities are ignored or ridiculed. Two young men, one a catatonic and one a spastic, are frequently joked about, sometimes in their presence.

The lower-class Vallecañese is dimly aware of the germ theory of disease and sometimes speaks of *micróbios*, but there is little either in his living conditions or his education to implement this uncertain knowledge. Thus one Vallecañese was ill for the first time in his life and had to go to a "real" doctor and spend much money on his sickness. He described it as a very bad cold. He said there was a coconut lying on the path which no one seemed to want; he took it, put some bicarbonate of soda in it, and drank the milk. Next day he awoke with his malady.

About 18 percent of all conceptions of Vallecañese mothers ended as stillbirths, abortions, and children who died of a variety of causes before two years. Several mothers who conceived ten or more times reported half their offspring dead before the age of ten.[9]

Common causes of death of children, according to the mothers of the village, are: *pasmo hincho* (a loosely used general term, usually referring to a spasm or paralysis); *alferecía* (symptoms are fits or con-

9. No comparable statistics for the island are available, but in 1950 the death rate for infants under one year from all causes was 68.3 per 1,000 live births. The death rate is nearly one-half of what it was in 1938 and the stillbirth rate is cut about one-third. (*Anuario Estadístico* 1950-51: 43, 44, Tables 22, 23).

vulsions; cause may be meningitis, epilepsy, or several other diseases); *sarampión* or colloquially *"sarango"* (measles); *hidropesía* (dropsy); *tifus* (typhus); *estreñimiento* (constipation); *hinchado irritación* (general term used to cover effects of cardiac diseases and cirrhosis of the liver); *raquitismo* (rickets); *fatiga* (bronchial asthma, which seems to the people like extreme "fatigue"); and *tos ferina* (whooping cough). However, the largest number of reported deaths of children, excluding accidents like falling or drowning, was from unknown causes, or if a doctor attended he did not inform the parents.

The town doctor did not know the meaning of several other terms so they are not included here, except for *mososuelo*, which was frequently alluded to by parents. It most often occurs to children, the people say. In some way the child is frightened, perhaps by some sudden noise like a clap of thunder or someone screaming close at hand. The child then swells up, "turns black," and dies within a day or two.[10] The doctor did not know anything about such folk beliefs. He is convinced the people are so ignorant that he pays scant attention to what they say nor does he tell them what the child's diagnosis is, since "this will just upset them." Even when a child dies in the hospital the parents rarely learn the true cause of death. Thus their traditional ignorance is perpetuated.

Another traditional belief, still widely held, is *mal de ojo* (evil eye), a power which is supposed to come to certain people whether or not they are aware of it. When they see someone, usually a child, whom they admire or envy, a look from their eye causes the child to become frightfully ill or die. One woman reported that two of her three dead children were stricken with the evil eye. One, a little boy, "threw up bile from his mouth and died." The other, a girl, "was nice and fat and pretty, but she suddenly got sick because someone with the evil eye envied her beauty, and people would no longer say 'Dios te bendiga' [May God bless you] when they saw her. But she had her 'santiguo' [rubbing or signs, sometimes accompanied by prayer] by a woman who could do this, and she did not die, but she is skinny and sick now,

10. This belief is as close as our investigations came to unearthing the kind of folk phenomenon known in Guatemala and elsewhere in Latin America as *susto* or *espanto* and which Gillin (1948: 387-400), who has studied the symptomatology and therapy closely, has termed magical fright or soul loss. It should be explained, however, that *susto* and *espanto* in Valle Caña are used generally to describe fright from most causes, the second word differing from the first in terms of greater degree.

not her old self." The ethnologist himself was cautioned that his two-year-old daughter was "too fat, white, and pretty; somebody will put the evil eye on her." Evil eye is, of course, closely related to witchcraft, which is also believed, though perhaps not as widely. A conversation in which the field assistant participated was recorded by her as follows:

And then they stated talking about Don Abelardo, that he was dying and that everybody said it was because of a *brujo* (witch's brew) a mistress of his had given him to drink. It had been some time that things were running badly for him, his store was nearly gone, he had been thrown out of his job as *mayordomo*, and then came this sickness.

The neighbor and Mariana kept on talking about witchcraft and they said they believed it sometimes, like when this woman put into a drink three drops of her menstrual blood and gave it to a man who did not return her love, and this made him tubercular, and he died. You can blind a person, they went on, if you take a big frog and you sew his eyes shut and you keep him in a can and say a prayer for several days. They told how a brother of Felipa's was bewitched by Pepita's mother because he once stole some meat from her. She turned him into a frog and he kept swelling up and would make noises like a frog until he finally died, croaking. "That Doña Anita [Pepita's mother] is a bad woman; she has the power to bewitch and some day she is going to pay off everyone [who has wronged her]." They said that if you put a frog on your stomach, it is good for *fatiga*. They also know that witches use scorpions, worms, and lizards. For this kind of sickness, they said, a doctor can do nothing. The neighbor commented that one of her sons who had been bewitched had been saved by a doctor in town who had been a Spiritist, also. He prescribed some Spiritist concoction to be put in an enema and some leaves to be placed on the child's stomach. He was cured and recovered quickly.

Here one may note many overlappings and mixtures between science, magic, and religion. I shall return later in this chapter to religion and one of its current varieties, Spiritism.

But in spite of all the folk beliefs about health and disease, the basic fact remains, as Manners (1950: VII/2) has put it, that "the health problems of the rural poor are frequently those of malnutrition—not enough of the right kinds of food." Many doctors and social workers have told the writer that they feel this is the point at which any real attempt to improve the health of rural Puerto Ricans must begin, since sickness not only occurs directly from sub-subsistence diets, but also, where the child is able to survive, a general lowering of constitutional resistance to disease takes place. A recent study (Seijo de Zayas 1955: 63) of Puerto Rican nutritional patterns and problems states:

In Puerto Rico poor nutrition is one of the reasons behind an infant mortality rate of 67 per 1,000 live births (1951) and a maternal mortality rate of 22 per 10,000 live births (1950-1951). Arising from serious deficiencies in the consumption of protective foods, it is also a factor in much of the morbidity on the island, including a high tuberculosis rate and a high rate of anemia among mothers and children. That it lurks, too, among those who are not included in the mortality and morbidity statistics can be assumed from the prevalence of conditions which are often symptomatic of poor nutrition—small stature, poor teeth, cheilosis or cracks around the mouth, toad skin, bleeding gums, poor visual adaptation to darkness, and low physical resistance. Height-and-weight studies have shown that Puerto Rican children are about two years behind children on the mainland in physical development.

According to this same study, several agencies are making a cooperative attack on nutritional deficiencies throughout the island, with some positive results.

Religion

In a formal sense, religion plays a minor role in the lives of the majority of Vallecañeses. Broadly speaking, theirs is a feeling of casualness coupled with tolerance for all sorts of deviations, even the embracing of other than the mother religion. A frequent comment in a religious discussion is "all religions are good." Catholicism seems to assert itself for most people of the lower class as a set of traditional beliefs and ceremonies rather than as an emotionally felt creed.[11] Thus it is not unusual for families to be mixed in their religious membership (Table 1).

Most children who go to church in the lower class attend the Evangelical church, even though their parents often report themselves as Catholic. As one mother said, "If there had been a Catholic church, I probably would have preferred it. But since it is far, I send her to this one; and my husband, who is also Catholic, doesn't seem to mind."

11. This is not to say that Vallecañeses are irreligious or even non-religious. Their belief system and vocabulary are heavy with the influence of the traditional religion. They are simply not formally observant of its dogma or proscriptions and not fanatical in spreading its gospel or in administering it to themselves.

TABLE 1

Religious Composition of the Families of Valle Caña
(as reported by themselves)

Catholic	47
Evangelical	22
Catholic, Evangelical	22
Catholic, Evangelical, Spiritist [a]	3
Catholic, Spiritist	11
Catholic, "Nothing" [b]	1
Evangelical, Spiritist	3
Evangelical, "Nothing"	2
Spiritist	2
Total Cases	113

a. Spiritist is used here when reported as a religion.

b. "Nothing" means one or more members of the family were reported as not having any religion.

Other mothers have said of their child's religious life: "The church is nearby, she should have some kind of religion, it might as well be *Evangelismo*"; or "Let him go there now. Later if he likes he can go to Catholic church." In addition to its proximity, adults give such reasons as these for switching to the Evangelical church:

I'm apt to keep out of trouble because I'm not supposed to drink or gamble.

The Evangelicos are more serious people.

One religion is as good as another, I suppose.

They have more faith in God and more goodness.

That church came to the people; they're not uppity like the town Catholics.

The minister visits us often; we never see the priest even pass our house.

A person may oscillate between church affiliations. A Vallecañese bachelor had been a Catholic, then an atheist, and then at 27 turned to Evangelism because he "liked the gospel" and "thought they would be serious people." Now he claims to belong to the Catholic church again, "although I'm basically an atheist and go to all churches." He said he reversed his entrance into the Evangelical church because they were constantly watching him and meddling in his affairs and "I don't care for nosey people."

Nearly every lower-class family has been visited by the minister, who considers this an important function, but none has seen the priest in many years. When asked whether they ever received church aid, not a single family in the village answered affirmatively. Some were very bitter: "We have to help them but they never give us anything"; "The priest comes around only when he wants some money or wants you to sign a petition for the church." Some literate adults say the best thing about the Evangelical church is that it encourages one to read the Bible, whereas the Catholic church forbids this. At one sermon at the Catholic church in Agua Lluvia, I heard the priest say angrily, "For the layman to read the Bible is like a child playing with a loaded gun. Sooner or later it goes off and kills the child. Reading the holy book is for holy men [priests] who are the only ones properly qualified to interpret God's word."

Spiritism, or Spiritualism, as some writers translate *Esperitismo,* is also believed in, tolerated, laughed at, and feared. So far it has not swept Valle Caña as it is reported to have done in many other places on the island (Siegel 1947). However, we found many men and women who believed in some aspect of Spiritism and used the services of a medium for curing or prognostications but did not report themselves as adherents when asked. One couple set themselves up as mediums and held regular sessions in their house.

Petrita was one of the oldest Spiritists in the village. When she was much younger she had been very sick. "Almost half-crazy," she said. She had been treated by many medical doctors with no cure, until she decided about ten years ago to take up Spiritism and since then she has been well, being cured through her belief and curing herself through seances. Her husband remained an unbeliever until less than two years ago but he "got sick and had many temptations to commit evil." But she took him to a Spiritist and he was cured. Since then he has been taking an active part in sessions which she leads.

The upper class and a few others think they are *un poco loco* (a little crazy) but they are not ostracized and have sizable attendances at their seances. Other mediums in nearby localities, some with island-wide reputations, are consulted for every variation of physical or mental illness, witchcraft, evil eye, advice, or consolation.

Some mothers prefer taking sick children to a medium rather than to a doctor. The cult may be believed in wholly or partially, as a religion in itself or as a supplement to existent Catholic or Protestant beliefs. Neither the priest nor the minister approves of the movement, but neither has suggested combatting it. Significantly, the wife of the minister, herself a devout Protestant, is a partial believer in Spiritism and says she had a terrible sickness which no one but a medium could cure. A likely hypothesis is that the Spiritist medium is the successor to the traditional *curandero* but compounds curing with the religion and counsel of priest and minister and the forecasting of the fortune-teller. Since he can siphon off so many anxieties at the same time, he becomes a much-desired person for many Puerto Ricans. To some extent Spiritism may serve the same function as witchcraft for the Navaho Indians (Kluckhohn 1944b) since Doña Petrita was a social misfit in the village before Spiritism and still is.

At both Catholic and Protestant services the most frequent church-goers, as in most Western societies, are women and children. The priest estimated less than 1 percent of the total attendance came from the village, though this may be exaggerated since he takes a "hopeless" view of the *jíbaros*. Few male adults go to either church, though pro-portionately more to the Evangelical, since it is the only local church. According to my informal count, children were less numerous than adults at the Catholic church, more numerous in the Evangelical. The priest and minister both feel attendance is extremely important but say there are too many outside attractions and the people are too indiffer-ent, though they also feel that if there were more men of the cloth available they could reach more people. The minister, more than the priest, is alarmed at the sinful lure of the little bars in Valle Caña, not to mention the evils of the city, and seldom misses an opportunity to sermonize against the jukeboxes, "those things that make the Devil's music." His preaching is usually done in competition with the blare and rhythm of the vicinal *velloneras* (coin-users).

Despite his casual religious values, the adult Vallecañese rarely takes unnecessary risks with his possible post-mortem fate. At a *velorio*, a singing wake held annually for seven years after a loved one's death, two men who were with me spent the evening fervently crossing themselves. We had earlier passed many hours in a local *cafetín*, each of them outdoing the other to claim how nonreligious he was. When I questioned them on this apparent contradiction as we were walking home, they said, again crossing themselves and kissing their thumbnails, as Vallecañeses do, "Well, you can't tell, something might happen; why take chances?"

In the next chapter we conclude our broad sketch of the cultural and social aspects of the Vallecañese way of life.

CHAPTER 3

Culture and Society in Valle Caña—II

Introduction

THE preceding account introduced the reader to the village of
Valle Caña, describing the natural setting of the community.
There followed an analysis of the composition of the community's
population, the orbit of geographic mobility, and the living conditions
of its people as social and environmental context for the discussion of
its culture. We have shown that while race does not appear to be an
important factor in child training the society as a whole is racially
conscious. The ways in which the people view and treat health and
disease have been discussed, and the chapter ended with a description
of the religious composition and beliefs of Vallecañeses.

In the present chapter the descriptive analysis of the culture and
social structure is concluded. Here we discuss the economic and social
relationships of the village and the division of the people into stratified
social classes. Briefly we scan the systems of kinship by virtue of birth
and by ritual after birth. We glance briefly also at the political life of
the community and its authority and legal structure, and we visit its
schools so as to see the modes of formal education. The chapter concludes with a discussion of the channeling of sexual behavior and forms
of courtship in the village society.

Economics and Livelihood

The range of reported annual income is from zero (unemployed,
too old to work, ineligible for public assistance) to the $12,000 re-

ported by two of the largest landowners. The average yearly income is $898, but 71 percent of the families make $800 or less and of this proportion the average income is $431.[1] Three pairs of old and abandoned parents receive no income, obtaining a bit of food and cast-off clothing here and there as their sole sustenance. Wives contribute a little to family income in 15 percent of the families and are the only breadwinners in 2 percent. Sons, daughters, and other adults contribute small amounts to the upkeep of 35 percent, and 11 percent are supported entirely by sons, daughters, or the old age pension of $7.50 monthly.

Since most commodities have to be imported and sold for higher prices than in the States, it is a constant source of wonderment to the outsider how these families manage to survive. Some of their comments provide an insight into the dynamics of the economic system:

We balance our budget by buying on credit—and we're always in debt.

My husband deserted me. He lives with a woman in the States but he sends me five dollars a month and that helps.

When my bachelor brother works in the cane, he gives me five dollars a week.

I cook for my neighbor and she gives me my meals in return.

Marina's old husband was a caneworker all his life. Now he's going blind and they won't hire him. Of course, they're making *cañita* (illegal rum)—either they risk that or starve. They give a bit to the policeman so he won't denounce them.

My daughter sends me food. When she forgets? I do without.

When there is a little money we always play the lottery. Why not? At least there *is* a chance to win something. If not, we have so little that the bit we spend for it is not missed.

As usually happens when information on income is sought anywhere, Vallecañeses tended to reckon their income downward and expenditures upward. However, I checked income for caneworkers by finding the average caneworker's wage rate during the preceding year and obtaining an estimate of the time a given family head worked during the last season. There was no ready check for landowners or storekeepers. One family who owned some cane land and a small business refused any figures at all, fearing, as others probably did, that I

1. National mean income happens also to be $898, and the median is $518, which compares with $3520 and $3000 for the United States (Federal Reserve Bulletin 1951: 920, Table 1). For a comprehensive discussion see Perloff (1950), especially Chapter II.

represented the government and would report their income to the Collector of Internal Revenue. A landowner whose holdings admittedly ran to at least the legal limit of 500 *cuerdas* (one *cuerda* equals 0.9712 acre), gave his income as $12,000, which seems unreasonably low in the face of much contrary evidence. His expenses were correspondingly unreliable. He reported giving the church $1200 yearly, but the priest complained that he is an irreligious man who does not contribute his rightful share. As with considerations of time, the *mañana* outlook precludes any kind of estimate for money over a long term or even relatively short periods.

The two highest items of expense are food and clothing, in that order. I was amazed to discover a family who reported about $400 annual income saying they spent $10 weekly for food. The storeowner gave us the clue: "Yes, they spend that much—during the *zafra*. When it is over, I give them two or three dollars a week credit during the dead season. Sometimes they pay it back. Sometimes not." As another storekeeper said, "If I don't extend credit, they won't buy anything from my store. I have to write off bad debts every year, but what can I do? It's either credit or go out of business. And sometimes it's both."

About 90 percent of Vallecañeses derive their livelihood directly or indirectly from cane. More than 62 percent of all working male family heads are employed in cane in the present or were in the recent past. Landowners derive their principal revenue from the sugar crop, as do the store owners via the workers. Many of the older lower-class men were literally born to the job and will keep working at the long green stalks until they are too old to swing a machete or are themselves harvested by the scythe of death. Carmelo, 67, has worked on the same *finca* (farm) for the same family for fifty-five years and claims he never missed a day. He was badly gored by an ox while I was in Valle Caña. He was brought home, but the next day (a Sunday) he went out to work over-time free for Don Pedro, whom he considers too poor to pay him (see next section). He could go to the municipal hospital for treatment but is afraid to lose a minute's work. "My work is my obligation," he says.

There are a few artisans whom only the middle class or upper class can afford to employ. They usually combine the skills of carpenter, brickmason, stonemason, painter, and so on, and often will work in the cane during the *zafra* as well. Most women are housewives, although a few take in some kind of sewing work contracted through small *factorías* on the island—gloves, slippers, trousers, etc.—on which they do a few or several operations. Generally, they must continue to fulfill their roles as housewives and mothers. A few girls and women work as domestics for middle- and upper-class families at $10 to $15 a month with their board and sometimes lodging. A few veterans of both World Wars receive pensions of some kind and do not work at all. There is one professional beggar who, the people say, has some land but is too lazy to work it. There are three school teachers (all the others live in town), the principal, and five storeowners who sell groceries, confections, notions, and hard and soft drinks.

There is one occupation which seems to be "caste" as well as class-determined. When an outhouse is no longer usable, it is moved ordinarily, and some earth thrown into the old location. Sometimes, especially in El Camino, the old outhouses have used up available space and the excavations must be cleaned and reused. No one in Valle Caña would do this work. Only two men who lived in Agua Lluvia would do it and then only after midnight when the village slept, "so that no one would complain about the odor" and especially that no one would see them.

Actually, manual labor of any kind is not looked upon as an honorable occupation by any class, including the lower which performs most of it. No self-respecting middle- or upper-class person will perform manual effort which might be done by a servant or hired hand. In the United States work helps to enhance one's status (Du Bois 1955); in Valle Caña it not only does not enhance status, but it may even devaluate it, in keeping with the Spanish tradition.

Social Class

While there are three social classes,[2] the bulk of the people belong to the lower class. This includes all caneworkers, *mayordomos*, and others who work for a living with their hands. The middle class is composed of the teachers, some storeowners and the small landowners. The three largest landowners (all related) and the school principal (also a landowner) comprise the upper class. Two storeowners who

---

2. Class was determined on the basis of observing behavior, occupation, income, house type, and other status determinants. As I saw it, people acted as though there were three classes.

come from the lower class are still part of it, two are members of the middle class but associate in a limited way with the lower class, and one comes from the lower class but having social ambitions tries to be accepted by the middle class.

Class membership is determined primarily by income, occupation, house type, etc., but only to a negligible degree by one's forebears. Anyone who can manage to get a high income eventually may become part of the middle or upper class. The wealthiest man in the *barrio* is so highly respected and feared that he is in a somewhat special category. All classes, including other members of the upper class, show him deference. Yet people say that Don Pablo once had only a tiny farm, hit it lucky on the lottery, parlayed his winnings, and thus began his career, buying up all the choice bottomland he could get. They also say they do not resent his riches because he is not too uppity to talk with *los pobres* (the poor).

As in all stratified societies, social class functions in Valle Caña as a set of reciprocating responsibilities and expectations. Upper-class people are expected to be "serious" and use conduct deserving of the respect of the subordinate groups. They are never expected to perform manual labor, but they are expected to consume conspicuously as befits their wealth and status. In reciprocation, the upper-class person is expected to treat his inferiors with a degree of respect, to exercise his authority, though not harshly, and to provide as much work as possible for them. Payment for work is of much importance, of course, but paternalistic employers are desired and if, in addition, they are circumspect in their behavior, are considered ideal people to work for.

Lower-class behavior is founded on three virtues: respect, humility, service. These are expected and usually characterize the behavior of the lower-class individual in his relations with the superordinate classes. He is supposed to behave with somewhat more abandon, say, on festive occasions, but this is only for intraclass conduct. The terms of respect, Don and Doña, are reserved within each class for those of superior age, but a lower-class person calls everyone of the upper classes, even his age-grade inferiors, by these titles. The "good" lower-class man is expected, in addition, to curb and limit his family's behavior in its relations with class superiors. Man, woman, and child are expected always to be at the service of the upper class, and while there is usually some type of recompense, however little, for most work, it is not unusual for lower-class persons to perform services free for middle- and upper-class members, because this is their *trabajo de compromiso* (work of obligation).

Lower-class men, especially older ones, commonly use this phrase, but even some of the younger generation seem to have fallen heir to this feudal service ethic. A striking example: One Sunday most of the husbands could not be found for interviewing. Not one was at home and we went through Valle Caña searching for them. We finally found them on the canefields of Don Pedro, a middle-class landowner who often made his contempt of the lower-class men emphatic to us and to them. He felt they were "no-good, spendthrift, shiftless, not very bright" and "would allow themselves to be worked for anything." Several of the men explained to us that they were helping Don Pedro since he was a poor man (he has fairly large holdings and his son had just built one of the best houses in the *barrio*) and could not afford to pay for Sunday work. He was their neighbor, they said, and further-more, since he was spending thousands of dollars on cortisone treat-ments for his arthritis, how could he pay them? Don Pedro's three strapping sons stood around and watched. Later we asked one husband we knew why he was not there. "In the past I have worked for him as my obligation many times. But for some reason he was angry with me last year and now I'm afraid to bother him—since otherwise I would have been working, too." It should be clear that in addition to their feudal heritage, the power of the landowner to hire or fire them is a realistic reinforcement of *trabajo de compromiso*. Tradition and reality support current practice.

Mintz (1951:IV/2,3) gives four reasons for characterizing the rural caneworkers in his southern coastal community as a "rural proletariat." They are: (1) landless and essentially propertyless; (2) wage-earners, not paid in kind; (3) predominantly store-buying and not self-sustain-ing; (4) "prevailingly employed by corporate entities rather than working for themselves or for an owner-employer with whom they might maintain continuous face-to-face relationships." The Valle-cañeses meet the first three requirements generally and in a basic sense the worker who lives on the owner's land (*agregado*) is not very dif-ferent from the landless laborer (*jornalero*). And yet there is a basic difference between the two villages, it seems to me, for while Mintz' workers feel little obligation to landlord or corporation, the Vallecañeses, as we have seen, still retain feudal ties with their employers, except for absentee landowners, of which there are two.

The difference here is undoubtedly due to the fact that most cane lands in Valle Caña are in the hands of individual, local owners, while the lands of Cañamelar are mostly tied directly into financial and absentee combines (a situation that has existed for a relatively long time, at least since the American occupation). There are functions in the quasi-feudal relationship which still operate for the worker, however. Since the landlords in Valle Caña are also in many instances politicians or friends of politicians, it is important to stay in their good graces. Then in the event of trouble with the law or getting a "government" job, like janitor in the school, the worker may seek the help of his patron, *con respeto*, and often he may be rewarded. Noblesse oblige.

The middle-class member is expected to show respect for the upper class but rarely associates with that class or the lower class. He has no ethic of service but pays even for small jobs, in money or goods. He is very anxious to please the upper class. Middle-class persons use respect titles when addressing upper-class persons, but occasionally use them for respected older men and women of the lower class. In turn they are paid the same kind of deference and respect shown to the upper class, though with a lesser degree of formal emphasis. Vallecañese class patterns are similar to those in other Puerto Rican communities (*ibid.*; Wolf 1951) and somewhat like those elsewhere in Latin America (Gillin 1949).

From birth the child is inculcated with the expectations and duties of his parents' class. The lower-class child is taught to show respect, deference, and humility before middle- and upper-class adults and children and is expected to perform all kinds of services, with or without fee, at the beck and call of any superordinate individual. This is especially the case in sharecropper-landlord relations, where the former's children are expected to do almost anything required by the landlord and often to perform services that will anticipate his desires. As with elders, the lower-class child may be called upon by a socially superior child of his age or younger for small services like running errands. The teaching of his class functions is an important aspect of the socialization of the Vallecañese child.

Kinship and Ritual Kinship

The kinship system is bilateral, with relationships reckoned collaterally as well as lineally, though hardly ever further back than two or three generations. Inheritance is normally through the male line, though the new legal codes give generally equal inheritance rights to females. Residence is nearly always neolocal, though several cases of matrilocality and a few of patrilocality were noted. Family names may be described as matro-patronymic, the individual retaining the surname of both parents in the ancient Spanish manner. A man, therefore, might be called Juan Fernández Ramírez, the first surname being his father's and usually the one by which he is best known. A married woman assumes her husband's name in addition to her full matri-patri title, thus: Señora Juana Fernández Ramírez de Fulano, the latter surname being her husband's, the first her father's, and the second her mother's (which usually is omitted after marriage). The customary emphasis on the extended family is partially disintegrating under pressures of culture change, although relatives still play some role, often an important one, in the socialization of the child (as we saw earlier, for example, in the case of *hijos de crianza*).

Compadrazgo "may be described as the system of social relationships growing out of the religious and ceremonial sponsorship of a child by its godparent or godparents" (Mintz 1951:VI/52).[3] But with the secularization of a formerly religious function, the increasing competition for available jobs within the lower class, and the precariousness of economic support, the emphasis on the institution, as Mintz has so clearly shown, has shifted from the godparent-godchild relationship to the godparent-parent or coparent relationship. Originally designed to provide a sponsor and economic guarantor of the religious education of the child as required by Catholic practice, these obligations have been weakened in Valle Caña although in a formal sense godparents are still ritualized for children. The act of baptism itself is still widely practiced, although some children are baptized *"de agua"* (originally used for sick or dying babies) at home without benefit of clergy,

---

3. For a historical and cross-cultural functional analysis, see Mintz and Wolf (1950). For an excellent analysis of the modification of the functions of this institution in a sugar cane community in Puerto Rico, see Mintz (1951:VI/52-80).

rather than at the church at Agua Lluvia, since there is a two-dollar fee and the distance is not convenient.

Several Vallecañeses did not know their godparents, because the latter moved away while they were still very young. When the godparent is present, however, usually he will give the child an occasional gift, will be affectionate with him, and will be sought by child or parent for advice. However, this is now of secondary importance to the *compadre* (coparent) relationship and, as in the case of Mintz's Cañamelar and other communities, *compadre* relationships may be set up between individuals for friendship, mutual respect, and economic advantage by a simple ceremony of declaration, *compadres de voluntad* (voluntary coparents), without a baptismal ceremony and with no children involved. There are still attempts to secure for children *padrinos* (godparents) who are advantageously situated on the social scale, but more frequently, and especially in the case of voluntary coparents, the *compadre* or *padrino* is chosen from within one's class. Colloquially, *compadre* is shortened to *compai* and *comadre* to *comai*, just as father becomes *pai* and mother *mai*.

Some Vallecañese children may yet find in their godparents an added, though not always dependable, source of security, but our impression is that the institution is somewhat debilitated in this community, and children, like their parents, are increasingly being thrown upon their own resources. However, to some extent it still obtains that "By making more interdependent and secure the adults in the social environment, *compadrazgo* gives to the child a firmer, more organized world. In a sense, *compadrazgo* constitutes a sort of age-grade grouping which lends social strength to the godchildren but in which they cannot participate" (Mintz 1951:VI/69).

It is interesting to note that aboriginally the Carib and the Arawak Indians often sought a friend to stand in a godparent relationship to a child at its naming ceremony and that to show friendship they would exchange names or presents. Hospitality was demonstrated by feasts and lending village women for sexual intercourse (Rouse 1948a, 1948b). While it seems apparent (Mintz and Wolf 1950) that *compadrazgo* was a European import, such a set of practices would find fertile soil among these Indians.

Political Structure

The Popular Democratic Party (PPD) controls the insular government and nearly all municipalities in Puerto Rico. Valle Caña's Don Pablo is titular head of the PPD and runs the government of the *municipio* with almost unquestioned control. He had the former mayor of Agua Lluvia, who had been elected with his original support, deposed because the latter insisted on certain independent courses of action, and he then had the present mayor named. The incumbent shows open deference for Don Pablo. Speaking at the school Christmas party, he told the people that he owed all to Don Pablo, Don Pablo never took a breath without thinking of the people's welfare, and therefore they should be ever grateful for his goodness. The new mayor deposed the doctor at the municipal hospital because, according to the latter, he was irked at the doctor's refusal to accept political favorites as public patients and wanted to set up a part-time private practice to supplement his moderate income.

Almost no action involving government or law is taken up by anyone in Valle Caña without the prior consent of the party through Don Pablo or his lieutenant, Don Arturo. The Socialist, Nationalist, and Republican Parties are dead or inactive. The Independentistas have an occasional meeting in Agua Lluvia. Around election time they send a sound truck to the *barrios*, playing music, calling Muñoz Marin (the governor) a dictator and his organization "the party of colonial slavery," and asking the people to vote their ticket. Vallecañeses enjoy the music but pay scant attention to the speeches, except to laugh at clever parodies of some local figure, usually Don Arturo. Three men in Valle Caña call themselves Independentistas. Two are old residents who are respected and left alone. The other, a middle-aged man, is something of a political scapegoat, even though he was originally a Popular who changed his mind. I was warned that he was a dangerous character. Independentista and Communista are used as interchangeable labels for him. Actually he is suffering from a bad heart, is socially and politically inactive, and wants only to be left alone. In view of their broad liberal approach to religion, Vallecañeses' intolerance of political heterodoxy is not easily comprehended.

Political deviance is rare. The middle class inveighs against the government for its taxes but most vote the party ticket. The lower class is almost without exception Popular; all vote the ticket when the party calls on them. Almost no one in the lower class I spoke with had fully read the new Puerto Rican constitution, but on the day of the 1952 referendum they turned out nearly 100 percent strong and under the watchful eyes of Don Pablo, Don Arturo, and others, voted en bloc for the constitution.

Doña Justa's son was planning to vote for the constitution, since it 'was made by the big ones.' He talked of the symbol for voting on the constitution, saying 'the sun represents the big government that shines over all of us—and the cloud beneath the sun—a black cloud—could hide all things that should not be shown to the public.' Then he said that every election year, when politicking begins, they always promise to fix their 'road' (a mountain path) and put up a bridge over the creek. Four years ago Don Pablo came up La Hoja and made a speech at this very house, saying that he would work on the bridge, even with his own hands. But the nearest they got to building a bridge was taking the measurements—the bridge has never been built. 'This year,' Doña Justa's son said, 'They have already taken the measurements again.'

Vallecañeses accept party rule as a basic fact of life and often speak of Don Pablo in terms highly suggestive of a father-child relationship: "He is good to us." "He is like a father to us." "He takes care of us." "He protects us." Some are disappointed when political promises, freely made before each election, seldom materialize, but their disappointment is expressed only in talking with other lower-class persons and they continue to vote for and support the party. Certainly it is true that the party has given them an increased stake in the government. Increased social services, especially medical care, almost universal suffrage for both sexes, improved educational facilities, and the appeal for their support give the lower class a feeling of new importance, however minor, in Puerto Rico's government. The writer believes that unless another political group offers a comparably comprehensive program and the capacity to carry it out, the people, whatever the dynamics of their motivations, will continue to support the party in power.

Few jobs of a governmental or quasi-governmental nature, no matter how lowly, are simply given to an individual. They are turned over to the local political leader and he dispenses them, even to a school janitor or cook, only after a political acid test. If the applicant is known to have any kind of animosity toward the party he will not be considered for the job. If while his application is pending he is heard to utter an "anti-government" comment (a broadly interpreted concept), not only will he not get the job nor any other government employment, but sometimes he will even be blacklisted by Popular private employers.

If one has a relative or friend in government or knows someone who does, it is helpful, almost indispensable, in getting these positions. If one has publicly supported and defended the party or performed some service for a party functionary, his chances are likewise increased. Nepotism, beginning with one's family and extending out to *compadres* and friends, is the rule. Even in nonskilled jobs like labor in the cane fields, kinship, friendship, and political service are important qualifications.

Police and Protection

The local policeman, Antonio, who is also supposed to service adjacent *barrios,* spends most of his time in Valle Caña but little on active duty because he feels the people are "mostly good and don't fight too much." Yet in the past year he had made more than eighty arrests, mostly for "robbery, property damage, fights and noisy jukeboxes." (If a jukebox is too loud, it is the user, not the owner of the *cafetín,* who may be apprehended.) Autos speed by his house and through the school zone but he says he is powerless to stop them because when he tried in the past he was reprimanded by his superiors. He comes around to elections and other community activities, and his presence is usually sufficient to stop any disorder before it occurs.

Antonio is considered, and considers himself, of the middle class; he shows much respect and deference for the upper class but often contempt for the subordinate class. Sometimes he acts on the basis of personal motives as when he arrested a young man for carrying a *machete,* a frequent sight in any cane community; the man was imprisoned for seven months. He was the brother of a woman with whom, people said, Antonio had had a frustrating affair. In other ways, however, he has shown some inclination to get just treatment for lower-class individuals who merit his respect. Once he made a young man, who had been drunkenly threatening several people with razor blades (a cheap, common weapon), do penance by walking a long roundabout way back to his mountain home—thus acting as judge, jury, and enforcer. He will seldom go up La Hoja alone, never after dark, and openly admits it is dangerous. Yet my female assistant and I went freely through the area, unmolested. After we left Valle Caña we learned that three young men beat up Antonio one night.

Unless it is a very serious case he is sometimes quite annoyed when he must leave his home to attend to someone's troubles; he says his rule is that if it is not an emergency he puts it off until he can get around to it. He never arrested a person of the middle or upper class in the village nor had anyone ever lodged a complaint against a person of these groups. But when complaints are made by middle- and upper-class persons against a lower-class person he acts at once. All crimes committed while we were there were by lower-class individuals against others of the same class. Lower-class aggression, especially, always seems to be intrapunitive with respect to family and social class. This is understandable since these are the objects most easily attacked with impunity.[4]

The policeman complained that with the best of intentions he was extremely limited by politics, which reaches into every facet of public action. He claims he has even been made to suffer himself when he ventured to "denounce" middle- and upper-class persons.

Mintz (1951) and Siegel (1947) mention a predilection by rural Puerto Ricans for doing things illegally. Illegal activity was found to some extent in Valle Caña but it centered mostly around illegal slaughtering, which everyone participates in, and illegal rum, which is much less openly consumed than formerly because of heavy restrictions against offenders. The illegal lottery, mentioned by Mintz, Wolf, and others, seems to have been stamped out in Valle Caña. I feel that what happens here is not so much a preference for illegal activity as such, but simply an illustration of the attitude that where something can be done to one's advantage, one does it, illegal or not, especially where there is a strong need and tacit approval of the community. Furthermore, being less under the watchful eye of nearby landowners, there may be less need for the people of Cañamelar to act in conforming, i.e., legal, ways. This is vividly pointed out in the very high proportion of consensual marriage in Cañamelar as compared with Valle Caña (see "Types of Marriages" in the next chapter).

4. Something of a cross-cultural parallel is seen in the aggression patterns of the Skagit Indians of Puget Sound, also confronted with intense acculturation and disintegration of traditional family patterns (Collins 1952).

Formal Education

Forty-one percent of all Vallecañese adults report themselves as illiterate. An additional 20 percent who did not go beyond the third grade probably no longer read or write because their schooling lost effectiveness through disuse. Thus about 60 percent of the adult population is functionally illiterate. Perloff (1949:52-53) quotes an unpublished study by the Department of Education of the University of Puerto Rico:

Literacy of the population ten years of age and over had increased from 20.4 per cent in 1899 to 45 per cent in 1920 and 68.8 per cent in 1940. But the fact is that some 30 per cent of the population is still illiterate, as compared with 6 per cent in the United States as a whole for 1940. But the past forty years Puerto Rico has expanded its educational facilities many times more than has any state of the United States. Yet half the children of school age are not attending school; a third of the children leave school between the first and third grades; only 36 per cent of the population (ten years of age and over) has an education equivalent to four grades or better.

With the middle and upper class excluded, the proportion of illiteracy in the predominant lower class rises even higher. But even in the superordinate classes, only school teachers and the principal have gone beyond high school. None of the storekeepers has continued beyond grade school. One of the teachers has a bachelor's degree from the University. One of the large landowners went through high school; the other stopped at or before the ninth grade.

Some historical causes may be suggested: (1) Until recent times there was little lower-class need for literacy, since it did not provide any promise of social and economic mobility. (2) During Spanish rule the *hacendados* (landowners) ignored and even discouraged education of lower-class workers, slaves, and tenants. (3) Even free education is an added expense for the lower class, increasing with family size. (4) Until 1948 most courses were taught in English with English textbooks. The paralyzing effect on a Spanish-speaking people would tend quickly to force out the least motivated. (5) Large low-income families require extra labor and when children are needed at home they are required to leave school. Students of Puerto Rican education can easily think of other historico-cultural reasons (see, for example, Mellado 1949) .

But the educational level of the community is changing with the new generation. There is both an elementary and secondary unit, the latter equivalent to junior high school, though of lower caliber than the school in town. In the school year 1951-1952 the enrollment was 752, compared with 925 the year before.[5] The school partially serves, especially in the seventh to ninth grades, three other *barrios* or sub-*barrios* besides Valle Caña. The principal, Don Carlos, estimated that only about 5 percent of Vallecañese children of school age are not in school, but our informal check and his own subsequent data tend to throw the figure closer to 20 percent, as compared with a national average of one-half (see Perloff quote above). The sex ratio of pupils was almost equal, with girls having a slight edge.

Like many rural secondary units, there are agricultural and mechanical training for boys and home economics and "native handicrafts," largely revived from folk crafts which had fallen into disuse, for girls. Principal and teachers report these more popular with the children than strictly academic courses, and they receive strong parental support.

The school is a group of old buildings, some of corrugated zinc, some of concrete and wood. In most rooms there is a seat shortage and some pupils have to sit on the floor or window sills. Often there are not enough textbooks and they have to be shared. Many books are still in English because there are no Spanish texts available, though some are supposed to be in preparation. Like most buildings in the tropics the structures are quite open, and children in and out of the classrooms give vent to much talking and other loud activities, often causing the teachers to have to shout to be heard. There are many external distractions, among which is a loud jukebox at the nearby *tienda* (store), played from early morning onward and heard over nearly all the school.

The government provides an adequate and balanced free lunch, but many of the children throw away greens and other things they do not like, though this may be the only full meal they get all day. Leftovers cannot be given to the people, because of federal regulations, and are

5. The principal attributes the drop to some decentralization of elementary grades as new schools were added to surrounding *barrios*. But in preregistration for the first grade for the next year (1952-1953) there was also a large drop which the principal feels is due not only to decentralization but a declining birth rate. If the increasing utilization of sterilization and contraception during the past several years has any effect, the principal's assertion may be justified (see "Birth Control," next chapter).

fed to the huge experimental hogs, also federal property. The federal government supplies the implements used in the tool shop, but when discarded they may not be given to people who might use them but are burned or buried according to regulations.

During the year there are thirty-two insular and federal holidays. The principal estimates about six or seven more due to unforeseen developments, but my own count (including teacher meetings, rainy days, illness, fiestas etc.) put the figure at more than double that amount. The normal school year is about forty weeks, which many "holidays" reduce to about thirty-two weeks. Absences are frequent. On several different occasions when the writer gave tests to children in the fifth through ninth grades the absentee rate averaged more than 20 percent. According to teachers the most common causes are: rain, illness, keeping children home to work, and lack of shoes and clothes.

Teachers feel discipline is good, but a strong fault of children is excessive talking. In the old days teachers were expected and commissioned by parents to administer punishment "when needed," but they are now prohibited by law from using bodily discipline. They take "serious" cases to the principal, who is permitted to use corporal punishment if two witnesses are present. He says he only has to resort to this about once a month and prefers not to use it, although his predecessor had a reputation as a severe disciplinarian. The students now respect him, he says, and know he means business. Instead of physical punishment he frequently metes out labor chores around the school for offenders. He feels this is useful and makes the children respect him more than if he whipped them.

There are several celebrations and fiestas and much preparation precedes a holiday affair at school. The year's high point is the Christmas and Three Kings season with several days of class parties and a program for the whole community. Except for the Evangelical church, there is little public "cultural" activity in Valle Caña, and what there is centers mainly around the school: showing of educational movies, sports, parent-teacher meetings, public fiestas, voting during elections, etc.

Nearly all teachers interviewed (eight plus the school principal, of a total of fourteen) teach at least one subject they have been specially trained for. Five of the eight prefer to be doing something other than teaching (three want to be social workers, two office workers) because the pay would be better and the work more interesting, but most important, they find teaching in Valle Caña beset with such difficulties as: (1) lack of interest by pupil and parent, especially the latter; (2) lack of proper equipment in quality and quantity, from books to classrooms; (3) insufficient pay; and (4) heavy work loads and not enough time to visit parents and involve them in their children's activities. Our general impression, nevertheless, is that the teachers enjoy their jobs despite these obstacles.

Older informants tell stories of the iron discipline of former days. Common punishments included: beating with a stick, belt, or hands; ridiculing before the class; kneeling the child before the class; rapping on the head with knuckles or fists; instructing children to bring pins to school and stick them into the elbows of the child in front of them when he relaxed too much. One woman told me her son had been made deaf by a blow on the ear. Another reported her son had died of a blow on the head with a heavy school bell. But this was many years ago. Physical punishment is rarely administered now and parents often become indignant when teachers lay a hand on their child.

There is a general trend toward making the classroom more democratic. In many classes children are encouraged to elect class leaders, and when the teacher cannot be present the class is turned over to the student leader to train him and the class in democratic procedures.

Teachers in the elementary grades are women. An equal proportion of men and women teach in the secondary unit. Male and female teachers agree that while boys often make as good students as girls, they prefer to teach girls, who "are more controllable, more answerable to their parents." They complain that some of the older boys actually go out and drink beer during class hours. Older children are generally considered less "controllable" and the teachers say that many boys and girls do "bad things" like having trysts in the woods and behind buildings, and teaching "ugly words and things" to smaller children. In cases where an older boy or girl is involved in a love affair or gets married, the principal's policy is immediate expulsion, "because they set a bad example for the younger ones."

Most teachers feel "bad" behavior is due to a "bad" environment: poverty, drunkenness of the father, parental irresponsibility, lack of interest. The principal, however, believes "bad" children are the victims of deficient heredity ("crazy parents") and therefore are probably incorrigible.

While not always convinced of the true worth or rewards of education, most parents feel it is good to send one's children to school. If the child can manage through school to get a good job ("stay out of the cane," "be useful to us," "help us in our old age") the effort will be worthwhile. Some become discouraged and allow or insist that the child leave school and prepare himself for a traditional job as cane-worker or farm laborer, or in the case of the girl, a proper housewife. Many assume that if they send the child to school, learning will come automatically, with no help from them, and are disappointed when this does not occur. And there are parents who cannot discipline their older children at home and send them to school "so the teacher will dominate them." For the materialistic Vallecañese, education is not a good thing in itself, but only if it brings definite remuneration.

Some parents have responded to the calls of the local Parent-Teacher Association, but attendance is sporadic, usually occurring when an issue of immediate importance is taken up. The tendency is to let teachers and superordinate class persons take over the meetings. The relatively authoritarian atmosphere in the home and field carries over into the school situation, though not because the principal and teachers prefer it that way. Parents seem content to let persons of higher social rank make decisions and feel they can do best by carrying out such decisions if they approve of them or simply assuming a passive indifference if they do not. There are some exceptions, as when a parent will disagree with a teacher's handling of his child and will come to school to complain to the teacher or principal. But in public functions most disagreements are kept to oneself.

Sex and Courtship

Marriage is accepted by everyone as the natural state for male and female, but apparent avenues to sex experience and courtship are often dead ends. In El Camino there are fewer opportunities than on La Hoja, but as compared with Agua Lluvia either place offers few chances for the sexes to mix other than in conformance with traditional patterns.

Even in Valle Caña however, there are some possibilities. Both sexes attend the same school classes and many school functions, including some mixed sports. After school, teen-age youngsters of both sexes may gather at one of the local *cafetíns* and on rare occasions, like graduation week, play the jukebox and dance. Formerly there were occasional Saturday night dances at the same *cafetín*, always involving only lower-class boys and girls, the latter mostly servant girls. They are the only ones allowed to come to such an affair unchaperoned after dark and the only ones who actively seek out male company, even in this limited way. They were therefore popular with the boys, even a few middle-class boys. But after one dance two couples were observed embracing on the porch of a middle-class home and "denounced" to the policeman, who arrested the boys. After that no more dances were held.

The girl is considered immanently weak and unwary in protecting herself from male assault. Men believe women are endowed with inferior mental equipment and some speak of males having extra "senses" as compared with females. From the time he is small the boy is supposed to be impelled by *malicias*, "vices" or "bad habits" with the Vallecañese connotation of a craving to violate sexual taboos. The older generation believes boys are worse now than ever. One middle-aged woman says:

... [Our dances] when I was a girl used to be decent and respectable. Girls all came with older women, were checked, and left only with the women. No girl was ever allowed to go out alone with a boy. We had good times but we did not trust the boys at dances the way they do now. Now they have nothing but *malicias*. I like dances, you understand, but since it is such an opportunity for the boys to do things to the girls, it is just as well we do not have them often. It is better for the girls to be home, where they belong.

In the evenings all females of whatever age are confined to their homes while boys and men frequent the *cafetíns*, drink when they have money, listen to the jukebox or an occasional guitarist, or gather in conversational knots along the road to talk. Once in a while a boy and girl who are interested in each other will walk along the road, not touching. They walk from the beginning of the lighted area to its end and back again, in the middle of the road, in plain sight of everyone, speaking softly. After an hour or two they separate and each goes his way. Or later at night some servant girls and caneworkers' sons may sit along the sidewalk under the streetlight, holding hands or "playfully" jostling each other with nervous laughter. I cannot say whether these meetings end in sexual relations, but if the sly innuendos of the youths are true, some of them may. One such affair ended in one of the two consensual marriages discussed in the next chapter.

The complex of attitudes and practices concerning correct female behavior has been termed the "cult of virginity" by Siegel (1947) and this seems an apt description of the behavior of the Puerto Rican female and the expectations of her community. "Virginity" as a desideratum here refers not simply to the intactness of the hymen in a young woman, but rather to "how a virgin should behave." Physiological virginity is not nearly as important as the ability to behave, before and after marriage, like a chaste and reproachless female. However, there is one difference between our findings and Siegel's. He says:

The adherence to this moral idea varies for the different socioeconomic classes. The middle class, upper and lower, have maintained attitudes and practices that conform closely to the established code, while members of the low income group largely honor it in the breach. . . . The class distinction with respect to prenuptial and postnuptial sexual morality may be stated as follows: the middle classes believe in the validity and in the righteousness of the code, and their members, particularly the females, are expected to conform to it; the low income group also recognizes the validity of the code, but a great many of its members follow, in fact, quite different standards (1947: 149-150).

It is our observation that just the opposite situation obtains in Valle Caña, with the lower class being the closest adherent to the code. They are extremely prudish, in theory and practice, with regard to the insulation and protection of the female, apparently even more so than the middle class. The latter often attend functions in Agua Lluvia where the sexes mix freely, an unheard-of occurrence for lower-class families, where sex separation lines cross every area of life. The difference may well be in the types of communities, since Siegel studied a town. But the puritanism of the rural lower-class family of our village, provided we do not call consensual marriage a type of sexual license, seems as rigid as that practiced by the people who settled New England in the seventeenth century. There are exceptions to this as there were also among the colonial Puritans (Willison 1945). An example is the traditional celebration called *La Candelaria*, when the folk of Valle Caña build huge bonfires. As they run around the leaping flames, the night air rings with obscenities shouted in honor of the *La Virgen de la Candelaria:* "Long live the woman with the long legs," "Long live the woman with the big breasts," etc. The women and children indulge themselves as much or more than the men, a rare public instance of vicarious sexual release. The general set of prohibitions and proscriptions for the Vallecañese female are pretty much the same as obtain in Siegel's community and in those areas studied by Mintz (1951), Padilla (1951), and Wolf (1951).

If a boy is "serious" with a girl he visits her at her home. After he has done this a few times the community expects them to marry and condemns them if they do not. In the family of many children and *poco dinero* (little money), no strenuous objections are offered when their daughter runs off with a boy; they hope he will keep and take care of her. This elopement pattern usually presages the consensual marriage, as we shall see in the next chapter. However, most parents will try to prevent the marriage of their daughter to a boy without *responsibilidad*. The daughter of one woman, for example, was sent to the States because she had fallen in love with a "lazy boy with no responsibility." Even when a girl leaves home to work in town her parents try to keep strict vigilance over her activities and will authorize employers and others to do so. Pita, whose daughter worked in Agua Lluvia as a student nurse, was not opposed to her having a boy friend because "he seems serious [6] and I think he has good intentions." But she made the daughter bring the young man home to be "inspected."

Some mothers, bitter with their own loveless and burdensome marriages, prefer to maintain a hold on their daughters to prevent their suffering a like fate and because they have become somewhat dependent on them. Doña Justa, in her late seventies, had wanted Juana, her only daughter, to be with her always and was angry when the girl defied her and married at eighteen.

In spite of obstacles, not all Vallecañese courtships are trysts in the night that end in consensual marriage. There must have been a great deal of meditation and premeditation before most couples decided to live together, since the average length of courtship is 1.7 years. The range is from three weeks to twelve years, and many couples have known each other since childhood. It is inevitable, furthermore, that

---

6. *Serioso* is mentioned frequently by the people to indicate a non-frivolous, and therefore dependable, approach to life. While a sense of humor is greatly appreciated, the man or woman who maintains a "serious" mien, even a dour outlook, is respected by community, mate, and children.

in a small community, most boys and girls will select [7] their mate from among their own acquaintances. Before marriage forty-nine couples were neighbors or "lived in the same *barrio.*" Another thirteen were interested in each other from childhood though their actual courtships were short. Three women married their cousins. The remainder met under circumstances such as these:

We met at a dance.
When I was married the first time, he used to visit the house often.
He visited Valle Caña and fell in love with me.
He was a cattle dealer and my family had a little store and he fell in love with me.
I met him at a party.
We worked together in a tobacco factory.
I met him at a *fiesta*—he flirted with me.
He used to work near my house, saw me, and fell in love with me.
We met at a *velorio.*
We were traveling in a *público* and that's how we met.

A one-sided approach to courtship is seen in these remarks. It is nearly always the man, they say, who falls in love with the woman, rarely vice-versa. Love on the part of the woman is seldom mentioned by her as a reason for marriage. Some admit frankly they married to keep from working or to get away from their families. The phrase "making love" has the connotation of sexual action, not the romantic notion conjured up by the term in the United States.[8] Even apparently happily married women will say: "I really do not have love for men," by which they mean not affection as such but the desire for sexual relationships.

When asked what they might be doing had they not married, twenty simply said they did not know and seven more sighed with resignation "*Sabrá Dios*" (God knows). Thirty-two said they would be working: washing, ironing, in a factory, or "at home with mother." Of two middle-class women, one wants to be a bank clerk, the other

7. "Select" is used advisedly. Unlike many other kinds of familistic folk societies, Vallecañese marriages today are not usually negotiated by parents or brokers, with or without the consent of the principals. The young man or woman usually selects the prospective mate and the parents hope it will be satisfactory. Parental protests, if any, are made after the selection.

8. Stycos (1952a) indicates that while Puerto Rican women may not always be in love when they marry, they have a definite idea of romantic love. In Valle Caña, it remains most often, though not always, an ideal for women, something that happens to the unreal characters of legend or movies, but not a reality for them.

(a teacher), a Ph.D. Thirteen feel they would probably be in the United States, adding qualifiers like "I always used to dream of it." Other kinds of responses:

Vistiendo santos (dressing saints—the scorned state of spinsterhood).
Vagueando (just wandering around, doing nothing).
Single, earning my livelihood as best I can.
What I'm doing now—nothing.
Without schooling there's not much I could do.
Probably alone, without so many children.
Working as a servant.
Not alive, because I was very sick and after I got married, I discovered Spiritism, and it saved me.
I was an orphan but perhaps someone—or some institution—would take me in.

Vallecañese courtship patterns contrast strikingly with those attributed by Waller and Hill (1951: 95-248) to the United States middle class.

As in all other phases of life, males have the greater sexual freedom. But in Valle Caña few women are accessible for sex or companionship, and the philandering man and youth must turn generally to the "loose" women of Agua Lluvia or Cañaveral. But even in these towns he is frustrated because prostitution has been legally wiped out and prostitutes operating covertly charge beyond his means. The lower-class male therefore suffers under the heavy paradox of high *machismo* (maleness) expectations from society and a paucity of opportunities outside marriage to demonstrate his maleness. His outlets become gambling, drinking, talking, and aggression on the one hand, and masturbation, occasionally bestiality, and rarely homosexuality on the other.

Juano, one of my major informants, mentioned that the twenty-five-year-old son of a local middle-class landowner had the year previous lured a little boy to an abandoned shack and attempted to have sexual relations with him. He was "denounced" and jailed and had just been turned loose on probation. But Juano does not think he is a real *maricón* (male homosexual) but just "crazy in the head for awhile." Juano thinks more such incidents happen nowadays than when he was a boy. He related several situations involving male homosexuality, all of them in the town, between adult males. He also told of sex acts by local boys with farm animals and says bestiality is fairly common. "How can you blame them when they build up so much of the natural feelings and cannot have a woman?" Juano thinks masturbation is probably the most prevalent form of sexual release, says it was and is quite common, and he recited incidents of group (but not mutual) masturbation in his youth while swimming in the creek. In his youth parents were so strict he did not learn to dance until he was twenty-one and away in the army, and he confirmed the testimony of many others about the strict chaperonage at dances and other social affairs.

Sometimes during a dry spell, he said, boys and girls were permitted to go up to a mountain well together for water, but while they played a good deal, "nothing bad ever happened." There never have been professional whores in Valle Caña and boys and men have always had to go into town. Juano's own initiation into sex came when an older man took him to a whorehouse when he was eighteen. Now the police are cracking down and a man runs a risk to try anything, even with a professional woman. He has to go to town and rent a hotel room, but must leave and separate from the woman very shortly. There are other places, however, like a beach resort near Agua Lluvia where cabins can be rented and easy women can be picked up, but this takes much money. He also mentioned places in La Perla (famous slum in San Juan) and other beach resorts but feels these are especially dangerous because "they have disease or they take shots of heroin in the arm or smoke marijuana" and he stays away from them.

[In the old days] the father would wait until a boy was twenty-one and then tell him the necessary things—how to get married, how to treat a woman in sex, and so on—but not a word until that time, the boy just had to pick up stuff from the outside. And the mother would tell the girl *poco a poco* [little by little], beginning when she was in her first menses, until she was a woman, so that she would not have too much dangerous knowledge too soon. Now at fourteen or fifteen they are ready for marriage, but before they were just learning how to control themselves.

Girls are less bothered by this confounding of roles and needs. Like her mother, the girl's place is in or near the home. She is not expected to go out very much, even with other girls, and never with boys. She is expected to be a mother-substitute to her younger siblings, caring for them and attending their wants, and helping with house chores. She is permitted to play with her friends, but after nightfall even this is discouraged. Except on special occasions as when a group returns from church services, no respectable girl or woman is seen on the street.

If females have a more restricted "living space" it is also much easier for them to live up to their expected roles. They have merely to be *de la casa* (a homebody) to prove their femininity.

Of course there are exceptions to prove the rule. Once in a while a female kicks over the traces. One girl in La Hoja, aged eighteen, who had been running around with men since she was fifteen, was constantly made pregnant and abandoned. She lived alone with two "natural" children and was pregnant with another when we were there. The wayward woman is much more likely to meet a tragic end than the man, for his loose conduct is usually ignored or sometimes admired, but hers is always condemned.

As we shall see in later chapters, the girl in general develops much more smoothly than the boy; her ego-structure is stronger and more intact in adolescence, and she approaches womanhood with a greater sense of maturity and responsibility. The boy is constantly trying, in the face of massive frustrations, to prove his masculinity, but seldom succeeds, except momentarily, and even marriage is often a disappointment.

CHAPTER 4

Marriage and the Family

Introduction

THE immediate context of socialization is the family. It is primary in time, and though later it shares honors with the child's peer group as cultural surrogates, its influence is felt to some degree throughout the individual's life-span. In this chapter we shall examine the relationships between marriage mates and the ways in which they are associated with culture, social structure, family size, and other factors.

The focus is on the eighteen families selected for intensive study. Observational findings are combined with results of rating the parents along many dimensions of family life and marital relations. Some comparisons are made with other Puerto Rican studies, as well as in-

TABLE 2

Types of Marriage for All Social Classes and for the Lower Class
of Valle Caña, Compared with the Lower Class of Cañamelar [a]
(in percent)

| Marriage Type | Valle Caña | | Cañamelar Lower Class Only |
	All Classes	Lower Class	
Catholic	22	18	11
Protestant (Evangelical)	6	7	5 (Pentacostal)
Civil	45	41	14
Consensual	27	34	70
Total	100	100	100

a. See Mintz 1951: VI/1-3.

ternal comparisons within the group of families for some variables along the variables of family size, location (road–open country), and sex.

Types of Marriage

While the island is traditionally Catholic, the church has married less than one-fourth of all Vallecañese couples (Table 2). The most popular marriage form is the simple, rapid, and inexpensive civil ceremony, and still viable is the traditional consensual union.

Causes for the very large difference between our data and Mintz' on the proportion of consensual marriage may be conjectured. One important difference is that Mintz' proportion is for all unions while mine represents only present marriages. Another is that his was a coastal community and he believes consensuality is more popular there than in the highland and inland villages. A third undoubtedly is that Cañamelar is a less feudally-oriented community, composed mostly of landless workers for absentee corporations (see pp. 48-51); and there may be less need to please the upper class by more circumspect behavior (see pp. 56-57).

Mintz' reasons for the popularity of consensual unions are worth noting: (1) There is the historical factor that the lower class descends from former slaves and *agregados* (roughly analagous to sharecroppers) of the landed gentry who did not pay too much heed to assuring the holy sacrament for their charges, though in other ways there was a paternalistic system resembling the plantation organization of the antebellum southern United States.[1] (2) Expense involved in religious rites may be a relatively minor reason in Valle Caña since the Evangelical minister and priest say they will marry poor couples without charge. The people say this is true only of the former. (3) Much more important is that in a consensual union neither man nor woman is bound to each other. If the man is a poor breadwinner, the woman may leave him and he has only the moral force of the community and her own needs to demand her return. Conversely, if the woman proves a

1. Similar culture patterns and historical factors may be found in the popularity of consensual marriage in Brazil among Negro families (Frazier 1942; Ribeiro 1942), and consensual or common-law patterns as well as philandering by the male (where the female assumes the greater responsibility) among Negro families in the United States (King 1945; Frazier 1934). Variations on the same themes may be found in most Caribbean cultures (Henriques 1949).

bad wife, he is also free to leave. (4) The Catholic church does not have a strong hold on the people, the Evangelical church (or other Protestant sects in other communities) influences only a minority, and in general even churchgoing people are broadminded and lax about their beliefs (see pp. 41-44).

If Vallecañese consensual marriages are fewer than in Mintz' village, they are not significantly removed from the Puerto Rican national mean of 23.6 percent. They are closer to the mean for urban families (24.5 percent) than for rural families (22.9 percent) (Bureau of the Census 1950:7). Siegel (1947:105-116) also found that his *municipio* mean was close to the insular mean, but in the lower-class sample of his town 52 percent of the marriages were consensual. Apparently in Puerto Rico there is a marked tendency in the urban lower class to have proportionately more such marriages than rural people of the same status. It is also important to note in federal census data that there is a general downward trend in consensual marriages for the island, although the decrements each decade have been small. It is our conclusion, in agreement with Mintz, Siegel, and the census, that civil ceremonies are taking up the slack, rather than a return to religious marital arrangements.

Mintz notes that the civil marriage is preferred increasingly by young women as a means of guaranteeing that no matter what the husband does, he must be legally liable for the welfare of their children. These ceremonies are also usually a little cheaper than paying a priest, and even more important, the bride's parents and the couple are not generally expected to sponsor a costly wedding party, as with religious marriages. The consensual union is consummated by little else than sexual union and common residence, although it appears that the cultural function of this act is to signify intention to cohabit and the recognition by the community of this fact.

No religious marriages took place during our residence, but two couples were united consensually and one by civil rites. In the latter case the couple went into Agua Lluvia, were married by the justice of the peace, and returned on the next bus. One hour later the bride was ironing her husband's clothes. They had taken up temporary residence in the house of the husband's widowed grandmother. Both consensual unions were by very young people. In one both principals were sixteen years old; in the other the husband was about twenty-five and the girl's age was variously estimated by her mother from fourteen to nineteen.

In general the pattern of the consensual marriage, particularly between youthful principals, is one of surreptitious after-dark courtships and sudden elopement, in which the groom takes the girl to some friend's house, or waits in someone's house while the girl is led there by an older female friend after her parents have gone to sleep. In the first of the two marriages, the couple moved in temporarily with the boy's parents and nothing more was said, since he was working in the cane and the boy's father was unemployed because of a skin infection. In the other case the parents weakly protested. The boy and girl promised to get married legally, but by the time we left Valle Caña they had not done so, and since the parents were themselves consensually united, they felt they could not urge legality upon their daughter (see pp. 62-69).

We agree with Mintz (1951:VII/2) about the general stability of consensual marriage. The statistics may show that more of them dissolve, but they are usually undertaken with as serious intent as any other marriage form; there is no discernible difference in attitudes toward children where the marriage does last; there is as much mutual respect between spouses; and the couple seems just as respected by the lower-class community.

Tenure and Responsibility

Each married adult in Valle Caña has been married an average of 1.6 times, a close approximation to the 1.5 times in Mintz' community (*ibid.*). Nevertheless, present unions have lasted an average of nearly twenty years, which seems quite high and may mean that earlier ones are a form of experimentation. Our mean would rise from 1.6 to 2.0 if we included a special case of a sixty-nine-year-old man who said he had been married forty-two times, of which all but three were supposed to have been consensual. We were wary of crediting this statement at its face value, though the man gave it in the presence of his current spouse with whom he has been living consensually for five years and eventually plans "to marry by the church." Before we could check his information he died. He reported he had been a "real hell-raiser" in his day, tired of women easily, caroused a lot. But in his senility he repented his sinful ways and became a leading member of the Evangelical church. He was quite self-righteous and virtuous, refusing a proffered drink though people say he died of stomach cancer caused by former excessive drinking. Wild youth and virtuous old age seem a fairly common pattern among Puerto Rican males.

No matter what the form, it is more often the husband than the wife who makes light of matrimony. If he abandons his family he loses little status, whereas if his wife does, she is almost universally condemned. The male may carry on affairs, sometimes in the same locality, and may even increase his *machismo* by demonstrating such control of his own fate, but the wife can seldom risk extramarital relations and has the most to suffer from desertion, separation, or divorce, since she is nearly always left with the children. For instance, Carmen Lydia was abandoned by her husband and she was glad to be rid of him, since he lived openly with other women, would abuse her in front of their children, and force her to go to bed with him while carrying on outside affairs. Nevertheless, since he was sending her a little money from the United States for the children, she bore him no particular ill-will. And Doña Juanita relates that her son

. . . has six children who are now living with their mother and being cared for by her. She works in the school lunch. They made a fine couple and were in love, but he drank so much she did not approve. They fought, had many separations, but she was constantly pregnant, he was constantly drunk, so finally they separated for good. Ai! It is too bad, but what can you expect? He was a good boy—but he is a man, and what can you expect?

Not only the man's mother but even his ex-wife continues to feel a curious maternal responsibility for him. Maria feels no animus toward her former husband.

Since he is the father of my children why should I? [She is bearing children to her present husband.] Well, I married this man when I was sixteen because my parents were poor and there was nothing I could do. He turned out to be lazy and a drunkard. He wouldn't provide for the children so I left him. He no longer drinks as much but he won't give me anything for them. Just the same, I give him all the money I can, I try to help him. I give him meals sometimes and fix his clothes, though of course Tino [her present husband] doesn't know about it. He would be very angry if he did. When my former husband was put in jail not long ago for carrying a gun, I went to see him. Tino knew about it but he didn't say anything.

It is not always the husband who goes off on an extramarital tangent. In several instances where old men married much younger women, the latter would grow restless and dissatisfied. Tomaso, in his sixties, had been married four times. His last wife was sixteen when they married and bore him three children, but she got restive and left him and the children after three years. The children—the smallest was an infant —cried for her for two weeks after she left. Tomaso had to give the infant to a friend. He lives with the other two and another son by a previous marriage. The last wife was "very nervous" and would swear at him and the children. He "tried to advise her maturely that she should be patient and control herself for the children's sake" and if she felt bored she should seek some work or outside activity to keep her occupied. She apparently took his advice seriously for she is now living with another man in Agua Lluvia. Tomaso says he does not want to "see the sight of her again."

In many cases former marriages were terminated naturally when one mate died. But just as frequently the following kinds of reasons are given: incompatible; he (she) was too young; drank a lot; fought a lot; found out he was married already; beat me constantly; didn't love him (her); another woman took him away; she had a terrible temper; she was ignorant; she would quarrel much; she was not congenial; he was *sin vergüenza* (shameless); she was wild; he had others; he was bad; etc. Regardless of tenure and other factors the woman usually bears the burdens of married life and manifests the greater responsibility.

Duty and Independence

The ancient dictum, "the woman's place is in the home," is to a large extent practice as well as theory among Vallecañeses. Even where in theory some husbands would permit a modicum of freedom for their wives, this is seldom practiced (Table 3). Except for an occasional trip to town, usually accompanied by one or more children (always with the husband's permission), and occasional neighborly visits, wives are securely bound to the hearth.

Most wives had never worked out before marriage. One washed for a landowner's family but has not worked since her first childbirth. Another takes in sewing because her husband will give her no money for the house beyond the grocery bills. At present two of the mothers

TABLE 3

Husbands' Expectations Regarding Wives' Home Duties

"Prefer wife at home, nowhere else."	8
"Prefer wife at home, but may go out a bit, after chores."	5
"Must stay at home until children are grown. Then she may go out to work."	1
"May work out a bit if not too far and someone can care for the children."	4
Total Cases	18

are working out, one as a laundress and one replacing her husband as school janitor while he works in the cane.

Nearly all of these women would like some diversion, however little, but it is apparent that they seldom get out (Tables 4, 5). One

TABLE 4

Wives' Policies Regarding Home Duties and Outside Activities

"A woman should stay home as much as possible. Extra work may be taken in, but no outside work, ever."	4
"Would like outside work if I could get someone responsible to take care of the children. Some diversion would be nice, but not at the cost of neglecting the children or the household."	8
"A mother should never work outside. But a bit of diversion like voting, school meetings, or visiting is needed, though not at the expense of household or child care duties."	5
"It's all right to work outside if one has dire need of money. And it's good to get out occasionally to change one's impressions."	1
Total Cases	18

TABLE 5

How Wives Solved the Problem of Home vs. Outside Activities

"I go out once in a while, not often."	10
"I never go out except on a household errand."	4
"I get out to *rosarios*, school meetings, some visiting."	2
"I get out to mother's, or to town. I get around quite a bit."	2
Total Cases	18

of the two who "get around quite a bit" has only one child. The lone
wife who appears to "get out when I want to" is a deviant who is
roundly condemned because she abuses her children. When she does
not lock them in, their caretaker is a ten-year-old aunt. Mintz (1951:
VI/19-20) feels that "there is a great deal of give and take in these
[marital] relations . . . [and] women do not appear to suffer any more
than their mates." Our impression of Valle Caña is that women generally are held to the traditional role and do indeed "suffer more."

Thus we have a picture of women who seem *conforme* (compliant,
resigned to one's fate), apparently accepting the customary wife-
mother role in belief and deed. But while these women are not independent or technically free and observe the traditional creed, their
hidden aspirations are for some independence and for contributing
financially to the family welfare (Table 6). One thing that apparently

TABLE 6

If Wives Could Be Doing Something Other than
What They Are Doing Now

"I would like to be working and earning some money."	11
"I would like to be working and I should have stayed single."	4
"If I could, I would stay young all my life and never marry."	1
"I feel all right being home with my children, doing my chores. Outside work is as hard as housework."	2
Total Cases	18

accounts for the greater independence of the women of Cañamelar is
that many of them earn a little extra money. Those few who have this
opportunity in Valle Caña achieve a limited degree of independence
as regards spending their own money, but ultimate authority remains
vested in the husband. Yet it is clear that if the objective conditions
were present—job opportunities and a way to care for their children—
their desire for work could very probably over-ride strong male objections. While seeing their own housework as their duty, most wives
do not view it as an especially dignified occupation and are scornful
of the role of paid domestics. We know of several who turned down
such opportunities even when desperately needing the money. But
they would work in factories. Thus frustrated by cultural pressures
and lack of opportunities, Vallecañese women accept, but do not

necessarily enjoy, the fact that they cannot "defend" [2] themselves as their husbands do.

Half of the men place their home interests above everything, including work; a third place home and job in equal importance; and the others feel that work should come first. This general predilection expressed by most men for being at home seems to contradict some of our own observations. But this is due to a road–open country difference. Open-country men actually are home most often. Many have a small plot and spend considerable time working it. During the harvest La Hoja men leave home at daybreak, walk up to five miles each way, and work all day under a broiling sun. By the time they force their tired bodies back up the mountain and have washed, rested, and eaten, about an hour remains till dark. They spend this time playing with the small children or visiting friends. After dark usually only unmarried males go down the rocky mountain in search of entertainment. The road men are not only closer to the source of entertainment but also to the bottomland canefields, the *públicos*, and the busses that rattle down the road into Agua Lluvia or Cañaveral where there are movies and other attractions.

When these men speak of "home interests" they are referring more to work on their garden patch, animals, etc., than to intrafamily activities. Even open-country men go out more than their wives. During *Navidades* it is the men who roam from house to house on the serial *asaltos*,[3] the women remaining at home to receive male guests and to retire with the children when the males, including the husband, depart for the next round. And if the men deem their wives too garrulous and quarrelsome, as old Don Raul feels about his young wife, they may take off to town at every opportunity. He often visits with his first wife, who wants him back, and after each quarrel with his current mate he is sore beset to yield to the temptation.

2. Used throughout Puerto Rico to mean "making a living," or "making one's way in the world." Use of the verb *defenderse* in this way signifies, as do many other things the people say and do and believe, a generally defensive, apprehensive outlook in a hostile, menacing environment. In the same way the verb *luchar* (struggling, fighting) is also frequently used to describe routine activities. When I would pass a male Vallecañese friend and say "*Qué pasa?*" or "*Qué hay?*" (how are you getting along?), he would reply "*Luchando, muchacho, luchando*" (struggling, chum, struggling). Even more often from women would come "*Pues, ya ve*" (well, see for yourself—you can see how I am), implying that the questioner should know their fate is unchanging.

3. Use of this term, which literally means assault or attack, may help convey the element of social aggression, ritualized and accepted, to be sure, which is implicit in this kind of foray against the hospitality of one's friends.

Division of Labor by Sex and Age

One might anticipate in this male-dominant society a sharp division of labor along sexual lines. And we do find that the traditional wall which divides male from female labor is only sometimes breached. The general pattern is that the man works in the cane and on his plot and the woman does the housework and caretaking of children. Boys run errands, tend livestock, and help the father, and girls help the mother. In seven families husbands refuse to help their wives under any circumstances, in eight they would help a bit in emergencies as when the wife is ill. In only three cases do we have something approaching what Herbst (1952:3-25) calls a combination between an "autonomic" and "syncratic cooperative" interaction pattern with the husband and wife performing their traditional tasks but also helping each other at times. Even when the husband condescends to help his wife, if she is indisposed, it is when relatives or neighbors cannot come in to take over. This aloofness of the male from domestic chores is not confined to the older generation; younger husbands often are even more prone to observe the differential.

A young husband who lived up La Hoja refused to pick up our laundry to be washed by his wife who could not leave because her child was ill. He came by our house to and from work each day but would not stop. He finally sent a ten-year-old niece. We felt she was too small for the huge bundle and sent word to him. A little later he sent his seventeen-year-old nephew, who was angry and chagrined at having to be associated with clothes-washing; but he had to carry the bag since he had been ordered to do so by an older man.

Add to primitive living conditions the apparent inefficiency of the Vallecañese housewife—who seems to take the hardest, most laborious way to do things—and one sees why most of them scarcely stop their chores all day. They were interviewed for the most part while they worked and often would not stop work while chatting with friends who dropped in. In this *mañana* culture, where a clock is a scarce domestic item, time is still the most precious commodity to the work-bound housewife. Thus, even with rare husbandly approval, they often turn down jobs as laundresses or servants no matter how badly they need the money, since there is no one to do their work. Water must be brought long distances; clothes washed in the stream; fuel gathered;

ironing done with heavy charcoal-burning irons; children taken care of; and often the husband may expect help on his tiny plot. It is not surprising that while marriage is still preferred to spinsterhood, more than one wife sighs, *"Es el primer matrimonio y será el último"* (It is the first marriage and it will be the last). Work in the cane and land patch is strenuous, but for the husband there are long respites during the dead season. He spends little of this extra time relieving his wife of any part of her burden and little of it improving his house or doing things like building a much needed bridge across the stream, which floods and is treacherous. A bridge could be built over the stream even with the materials at hand, but no one does anything about it. Children lose many days in school when they cannot ford it, as adults do.

Balance of Authority

Along with his generally superior status the male expects, and is expected, to have commanding authority in the home. To a large extent this is carried out in practice, and while the wife is permitted to run the house when the husband is away working or entertaining himself, she is really running it in his name and for him. My observations tend to strengthen the balance of authority even more on the husband's side than the preponderance indicated by wives' views on the subject (Table 7). For example, of three women who claimed they

TABLE 7

Balance of Family Authority

	Children	Money	Leisure Time Activities	Moving to New Location	All Other Matters
1. Husband nearly all	10	13	7	15	7
2. Husband mostly, but consults wife	5	—	—	1	6
3. Husband and wife, but she gets his permission on important ones	—	5	—	—	4
4. Husband and wife jointly, more or less equally	—	—	2	2	—
5. Wife mostly, but consults husband	—	—	7	—	—
6. Wife nearly all	3	—	2	—	1
Total cases	18	18	18	18	18

made most decisions regarding what to do about their children, one was the deviant "independent" mother mentioned earlier, another added bitterly, "I make the decisions because he never goes out with us, he is hardly in the house, he goes only with rum-drinkers," and the third added a hasty "mostly" to her response.

There is little display by these women of the sharing of authority noted by Mintz (1951:VI/20-21) in Cañamelar: ". . . women appear to share equally in familial authority and do not seem to fear the breakup of their marriage as much as might be expected. While this equality may allow for easier dissolution of common-law unions, it also appears to reduce the tensions between husband and wife, and to permit greater freedom and security in the home than would be the case otherwise."

Nearly every Vallecañese woman takes it for granted that her husband wields the main switch in the powerhouse of familial rule. There is a good deal of variation in the actual extent to which she consults him only for "important" decisions. Nevertheless, it is still safe to conclude with Wolf (1951:94) that "this partnership requires the subordination of the woman to her husband." Wolf's data seem more heavily weighted in the direction of male supremacy than ours. Vallecañese families stand somewhere between these and those of Cañamelar. Acknowledgment of the man's supremacy and authority openly or tacitly colors many aspects of socialization. Within the sphere of child-rearing practices however, as opposed to policy decisions, the wife usually depends upon her own judgments and seldom consults anyone except her husband. Vallecañese children are raised, not "by the book," but by the dictates of tradition and the whims, caprices, and "common sense" of their parents and other caretakers, especially their mothers.

Responsibility for Discipline

An area apposite to the problem of authority is the responsibility for day-to-day discipline of the child. In a subsequent chapter it is shown that the mother is the most frequent agent of punishment, since she is at home more and the father's authoritarian status makes it less necessary for him to resort to punishment. Even when the father is home the mother often acts as executor of punishment, enforcing his or her own authority or punishing the children to forestall his displeasure. Unlike the older generations, when the division of labor was such that the mother punished the girls and the father the boys, today the wife usually punishes both sexes, although she and her husband tend to be more severe with the male child (see Chapter 6).

Regarding severity of discipline, husbands think of themselves as somewhat more lenient than their wives do, though neither feels the husband is very easy-going. As indicated later, this may reflect the image of the father as held by both mates rather than his actual sternness. Five wives feel their husbands just as strict, three less strict, and ten more strict, than they were themselves. Nearly half the wives and most of the husbands approve of each other's way of disciplining their children. Generally husbands approve much more of their wives' modes of control than vice-versa. Among the things each disapproved in the other are: kinds of physical punishment (hits too hard, wrong places); too hasty (doesn't stop to learn cause of trouble); unreasonable demands; withdrawal of love; too many threats; loud yelling; place of punishment (in street, in front of others); and too lenient.

Twice as many husbands as wives feel the former are more often the recipients of good child behavior. In about half the cases where wives rate "both" as receiving good behavior, their previous statements implied that this was more often true with the husbands. This inconsistency may be explained as wishful thinking by the lower-status, harassed wife, as a means of asserting her pride by creating a situation of equality with her husband which does not objectively exist. Nearly twice as many wives as husbands feel the woman is more often fortunate in this respect, while six husbands and seven wives deem both equally fortunate. The child may be thought to behave better with either parent because he respects that parent less or more or gets punished by that parent less or more. But the reason most often given for good conduct is that the parent is more respected and more loved. Here, as in many other instances, it is always made clear in context that when these parents speak of love, they include a large component of dependency, and when they speak of respect, they include a large component of fear.

Bearing Children

Wives were generally unhappy about the coming of the child about whom they were interviewed. The cultural ideal of the pleasures and virtues of motherhood is restricted to two small and three large family mothers. The same number also approached impending childbirth with mixed feelings: "I was frightened, but happy"; "I was happy because he didn't make me sick"; and four each of small and large family mothers were simply unhappy. For half of these wives their first re- action was prolonged illness. Two of the mothers whose feelings were mixed mentioned being frightened but wanting the child, nevertheless. A third of the group used expressions of outright rejection; several more rejected the child by implication. Family size seems unimportant here. One rejecting mother unsuccessfully tried to have an abortion; others were very angry and physically ill and turned on their husbands, whom they hated during pregnancy.

One "could not stand the sight of him," one "could not eat when she looked at him." They quarreled often and rancorously. In both cases the husband temporarily had to leave the house to escape the lashing tongues, but both husbands easily forgave their wives and now seem to be enjoying a relatively happy life. This emotional turning on the husband could be a tentative rejection of both husband and child, which comes to the fore during the stresses of pregnancy when ordi- nary inhibitions are forgotten. I am told this syndrome occurs fre- quently among middle-class Puerto Rican wives. It seems to be a culturally approved outlet for an emotional attack on the husband and ultimately on strict sex demarcation itself.

Yet most mothers express no deep dislike of children in general and in other contexts speak of their usefulness as additions to the family labor force; many of them speak with affection even of the child whom they rejected at conception.

There are some cases of parents deserting or "giving away" their children either because they do not want the child or are pressed by economic necessity (see pp. 25-27). Doña Ana, for example, a widow who had seven children by two marriages, had to give away a boy at the age of five because she did not have the means to bring him up. She says she misses him now, but since she cannot have him and he is better off she is resigned to God's will. The boy is now fifteen and she is presently raising one of her grandchildren. In other in- stances, however, such affection for relinquished children is not always evident. One woman was reported by her neighbors to have had nine children which she did not mind bearing but did not want to raise. She has given up all but two. When her last two (twins) were born, she took home the girl but said the nurses at the hospital would not let her have the boy. Shortly thereafter she gave away the infant girl (the boy she had given away too), but the foster mother discovered she was crippled at four months of age and returned the child to her unwanting mother.

Perhaps the most important thread running through the husbands' reactions to pregnancy is indifference about the event on the one hand and concern for adequate finances on the other. Only two fathers seemed genuinely happy, both of them from small families. Fathers of small families in general fear the birth least, or, put another way, families, when small at the incipiency of the family cycle, fear having children less than large families, which have already experienced the material and psychological costs of several children. Five husbands seemed more concerned with their wives' health than the unborn child.

Some husbands, with their greater freedom and irresponsibility, will desert mates and children. When they remain with their families, some abandon the husband-father roles, ignore the needs of wife and children, and assume the role of a privileged guest whose slightest whim and need must be complied with. A case in point is Anselmo, who paid not the slightest attention to his wife when she returned from the hospital, weak and ill, with their tenth child. (Two had died of malnutrition and neglect, according to their neighbors.) Anselmo is a stranger in his own home. His aged mother takes care of his children with his wife. An intelligent timekeeper in the cane, Anselmo spends a large part of what money he seasonally earns on rum. His family is scarcely considered. However, there is one culturally extenuating circumstance. All of Anselmo's children are females. This is a cutting blow to his *macho* pride. Before his last child was born he told us how desperately he wanted a boy and promised to name the child for the ethnologist. It was a girl. He is also very frustrated by his meagre earnings and feels his intelligence should be better rewarded. He occasionally boasts of the scholastic achievements of his oldest girl in the eighth grade, not as they reflect her abilities, but his own, as her father.

Communication between Marriage Partners

That many fathers were preoccupied with the additional expense of another child is easily understood (see pp. 87-88). The amount of food they are able to buy and raise is precariously close to the starvation level, and more than one parent has seen his child die of rickets or malnutrition (see pp. 35-41). Newborn infants are often extremely undersized. The pregnant mother simply cannot obtain sufficient or proper food. Wives in their thirties look emaciated, drawn, and ten years older than their actual age. Loss of teeth due to calcium deficiency is common among mothers and children, and the latter often have swollen stomachs due to worms and near-starvation. "Another mouth to feed" is often the attitude toward a new child.

But what is not so readily comprehended is how these men and women live together, often for many years, with a broad communication gap between them (see Table 8). Two facts stand out: (1) the

TABLE 8

Wives' and Husbands' Estimates of Each Other's Reactions to Pregnancy

	Wife's Reaction (according to husband)		Husband's Reaction (according to wife)	
	S[a]	L[a]	S[a]	L[a]
1. Completely accurate	1	1	2	—
2. More accurate than inaccurate	2	2	—	3
3. Equally accurate and inaccurate	—	—	1	1
4. More inaccurate than accurate	—	1	1	—
5. Completely inaccurate	3	3	3	4
0. Does not know, or "He (she) didn't think anything."	2	3	1	2
Total Cases	8	10	8	10

a. S = small family, L = large family.

husband shows much less knowledge of his wife's reaction than she of his; (2) family size does not seem to be important in determining the degree of communication, though there is a slight tendency for small family spouses more accurately to gauge each other's feelings concerning pregnancy. The first may be understood if we bear in mind the sharp sex differential, the father as authority figure (the wife would thus be more interested in discovering his reactions than vice-versa), and the father's scant participation in family affairs. For the second we may hazard this speculation: (1) a larger group than our sample might have registered more small family wife-husband communicability, decreasing with growth in family size because of added economic problems, increasing complexity of intrafamilial relationships, and routinization of wife-husband relationships; (2) strict sex demarcation, father authority, and minor paternal family participation may make for a lessening of communication from the beginning of a family's history, and size may actually be an unimportant determinant of attitudes. Bossard's (1945:292-294) "law" that "the number of persons increases in the simplest arithmetic progression while the number of personal interrelationships within the [family] group increases in the order of triangular numbers" may account for the quantitative aspect of family size and interaction, but it does not explain the nature of family relationships, which is heavily influenced by such factors as parental roles.

Pregnancy, a subject of lively discussion and interest in some cultures, is no cause for excitement in Valle Caña, nor in many other Puerto Rican communities. It is accepted as something which just happens in the natural stream of events, and for many families it may arouse no more interest, as Wolf (1951:87) puts it, than to herald the cessation of the wife's menstrual flow so the husband may proceed with intercourse without worrying about reproductive consequences. He adds, ". . . it is believed that it is actually beneficial for the development of the foetus." I did not hear of this belief, but it may nevertheless be held among some Vallecañeses. It is worth noting that when the writer's wife became pregnant while in the village, few women were surprised or moved by the announcement, some hinting that this was an unexciting topic for conversation. Pretty much the same reaction ensued from my male friends. Wolf also found this indifference in his lower-class community.

Nevertheless, such frequency of ignorance about each other's feelings concerning something as intimate and apparent as pregnancy seems to demonstrate that the male-female division extends to communication itself. Alternative explanations could be suggested: if the coming child were not welcome the wife may fear even to mention it, so as not to arouse her spouse's anger; and the husband may not wish to discuss an event which will inevitably make his own lot more difficult. But a similar lack of mutual knowledge will be evident in other aspects of family living where each mate normally might be expected to know something of the other's attitudes.

The Economics of Fertility

When there is no work during the long *tiempo muerto*, there is no money for anything. Little can be saved from the harvest season when income is immediately blotted up by last season's grocery debts, a few clothes, and a bit of entertainment. But when the *zafra* returns a man can somehow find money for many things, even the arrival of a baby. A "good" or "bad" time financially for having a child is defined by when it comes insofar as cyclical employment is concerned. A few months or weeks either way may make a great deal of difference. Only a few husbands mention savings and they imply that this began when pregnancy was certain, if there was something to save. But the small and precarious earnings of Vallecañeses and their economic way of life are not ordinarily conducive to savings.

About half the wives and husbands in each of the two family-size groups feel the economic situation at the time of having the subject child was bad; so for them, at least, family size is comparatively unimportant in determining desirability of pregnancy. But five of the men who felt the time was financially right were worried about money on other questions related to pregnancy. Added to the first group, we find two-thirds of the fathers preoccupied with economic considerations. Thus husbands think about money matters more than their wives.

However, several husbands are concerned not merely with the necessity to provide but to buy "special foods and things a child needs," a clue that they are thinking in terms more considerate of *los pequeñitos* (the tiny ones) than their responses otherwise indicate. Mothers are more sanguine than their mates that a new child somehow will be clothed and fed. They hope, as one expressed it, that *"Cuando Dios según da la llaga, da el remedio"* (When God gives one a sore, he also provides the remedy).

While economics is a significant factor in fertility regardless of family size, the extent of its importance cannot be determined from our data, since its relative role alongside other determinants has not been studied. We do not know whether our families, given a satisfactory income, would be in favor of large or small families. In another Puerto Rican study (Stycos 1952a) a sizable minority of twenty-four each of town and city families wanted more children if they had the

money for them and did not differ significantly from those who would
be satisfied with the same number of children. However, since this is
not a rural sample, we do not have strictly comparable data.

Family Size

Nevertheless, Vallecañese parents exhibit an extremely strong belief
in small-family mindedness. The traditional desire for large families
because "children are the capital of the poor" has given way to "the
new mentality" (Stycos 1952b; see also Hatt 1952, Hill, Stycos, and
Back 1959). The median ideal number of children for wives is 2.3
and for husbands 3.3, while the actual median is 6.0. The latter statistic
includes only biological children and *hijos de crianza* that survived to
five years on the assumption that those dying under that age would not
be a major influence on the rearing of current children nor a long-
term drain on family resources. It excludes stillbirths, abortions, and
miscarriages, though for several mothers as many as half of their conceptions ended in these ways. Also excluded is the previous childbear-
ing record of these women.

Existing family size is an important determinant of ideal family size.
Wives in small and large families consistently desire fewer children
than their husbands, the median being slightly lower for large family
wives (2.0 compared to 2.3). This trend is intensified by the husbands,
those from large families desiring an ideal median of 2.8 compared
with 4.5 for small family men. We would predict, however, that these
small family husbands, with incipient large families, would in several
years desire fewer children. While as a group husbands understandably
would like more offspring than their wives, little difference was found
by Stycos in male and female median ideals, but with a slight difference in favor of the men on the average. In island-wide research
Hatt (1952:Ch. 1-2) found that men expressed an important, though
not large, difference for greater ideal numbers of children.

Desirability and Rejection of Children

Though without enthusiasm, most wives prefer having had their
child when they did because, among other reasons, "it was during
harvest"; "we were still young and strong"; "the child is now grown
and can help us." Husbands generally would rather have had the child

later, though nearly a third were indifferent about its time of arrival. Parents of both sexes who wanted to put off the child have such motivations as: "No money"; "The later the better, for then there are fewer"; or "The children will be too close together." It is interesting to observe that there is substantial disagreement between nearly all couples on this factor, another possible indicator of the communication barrier between them. Almost half of both spouses demonstrate rejective attitudes toward having not only the specific child but children generally. In view of their inferior status, domestic and child-rearing chores, and the physiological and psychological strains of childbirth which plague most Vallecañese women, it is not surprising that wives display stronger rejective feelings than their husbands.

In the following incident related by a *comadrona* (midwife) it is easy to construe that the attitude of the mother, whether motivated by fear or by a refusal to cooperate as the *comadrona* charges, was tantamount to killing her offspring:

Well, I was called in at the last minute and when I got there the child was halfway born, the leg was protruding. I told the mother to try to hold on and I went back into the kitchen to talk with the husband. I told him it was going to be a difficult birth and it would be better to get her in a hammock and down the mountain where they were living, and to the hospital. [Sick persons must be carried down mountains this way.] But there was another woman in the room with the mother who was telling her to bear down and push so that by the time I came in again the child was more than halfway out. Only the head remained to come out. So I told the woman to bear down again, but she said she did not feel like it. I worked on the baby a long time, moving it from side to side, and kneading it, and finally got it out and rolled it and patted it some more, but the child had already been asphyxiated and was dead. I was so angry with the woman's negligence I wanted to hit her, because the child could have been born alive. I knew when it came out and spit out bile the way it did that it was already dead. I also told the husband that the child could have been born alive but it was dead because of his wife's refusal to cooperate. . . .

Two obstetricians on the island have told me that in hundreds of cases they have handled, lower-class mothers show less fear and scream less than middle-class mothers. The latter, they say, exhibit extreme hysteria. But it is a lower-class ethic that the woman not show pain in childbirth, especially in a home delivery which is almost a public affair.

Birth Control [4]

The most popular way of avoiding children by desire and deed is sterilization of the wife. With the tacit cooperation of the government most wives may be sterilized at government expense at the district hospital, provided their case may be shown by the physician to be one of physical or other need. Many women say they were sterilized and name neighbors and acquaintances who were. Many others desire to be sterilized but have had to put it off for one or more of several reasons: (1) could not get the doctor's approval; (2) therefore, could not afford to pay for the operation (there is a special rate for poor women of about forty dollars); (3) afraid of the operation; (4) afraid to broach the subject to their husbands; (5) afraid of the after-effects of sterilization.

It is a rare man or woman among the lower class in Valle Caña who uses contraception. Although no instruction is currently given, the local health unit dispenses contraceptives free for the asking. A few women got them, their husbands being too embarrassed, but did not generally benefit by their use or said they were "ineffectual," which may mean they were not properly used, that proper instruction was not given, or that they were taking away from the pleasurable sensation of the husband. The men object to contraceptives even more than women and withdrawal is considered unmanly. However, they also favor sterilization of their wives as a way of surely stopping further insemination without sacrificing their *macho* pleasures, and wives for security also favor this method. It has been mentioned by Mintz and by an island physician to the writer that the sterilization of the male has never been suggested although it is much simpler and less expensive. But the position of the male in Puerto Rican society throws the onus of having children and the responsibility to do something about it on the already sagging shoulders of the female.

4. It is not an objective of this study to investigate in depth the patterned attitudes toward reproduction in our community. This is the primary objective of Stycos (1952a, 1955b) and the island-wide survey by Hatt (1952). The reader is also referred to King (1948) and Cofresi (1951). Final results of the fertility study by the Family Life Project will be found in Hill, Stycos, and Back 1959. A few differences between the lower-class group of that study and the present one may be attributed to the probable subcultural variations in the subject communities. That such differences may loom large is amply attested in the subcultural series researched by Steward and his associates. See Steward, *et al.* 1956, and Wolf 1952.

Candida, who has six children, had been "warned" by her husband to be "operated" after her second child, but "I was so scared it would keep me up nights just thinking about it." But after having children every year she decided to go through with it. Now she is not sorry for the operation or for the children she already has. It is also significant, however, that she is often "sick" and frequently has to go to the hospital. At least three other women who also were sterilized reported they did not feel well afterwards. Whether these deleterious after-effects are of a psychological nature or postoperative physiological reactions to surgery the writer is not prepared to say.

Two or three women volunteered that they knew nothing at all about contraceptives. Until a systematic effort is made to educate the people about the known facts and proper instructions in birth control methods, they will continue to be surrounded with ignorance, misinformation, suspicion, and fear. We are told that in the school's home economics course some facts concerning conception are given. This may prepare the female with more adequate knowledge than the traditional ways of mothers not saying anything, giving misinformation, or even punishing the child when asked about such things, but nothing is being done about birth control methods as such. Therefore common methods of controlling reproduction are not being used, only the drastic resort to sterilization.

Only two Evangelical respondents are against birth control for religious reasons. No others, and no Catholics, mentioned religious sanctions on contraception or sterilization. An anti-birth control campaign has been conducted by the Catholic church on the island against even the modest beginnings undertaken by the government, but few people in Valle Caña have been touched by this movement, which seems to be confined to prominent laymen and clerics in the towns and cities. The priest in Agua Lluvia is strongly against birth control and believes in continence or the rhythm method.[5] "The crux of the problem, I believe, is in moderation and in curbing one's passions," he said. "Even the problem of overpopulation on the island could be solved if the people were educated to the ethics of continence."

The Evangelical minister is ambivalent on the subject. His former Catholic background pulls him in one direction, but he is concerned with the necessity for limiting family size, though he feels this is best

5. This was in 1952, just before the Pope issued a decree against the rhythm method except in cases of illness.

done by abstinence. He has never preached against birth control and says his church organization has not mentioned it to him in any way, though he is personally opposed to it. He does not ostracize women who are sterilized, as has been reported for another community (Stycos 1952a:12), but says that if he hears they are going to be "operated," he visits them and attempts to dissuade them. Unlike the priest, he does not think merely "uncurbed passions" are involved in prolific fertility but also "poverty, ignorance, and ill-treatment of the family by the husband." He says that he has "been able to solve these problems for a few families and prevent their being sterilized."

Boy or Girl?

In Valle Caña half the wives prefer girls and half the husbands prefer boys. Additionally, while one-third of the wives prefer boys, only one-sixth of the husbands prefer girls. Boys seem to be the preferred sex, although not overwhelmingly, since one-third of the husbands and one-sixth of the wives consider their advantages equal with those of girls. Most parents make a choice which either agrees with present sex distribution or with the predominant sex in the home. The minority prefer one sex when the other predominates, both when one only exists, or one when both exist. Thus current male-female ratio affects parental choice of children's sex in a positive manner. As family size increases, boys become more popular, probably not least of all because they are an addition to the labor force and are not as expensive to maintain in terms of clothes and shoes. Our data bear out precisely the observation of one anthropologist (Mintz 1951:VI/28) that ". . . on a verbal level boys are preferred, particularly by fathers; nevertheless every father wants at least one *mujercita* [little woman]."

There are practical reasons for their choices which revolve around the division of labor and other cultural factors:

I like them both the same. The girl will help me in the house and the males will help their father.

The males work harder and do not demand so much care and problems as the girl. When the male works he will give me money and help me. Girls you must buy many things for, but boys you can clothe in any old thing.

Girls are better to take care of. . . . They are more obedient and humble and *de la casa* [literally, of the house—homebodies]. They are always in the house, they ask permission of one, and one does not worry as much with them.

The son "defends" himself better. When daughters are married they sometimes suffer very much if their husbands don't pay attention to them and their children. As to the male child, if something happens to him, it is his own fault. Women have 90 percent more disadvantage than men.

Girls "yield" more than males. When they are big enough, the *machos* start drinking rum and looking for fights and one day when one least expects it, they come and tell one that he has been killed in a fight. Not the *miña mujer*. They are *de la casa* and keep one company and do not give one so many headaches.

In a community of smothered tensions which occasionally break out in the open, it is more often the male who is involved, who gets "mixed up with the law," and more often the female who is the object rather than performer of aggression, since family members are apt to retaliate less than nonrelatives, strangers, and upper-class persons. This is not to say that the female does not aggress, but in different ways, as we saw in Chapter 3.

The female is cloistered and closely watched. She provides companionship for the mother, while boys, once they have passed the "fondle-able" age, become more and more outgoing, have greater and greater freedom. The male will help with the harder chores and is a necessary errand boy (a frequent description of a "good boy" is *buen mandadero*—good errand boy). Especially for mountain families, a boy to run errands, tend animals, and perform the harder domestic chores is almost indispensable.

It was traditionally hoped that children, more especially the male, would help out with monetary and other assistance as they grew older. The young man used to be required to turn over most or all of his money to his parents. Only marriage set him free from this traditional obligation. But in a world of raised levels of aspiration and greater desires, traditional family obligations have given way to a more self-oriented attitude. Once he grows up, the male often ignores the family almost completely. Thus the boy is not as overwhelmingly desirable as he was in former days, though he still maintains an edge over the girl.

Even the time-honored respect and veneration for the aged seem to have evaporated in the face of acquired needs for the wonderful things from the United States and increasing insecurity. Cases are not rare where, living in the same household, adult wage-earners will not contribute anything to the general welfare and, on the other hand, will expect when they have no money to revert to their child roles and be given food and shelter by parents, no matter how badly off the latter may be. This change has made old age, almost completely lacking in security, feared by most men and women. When they are too old to work they may apply for old-age assistance, but if they are fortunate enough to get it, the $7.50 per month scarcely keeps them alive. Many elders are forced to beg or otherwise impose themselves on the charity of others. On the other hand, it is the old parents who are often saddled with responsibility for taking care of children, no matter how grown, who have no income.

In spite of what has been stated, this does not mean that parents consistently confer their nurturance and love strictly according to preferences. Some mothers who say they prefer girls treat their boys with much love and affection, and where fathers prefer sons, they often are kind and affectionate with their little daughters. Perhaps general treatment of the sexes may be framed in these terms: The mother prefers girls, because of their stated advantages, but also is often quite close to her sons and may even, to please herself and/or her husband, accord the boy privileged handling. But she knows the boy is more likely to leave her and there is little she can do about it. However, she does succeed in making the boy as well as the girl dependent upon her, so that there are strong ties which may be difficult to sever and which the boy will frequently maintain even after marriage.

The father prefers boys because of their stated advantages but is also considerate and affectionate with his girls. With strong puritanical suspicion of male intentions, he tends zealously to guard the girl from contact or "contamination" by males. The boy is his companion (more in the sense of tagging along than as an equal); the girl is his ward. Once she passes the age of six he may retain his affection for the girl, but he will no longer demonstrate it. Perhaps he does not even trust his own feelings where the *ninas mujeres* are concerned. Neither son nor daughter is as dependent upon him as upon his wife. But father and children are all dependent upon the wife-mother, though this dependency may not be characterized by affectionate acts and there may be much abuse of the mother, in spite of or because of their dependency.

Marital Relationships after Children

In most families no changes occurred after the arrival of the child in the amount of time husband and wife spend together, though in a few cases changes of more or less time were involved. Four small and six large family husbands also feel there were no changes in the relationship itself, while three each feel changes for the better took place. Those where no changes occurred feel, with an air of fatalism, that "we have always lived in the same way," or as one expresses it: "When the baby arrived I went to see her. I looked at the baby and my wife said to me, 'Here is the child you have wanted.' The relations have been the same." Most of those who experienced changes for the better had quarreled before but now live peaceably: "The child brought a certain degree of affection and strengthened our relationship; I don't like that she see us quarrel." And as one traditional-minded husband put it: "There has been more love, because after having children the wife is loved with more pity. Although we may quarrel, still she is loved with more pity. If there are no children, there is no affection." One of two husbands who got along worse with his mate told us, "No, señor, when there is no family one lives more peaceably."

Most changes or lack of them were expected by these men, either by example of other marriages or in their own family of orientation, or, as one husband said, having had several children he now had more experience and more *capacidad* (sense, maturity). Furthermore, the arrival of the child was usually expected. The bland assertions of some fathers that they had not expected this child one is apt to take with a large measure of reservation.

Two possible exceptions never mentioned by any of the husbands might be: (1) They may have been using contraception and it failed. (2) As a doctor in the American missionary clinic in Cañaveral told me, there are many unmarried girls and women (perhaps this had some relevance for naive married ones, too) who come to her with all the symptoms of pregnancy yet insist they have not had intercourse. Though they are still technically virgins, and there was no penetration, they were apparently unaware of the fact that the spermatozoa may reach the ovum without intromission. This ignorance may be shared by some of the males, also, but would hardly account for so much "surprise" from a married man at the onset of pregnancy in his wife.

In only one of our cases could there really be honest astonishment: a wife who was supposed to have been sterilized but then became pregnant. Since she had a multiple operation (cyst, tumor, sterilization), it is possible that the surgeon may have told her he was going to sterilize, then finding it unfeasible while she was under anesthesia, neglected to tell her. This "less-they-know-the-better-off-they-are" attitude of doctors toward the people is quite common in Valle Caña and Agua Lluvia (see pp. 38-39).

Role Evaluation and Self-Esteem

To round out this consideration of wife and husband relationships and bridge over into parent-child relationships and training, let us examine how our married pairs rate their own and each other's roles. The role balance of his parents will crucially affect the socialization environment of the child and will be part of what the child introjects in identifying with them and building his own ego and superego.

No couple seem completely satisfied with each other, and four wives and one husband are completely dissatisfied (Table 9). Wives are more

TABLE 9

Wives' and Husbands' Evaluations of Each Other

	Mother's Evaluation of Father	Father's Evaluation of Mother
1. Highly critical; holds in low regard, no admiration	4	1
2.	4	4
3.	4	4
4.	6	9
5. Highly admiring, commendatory; high regard	—	—
Total Cases	18	18

critical of husbands than vice-versa, though there are strong instances of each. But while these women do not admire their husbands a great deal, they do fear them, and it is this fear which they translate as respect and transmit to their children and by which they control them.

As to their roles as mothers, however, these women value themselves very highly (Table 10). Most of them generally accept life as they find it, although four are pretty much dissatisfied. However, as shown

TABLE 10
Parental Self-Esteem

	Mother's Self-Evaluation	Father's Self-Evaluation
1. Deprecates self in many areas; "I'm a poor parent," "People don't seem to like me"	—	—
2.	2	1
3.	1	2
4.	7	8
5. Praises self in many areas; "I know I'm a good parent," "People all like me"	8	7
Total Cases	18	18

in Chapter 3, while they accede to their laborious and often emotionally painful roles, there is a repressed desire for more independence which could materialize with the right conditions. The wife-mother's satisfaction with her own roles is shared by the husband-father (Table 10), though they do not esteem each other very highly.

They do not appear to be troubled about raising their children insofar as their own roles are involved. It is not that they do not have many self-admitted problems and anxieties concerning their children. Speech and actions are fraught with anxieties of all kinds. Nor is it that they are not concerned at times about the behavior of their child or how he is growing up. It is that somehow they feel that when something is amiss in the parent-child or wife-husband relationships, it is due to the inherent *carácter* of the child ("that boy was born bad") or things they cannot obtain by way of material satisfactions for the child. While the latter is more realistic objectively, the former is given more emphasis. In any case the wife and/or husband will almost never blame himself for this or for their own relationship conflicts. Guilt in these areas is not frequent. Perhaps a third reason would be other children being held to blame, but parents guard against this possibility, as we shall see later, by insulating their child from most outside contacts.

In the account which follows we shall investigate the modes and means by which these husbands and wives, in their roles as fathers and mothers, go about the process of making little Vallecañeses into big ones.

CHAPTER 5

Bringing up the Child—I

Introduction

Now we shall describe and analyze some areas of child care and training in Valle Caña which seem common to all societies. The wider scope of the village is narrowed to focus on the role of the parents and their surrogates in rearing the child, but the interrelationships between the culture and the family and the ways in which each defines and influences child training will be apparent. Through the screen of the family the culture is uniquely interpreted and transmitted to the infant and small child. As the child grows older, peers and extrafamilial cultural agents like the school exert increasing influence, and the family's importance diminishes somewhat. Culture, family, society, and "natural" environment are antecedent conditions whose consequents are seen in the behavior of the child.

There is no clear chronological delineation between infancy and childhood; the determinants are cultural as well as biological. Whether it is true that the mother-child relationship begins at conception as one psychoanalyst (Benedek 1949) claims, it assuredly commences at birth, and it is from the care of the infant that we begin.

Adult View of the Child

The infant and small child is seen as a kind of doll, an enjoyable, pleasure-provoking plaything. Babies are affectionately regarded more for their entertainment value for parents than because the latter enjoy amusing them. Commonly voiced by the mothers in our sample were such attitudes as the following:

I would lie down on the bed and play with her, making noises for her, caressing her. I would give her a little rattle to entertain herself with. I would dance her the way you do with dolls. . . .

I am a woman who works much and I hardly have time for anything. So mostly I have never been able to entertain myself with my children.

I would throw her up as if she were a doll. I would make noises and teach her how to do *tortita* [a clap-hands game]. I would caress and kiss her much.

The infant and small child are regarded as *sin capacidad*, which means not merely "without capacity" but lacking the ability to think for himself. One result is that the child is seldom taught anything deliberately, is never, until maturity, considered really capable of acting independently. He is assumed to be, and is disciplined into being, a passive creature for whom things must be done and decisions made, one who, if he acts alone, acts from instinctual (ergo, bad, evil) desires rather than by reasoning. So a dependency relationship is often maintained and encouraged long after the child maturationally could behave with some degree of independence.

In line with this view, a child is considered *inocente* and is likened to the angels. When a child dies, friends and neighbors gather at the house, decorate the corpse with flowers, and sing, eat, drink, and make merry all night. For this is a *baquiné* (in some areas called a *florón* after the tradition of making floral wreaths to decorate the coffin), a time for rejoicing; the child's soul, unblemished as yet by the sins of the wicked adult world, is returning to its place among the heavenly hosts. In any funeral procession, child or adult, a row of children lead the mourners. These are religious manifestations of the child conceived as *tabula rasa*.

However there is a counter-belief, as we noted in the last chapter, that the male is born with *malicias*, while the girl is born defenseless and corruptible. It represents a basic split in the outlook on child-world relationships and may help explain some otherwise seemingly contradictory behavior patterns and attitudes. Among other things, it aids us in understanding the frequent caprice and whimsy with which the child is treated by the parent on the one hand, and the often violent restrictiveness and punishment on the other. In his or her fundamental ambivalence, the contemporary parent often does not know with assurance which approach to take. And of course one result is the assumption that as long as the child remains in its place and "out of trouble," the parent himself will not have to bother to resolve the conflict, since there will be a minimum of situations requiring careful and considered judgment.

Separations from Parents in Infancy

Children of Vallecañese families seldom leave their parents or are left by them, either in the period before two years of age or from two to six years. Exceptions are those who become *hijos de crianza*. Work patterns do not necessitate fathers leaving home for long periods, as in some communities where they alternate between coffee and cane seasons, or rarely when a Vallecañese father goes to the United States for temporary farm work. But the cultural definitions of the father's role involve a good deal of daily absence from the child even though the father is "in residence."

Infant Caretaking Agents

As in most cultures, Vallecañese mothers are the chief caretaking agents (Table 11). Their duties and responsibilities increase with the

TABLE 11

Amount of Infant Caretaking by Mother

1.	Practically none	—
2.	Less than half, but some	1
3.	About half	2
4.	More than half, but considerable help	2
5.	Most, but some help	6
6.	Nearly all, rare help	6
7.	All	1
	Total Cases	18

child's age, while the father comes to play a minor role in day-to-day care. Where the mother, because of illness or temporary employment, cannot fulfill her caretaking responsibilities, usually this is done by a third surrogate.

Caretaking agents other than parents participated in some infant rearing but not usually to a large degree. Seventeen of the eighteen families utilized a nonparental surrogate as follows: eleven older siblings, one friend, two grandmothers, three other relatives.

Maternal Nurturance toward the Infant

Most mothers feel their children did not cry much in infancy, but when they did cry mothers were generally responsive, half being highly responsive. The most frequent reasons given by the relatively unresponsive mothers were that they could not get their chores done and too much picking up would spoil the child. Two also felt that crying "helps to develop their lungs."

The responsive mothers seem to be motivated by many fears due to what Gillin (1948: 313-318) terms an "unrealistic belief system." They feel that crying will rupture the child's navel ("make it stick out long," "make it grow with the child's growing," "look ugly"), or else make the child nervous, sick, asphyxiated, or hoarse.[1]

Considering their endless round of onerous and time-consuming tasks, these mothers give a fair amount of time to being with their infants. Yet, since affection for children is taken to be traditional, this is not surprising. What is unexpected is that two mothers spend practically no time with the child beyond that of daily caretaking necessities.

Mothers attend frequently to their infants, though it is often the most cursory kind of attendance. However a good deal of affection takes place, with much fondling, caressing, and carrying about, even by the smallest siblings. Many of these children were unwanted (see Chapter 4) but this does not imply that rejection at conception carried over into the postnatal period. Much apparent neglect may be due to ignorance of what constitutes an objectively dangerous situation (disease, injury, etc.) for the child, the pressing burden of household chores, and economic poverty itself, which may create a generally hopeless outlook.

These mothers are fairly warm toward their infants, though not excessively so (Table 12). In general they seem to enjoy moderately the duties of infant care and think babies are more fun than older

1. This phenomenon illustrates how folk beliefs probably arise. In the past or with earlier siblings, deaths, sickness, or disease may have indeed been preceded by crying, and coming first in the time sequence, crying is taken to be a cause rather than an effect of whatever is wrong with the child. Several said they received this knowledge from their own mothers or midwives.

TABLE 12

Warmth of Affectional Bond, Mother to Infant

1. Mother cold, matter-of-fact; little cuddling or play; did not particularly enjoy baby	1
2.	3
3.	6
4.	4
5. Very warm, affectionate; much cuddling, holding, admiring	4
Total Cases	18

children, but a sizable portion have little liking for these duties and prefer larger children.

Family size seems to make little difference in the quality of affection, although one would have supposed that affection might be less in large families because of additional burdens. However, it could be argued that people have large families who like children, and that small families might be in part due to a dislike of children.

Infant Feeding and Weaning

When food is available, Vallecañese mothers permit children to have as much as they can. They fear that if the child loses his appetite he will become seriously ill. The cultural ideal for child and adult is fatness, as among European peasant families. The highest compliment one's child may receive is to be called *gordito* (little fat one). Such a child is beautiful and a mark of the care, consideration, and food resources of the parents and therefore enhances the latter's prestige. However, fats and meats are not regular fare, and Vallecañeses, though occasionally starch-fat, are not necessarily resistant to disease.

Most infants are breast-fed—upon demand and/or when their mothers think the child wants or needs to be. Rigid scheduling is generally absent. Mothers feel that to insist on feeding a child when not hungry, or too hungry because of long waiting, "would cause the food not to agree with the child." Even if they preferred it, they would probably not schedule-feed, since clock time does not govern Vallecañese life. Only one mother tried scheduling.

There is no common weaning pattern. The central tendency of the distribution is bimodal; mothers tend to wean either gradually or abruptly, with scant middle ground (Table 13). However, there is a fairly common pattern for preparation for weaning which runs about

TABLE 13

Severity of Change-of-Mode Weaning

1. Child weans self, refuses bottle or breast	4
2. Mother weans gradually, trains in other modes before transition, no punishment; allows return to breast or bottle at will	4
3.	—
4.	1
5.	2
6. Weans very abruptly, usually without cup for supplementary feeding; does not allow sucking, no night bottle	5
0. Not weaned	2
Total Cases	18

as follows: The baby is breast-fed for a few months, then the bottle is introduced for daytime feeding and the breast saved for night feeding or withheld if another baby is coming. Through the bottle mothers introduce to the child dried milk from the public milk station or store, "teas" made of native herbs, and fruit juices. Any soft drink or rum bottle to which a small nipple may be attached is used. Cooked cereal and the cup or can are also introduced after a few months. In a year more or less the night breast-feeding is dropped. Where gradual weaning takes place the bottles decrease as cup feedings increase. Where abrupt weaning occurs, bottle or breast is suddenly discontinued.

The decision to wean is usually fortuitous. For instance, if the mother wishes to wean but fears to take the bottle from the child, she may seize upon a sudden event like the disappearance of the nipple as an excuse. Several either hid the nipple or said it was taken by a rat or dog, which often is the case. None applied physical punishment in change-of-mode [2] weaning, but two admit smearing bitter substances on their nipples and another frightened the child by pointing to her breasts at each feeding and exclaiming "*caca!*" (filthy) until the child came to abhor the breast. One boy who persisted on the bottle until six years old, having been weaned from the breast abruptly, was bottle-weaned by friends and siblings who shamed him until "he came to hate the bottle."

The wide variability of change-of-mode weaning illustrates how the end of infancy patterns is determined as much by individual choice

2. Change from breast to bottle is not change-of-mode weaning, but change from either to cup drinking is. Sipping sporadically from a cup along with bottle or breast is preparation for change-of-mode. A child is counted weaned who has completely relinquished the nipple except as a pacifier.

and culture as by biology. These children were weaned as early as seven months or as late as seven years (carrying their bottles to school!). Most had a fair amount of preparation for weaning, but the decision to remove the sucking medium depended upon maternal whim and might be slow or sudden.

Child Feeding and Eating

Eating problems do not center on whether a child will eat but whether his mother can keep enough food in front of him. The children are heavy eaters. It is not at all unusual to see a large plate of boiled, starch root vegetables placed before children of five or six who bolt it down and ask for more. If there is more the child will get it. If he eats only part or does not want to eat at all, nothing is usually done. He may even be allowed to toss part of it outside to the pigs and chickens. If other things are available, the mother frequently will prepare a more desired substitute. Usually, however, *"El hijo del pobre no puede pasar como el hijo del rico"* (A poor child cannot get along like a rich child) and therefore will not be finicky since there is little choice. If a child undergoes persistent loss of appetite the mother may apply a home remedy or perhaps take him to the doctor.

Eating in a Vallecañese household is not a social occasion. The mother serves the children first, then herself. The father's food during cane season is brought to him in the fields by a son, or if none is old enough, by a neighbor's boy. If he is home he is served first, then the children. Once in a while the mother may eat with the others, standing or squatting somewhere, but usually she eats alone. Small children are served together but often their older siblings wander into the house and are served on demand, especially older boys.

If there is a table or bench, it usually seats the father or older sons. Most often children sit on the floor with their plates on their knees. There is little conversation between spouses or between them and the children. Children may speak quietly among themselves; playing or making jokes is not permitted, though occasionally honored in the breach in the father's absence. When each child has finished he brings his plate into the kitchen to his mother. The father's plate is kept filled and as soon as he finishes the mother hurries in to clear the table. Once in a while an older daughter will help the mother clean the dishes.

Most parents feel that children between the ages of four and seven are too small to adhere to severe restrictions on eating practices, but nevertheless generally express high demands regarding eating behavior (Table 14), fathers being somewhat stricter. Little emphasis is placed on eating manners as such, and in fact it is difficult to communicate the concept in English (Appendix C). But health is a primary concern.

TABLE 14

Restrictions on Eating Behavior

Physical Movement
1. Child has much freedom, may leave table at will	6
2.	3
3. Child must remain at table through meal	9
Total Cases	18

Use of Fingers
1. May use; no restrictions	3
2.	2
3.	9
4. Severe restrictions, much emphasis	4
Total Cases	18

Interruption of Adult Conversation
1. No restrictions; parents give attention whenever child talks	—
2.	—
3.	2
4. Severe restrictions; much emphasis	16
Total Cases	18

Eating with fingers is bad because their hands might be dirty and infect them, not because it is impolite. Moving about is dangerous for the child's digestion and interrupting the conversation of elders is bad anytime, rather than merely poor etiquette. Since parents feel the way they do, in spite of high demands, one sees much of children eating with fingers and moving about, though generally they will not interrupt adults.

When parents punish children about eating, it is because they ignore parental demands, not because they have bad manners. Often such punishment is quite severe, but like punishment in general it is apt to be capriciously administered. Therefore, while there are many parents who resort to such punishment, general pressure for conformity with eating standards is relatively moderate, especially as compared with verbal expectations. Mothers pressure their children for adherence to these rules more than fathers because they are more directly concerned with the child's eating, being with him all day and being most responsible for his welfare.

For violating eating rules, twelve mothers and seven fathers use scolding and physical punishment; five mothers and five fathers scold only; one mother and six fathers use calm explanation. Praise or any other indication of pleasure is seldom expressed by these parents, who expect conformity as a matter of course.

Parents consider eating, "like praying, a time for seriousness, quiet, and devotion." As one phrases it, "the guardian angel is with one when eating and one should be quiet." Like praying, proper eating should not expect rewards on this earth. The good child eats *con vergüenza* (with shame, humility). The kind of completely permissive situation for eating experienced by Mintz (1951:VI/39-41) is not quite as true in Valle Caña. It is true that children are allowed to eat at any time, to eat without punishment whatever they can obtain, and are permitted much freedom while eating within the limits we have outlined, but our parents seem more restrictive in principle than those of Cañamelar.

Sphincter Control

Letrinas (outhouses) are owned by about half the families. Most open-country folk use the countryside itself. Frequently, especially on rainy days, small children are permitted to urinate through cracks in the floor or dash under the house; they are permitted in good weather to use the grounds nearby. As they grow older they are asked to use a place removed from the dwelling, usually an area which adults frequent also.

Mothers do not feel that the child can train himself or that sphincter control comes with maturation. They usually want to do something active about it and may become quite emotional. The usual method is to use a potty in the beginning and, after the child has learned to use it himself, to wean him to the outhouse or outdoors. The mother sets the child on the potty, holding him there if he attempts to move "until he has done something." When the mother becomes irritated, usually in a short time, the child is harshly scolded or spanked.

Well, at first I put her on the potty; I had to force her to sit down and she cried much and did not want to sit down. Well . . . I took her and sat her down and forced her. I watched her and when I saw she was going to do it on the floor I would run and sit her on the potty. She cried much and I would tell her angrily: "Sit down here and do not do it on the floor or

I'll hit you." And I hit her. After four or five days she did not cry any more when I sat her down. She knew I would hit her.

Most children are trained in six months or less, but the range is from a few months to 2.5 years. Median age for beginning training is 12 months for girls (range 7-24 months) and 21 months for boys (range 5-36 months). Like Mintz (1951: VI/41) we find that girls are trained earlier and more severely than boys.

Children are also frequently cuffed, spanked, and scolded for wetting the bed, which persists long after anal control has been accomplished.

Q. Could you tell me what you have done when he wet his bed?
A. He still wets his bed. And I hit him when he does it.
Q. What is his reaction when he wets the bed?
A. He calls me and I get up and I scold him and hit him, but I have not been able to rid him of the habit.

How may one understand these sharply restrictive practices to achieve waste control? It seems to fit in with the general value of "cleanliness but not sanitation." There is abhorrence of filth but only when it is directly on or near the person. If it can be circumvented or shoved away from one's presence, one feels rid of it. Thus houses themselves may be quite clean and the bodies of individuals even cleaner, but under and around the house all kinds of filth and debris accumulate. The mountain path may be spotted with human and animal excreta. The child is constantly warned about getting dirty or contaminated (anything the mother does not want the child to touch she calls *caca* [filthy]). The common colloquial for defecate, *cagar* (the only literal English equivalent is a vulgarity), is used by adults and children more frequently than the somewhat more polite term *ensuciarse* (to soil oneself), providing an interesting linguistic clue.

Modesty and Sex Training

Differential practices and policies toward male and female children are manifested prenatally and shortly after birth become greatly emphasized. While all children receive modesty training fairly early, strictest emphasis is on training the girl properly to conceal her body. Median beginning age of modesty training for boys is 24 months (range 10-48) and girls 18 months (range early infancy-36). One boy is untrained at 7 years.

A girl is almost never seen without a dress and loin covering, even during infancy, while boys go about nude or with just a short shirt, genitals exposed, until five or six years normally and occasionally as late as eight or nine. Jokes may be made by parents and elders about a boy's sexual organs but I have never heard joking references to girls' organs, at least not in their presence. But boys and older males often joke in male company about female genitalia. A kind of invisible wall is built up around the female which begins in infancy and lasts with increasing stress until the climacteric. Older women sometimes cast aside their "virginal" behavior and make ribald jokes with the men, but these are women who could no longer even remotely be considered potential sex objects. So long as a woman is so considered, however, she maintains the lady-like qualities which husband and society expect of her.

But while boys are often permitted to display their penises, this is not always approved as a policy by mothers. There is almost no permissiveness for children going without clothes (mode and median of 1 on a 5 point scale). Some mothers do not in policy or practice permit boys to go without clothes, but the latter often break this parental prohibition, especially out of sight of their mother. I have never observed opposition by fathers for boys under six, although mothers have occasionally become angry enough to strap one or two in my presence for going nude outdoors. On the other hand, male nudeness is somewhat more sanctioned indoors, and I have several times seen a mother fondle a naked boy of four, playfully caressing his genitals and smiling proudly at her visitor. It is also not unusual to see a man suddenly grab the penis or scrotum of a little boy and jokingly threaten to pull, bite, or cut it off. A few mothers also reported they sometimes used castration threats with their little sons, something which, according to several male informants, was considerably more frequent a generation ago.

One father in his late sixties said that men constantly used castration threats with boys when he was a child. Several times he had been told a story by his mother in which an old man would lie in wait in a canefield for unsuspecting boys. When they came close he would lure them with a loaf of bread, then grab them and cut off their penises with a sharp machete. He still gets a twinge of fear when passing a canefield alone at night and always wants to run past them. He says it makes him fearful even to hear men joke about these things and he has never threatened his own sons with this fate.

Mothers feel very strongly about modesty standards (Table 15), yet the pressures of housework and child rearing may often prevent their administering punishment for nudity as much as they would wish. There is a general nervousness of tone in regard to maternal statements

TABLE 15

Maternal Pressure for Maintenance of Modesty Standards

	Boys	Girls
1. No pressure, though instances have arisen	1	—
2.		
3.	1	1
4.	2	3
5. Severe pressure; punishment, anger, emotion	6	4
Total Cases	10	8

on boys which accounts for the variance between what they say they do and what observation indicates they actually do. A large portion of their concern is based on "what other people will think." People, they feel, will think they are bad parents because they permit their children to be immodest. People will think their children are bad. People will think they are worse off than they actually are if they cannot afford even a simple garment for their children. It may get the child into "trouble" with the opposite sex, causing shame and embarrassment to child and parents. As one mother says of her son:

He never goes around nude. In former times . . . there was not that evil intent so much, and men, women, and children would even bathe together. But today a boy, from the time he is in his mother's womb, has *malicias*—dirty things they say, like *chochita* [little vagina], *pinguito* [little penis], *huevitos* [little scrotum, little eggs], and the way they look at each other and say "Look what that one has," or "How big that one's is." People pass by and hear them and that is ugly. And if other persons hear one is embarrassed. So, covered up, they do not give the opportunity to anyone to say these things . . . Boys must not let themselves be seen by girls. They must bathe alone, not with girls . . . If I see him taking off his clothes, I scold him.

And the mother of a little girl says:

I do not like to have her go around without clothes because that is the way they can get sickness. Because that is ugly—girls being nude, that does not look well ... Because it doesn't [embarrassed laughter]. The *muchachas mujeres* [girl-women] should cover up more than a male because—I don't know—a nude boy does not look well either, but it is not so bad because he is a *machito* [little he-man]. But a girl should cover her parts [more nervous laughter]. In the morning when she gets up and takes off her nightclothes I make her put on her dress and panties—and she must stay that way all day ... Since she started walking I took good care to see that she would always be clothed. She still takes off her dress but I put it on again and scold her harshly.

Aside from other dangers lurking in the masculine world, a note of incest fear creeps into the testimony of more than one mother: "I do not let her undress in front of anybody. She does not undress in front of her brothers or even her father. ... A boy today is very evil ... I can believe anything of a boy ..."

Mintz (1951: VI/43) says of Cañamelar:

The first and most pressing peril is that of incest ... It is this possibility that parents strive hardest to avoid. As a result, the desire for their own privacy is sometimes thwarted. Attitudes toward incest are frank and realistic. ... There is a tying in of maleness with a local cultural assumption that men are sexually irresponsible and cannot be expected to show restraint. This feeling, which is shown most clearly in the frank efforts to avoid the possibility of incest, pervades other aspects of child training, and is part of the process of sex differentiation.

In Valle Caña, mothers commonly sleep with children, especially girls, while fathers are usually confined to the hammock. Presumably, however, a change must be effected each time there is sexual intercourse between the parents. It would become impossible, in spite of parental precautions, to hide the sex act from at least the hearing of children.

Lita represents a deviation from the norm. Her son is seven, but she feels he is too young to be made to wear clothes; yet even Lita must bow to public opinion at times:

Well, he might as well be cool. He is still small and can be around without clothes. I do not mind ... It is good for his health. Now if he has grippe it is good that he covers his chest, but if not, he may walk around nude.

When he is nine or ten I will tell him not to take off his clothes, but then he will be getting big . . . I've never told him anything about his clothes . . . Outside, though, he should have clothes . . . if far from the house . . . because there are *muchachitas mujeres*. Today you don't bring up children . . . what you bring up is hell. Maybe nothing will happen . . . but since there are *malicias* mothers do not like to send out their children nude.

Autoerotic and Group Sex Play

Most parents deny they have ever noticed autoerotic play in their children and view it with a jaundiced eye, handling it severely where it occurs. Both parents in all families scale extremely restrictive toward boys and girls as regards masturbation. Mothers admit the occurrence of masturbation more readily than fathers, but this may be due to a freer attitude on the part of all children in the presence of the mother alone and the fact that she is with them more.

In line with what has been said of incest fears, none of the fathers admits noticing masturbation in their girls, but they are more permissive with boys than mothers (Table 16). Ten fathers but only one

TABLE 16

Severity of Parental Pressure against Child Masturbation

	Mothers		Fathers	
	Boys	Girls	Boys	Girls
1. No pressure, though has occurred	—	—	—	—
2.	—	—	—	—
3.	—	1	1	—
4.	2	4	3	—
5. Severe pressure; punishment, anger, threats	7	2	1	—
X. Issue hasn't come up; parent hasn't noticed	1	—	3	8
0. Insufficient information	—	1	2	—
Total Cases	10	8	10	8

mother deny noticing juvenile autoeroticism. Such denials of masturbation were followed with the assertion that while the parent had not noticed it in his child, he was sure it took place among neighbor children. Here again, however, we have evidence of "plurality of denial plus noticing it in other's children." Several mothers give examples of how they saw *fulanos'* (so-and-so's) offspring ("everyone around here talks of how bad her children are") engaged in mutual sex activity.

Parental fears underlying opposition to child sex play, besides shame, include:

> The child becomes pale and sick when he plays with "that." If she plays with "that," then gets her hands on a skin sore, she will become infected.
>
> If she does it when she is small, she will do it when she is big.
>
> Urine contains disease and he takes his hand to his mouth and can get sick.
>
> They would then go on and try to have the relations of male and female.
>
> Sometimes they pull it and twist it . . . and can hurt themselves; a dreadful, tragic thing happens to them . . . the cause of a hemorrhage. . . .
>
> . . . Turns pale and sick-looking because he takes his hands and carries them to his nose.[3]
>
> His urine could stop so he couldn't urinate.
>
> He may be ruptured . . . and the *huevos* (testicles) will get very big. . . .
>
> They thrust sticks inside—I have seen them—and can get hurt.
>
> They make it long and stiff; it will grow big and then not fit into his clothes.
>
> They get sort of *emboban* ("dopey").

Sex Education

All mothers and all fathers without exception aver that their children have never asked them questions regarding sexual relations and reproduction. When his little boy asked one father why he kissed the boy's mother, he replied it was because he loved her, but prohibited further questions. When her little girl asked a mother where she came from she replied that the child "came from the States." Another mother says her little boy did not ask, but his two-year-old sister said to her (the mother was noticeably pregnant), " '*Mami,* what you have there is a child.' And when she gets angry she hits me in the stomach and tells me, 'I will kill the baby.' I do not know who told her this. I do not tell her anything. I laugh. Sometimes I tell her, 'What if the child dies?' and she answers, 'You will buy another one.' Since I go to the hospital she believes this."

The gist of parental responses to children's "facts of life" questions

3. When a pale, drawn person (*una persona hinchada*) is seen, people sometimes say of them they smell their sexual organs too often.

is that they would consider them a terrible affront and a sign that they had lost the child's respect or an indication that they had probably picked up bad ideas from other children. A few fathers but no mothers said they would talk about sex to the boys when older (14-21 years). On a scale of parental sex anxiety with 7 as the high extreme, the median for mothers is 7.0, and for fathers 5.0.

While parents occasionally may joke about sexual affairs in front of children, in "serious" discussions about sex, children are always excluded, especially girls. Yet children pick up ideas about sex, especially boys. In the first instance, they observe farm animals, the means of sex education of rural children everywhere. Groups of men are not wont to dismiss the company of boys, no matter how small, when talking about women. Some men and older boys deliberately take it upon themselves to inform boys (not their own sons), usually to "do them the favor" but also because they enjoy watching the child's reaction and joke at his expense. Older playmates may be counted upon to initiate younger ones into the mysteries of sex or at least their perhaps distorted version of it. The last point is significant in the case of girls. The case of Felipa is illuminating. Her seven-year-old daughter, she says,

... does not know anything about this. These kinds of things have not crossed her mind. Not even Luisa [age eleven] or Lucia [age twenty, also her daughter] have talked to me about these things. If Lucia knows, she found out on the outside.

... It is bad to tell them because they are small children and innocent; they should not know about this. Their *capacidad* is not like ours. We have secrets about that. A child tells everything.

.... I have never had to explain it, even when Lucia got her first period [fué señorita]. She did not tell me about this, I found out from a friend. Only as general advice, when she was about twelve or thirteen, I told her not to eat oranges and sour things. But I did not tell her why. If I told her suddenly she would have gone to her friends and she would understand what it is all about. I found it out from my friends.

Many mothers might tell their children about births and such but I don't. If she asked me where children are born and how, I would give her a slap in the mouth and tell her, "Children do not ask that...."

Thus the woman builds up a network of defenses to cover her anxieties and guilt over not meeting the problem of her daughter's sex education.

Aggression Control

Adult Vallecañeses seem to be characterized not so much by fear of personal injury as of the social consequences of aggression. Most of them prohibit and punish aggression in their children not only because fighting itself is "bad" but because parents are afraid they will "get into trouble." They have often seen aggressive persons, especially males, end up seriously wounded or in jail. They are not abhorrent of overt aggression per se—they often gather around to watch "trouble," a cockfight, animals attacking each other, or children attacking animals —but it is the punishing effects in the culture for interpersonal aggression which deter them and make them extremely anxious about it in their own children. Both parents place a high restriction on all forms of aggression (Tables 17-21). Not only offense-wise, but even in self-

TABLE 17
Permissiveness for Sibling Aggression

	Mothers	Fathers
1. Not at all permissive; punish, stop fighting	9	3
2.	6	5
3.	1	8
4.	—	—
5. Entirely permissive; never interferes; "fight it out"	—	—
o. No siblings	2	2
Total Cases	18	18

TABLE 18
Parental Demands for Child to Be Aggressive toward Other Children

	Mothers	Fathers
1. None whatever; explicitly does not want child to fight; come back home when attacked	9	13
2.	—	1
3.	1	1
4.	6	3
5. High demands for fighting; important for child to hold up his own end, not ask for help	2	—
Total Cases	18	18

TABLE 19

Extent of Pressure to Encourage Child to Fight Back

	Mothers	Fathers
1. Never has encouraged child to fight back under any circumstances	9	14
2.	—	2
3.	7	1
4.	2	—
5. Strong encouragement; punish if asks for help	—	—
0. Insufficient information	—	1
Total Cases	18	18

TABLE 20

Parental Permissiveness for Antiparental Aggression

	Mothers	Fathers
1. Not at all permissive; stops at once	18	11
2.	—	2
3.	—	1
4.	—	3
5. Completely permissive; no attempt to stop	—	—
0. Insufficient information	—	1
Total Cases	18	18

TABLE 21

Severity of Punishment for Antiparental Aggression

	Mothers	Fathers
1. Has never been punished	—	—
2.	—	—
3.	1	4
4.	5	1
5. Severe punishment; parent angry, hostile	7	—
0. No issue; child has never attacked parents	5	13
Total Cases	18	18

defense, they seldom encourage their children to fight back. More generally, parental rules are for the child to come home at once when attacked by another child, complain to them, and have the parents, usually the fathers, settle it at the higher level. Since they are more involved in adult aggression and are also more concerned with *respeto* than the women, the fathers' participation in this aspect of socialization is expected.

The general governing maxim seems to be: "Keep your nose clean and out of other people's business. When trouble starts, leave it. No matter whose fault it is, you probably will be blamed." True, there is sometimes thinly concealed admiration for an aggressive man (*guapo*) at a distance. The man is given a wide berth, and his prowess may be commented on with envy, but at the same time he is also called a bad fellow and the people feel pity and sorrow for his parents and family. Sooner or later, they know, he will "get in trouble" and bring them disgrace and worry. And while they may applaud occasional outbursts of aggression against authority figures, particularly the policeman, little sympathy is shed on the aggressor once he is arrested. The rationalization becomes "He had no business doing that. He deserves what he got. We don't like the policeman but he must do his duty."

When children do play together harmoniously, they are not usually rewarded with any indication that this is proper behavior. As in other areas of child training, it is felt that praise does "more harm than good."

The typical way of handling a fight when the parent is nearby is to extract the child from the imbroglio, take him home and punish him whether or not it is his fault, since his orders are not to fight under any circumstances but to run home. In intrasibling battles, the general procedure is to call once or twice to "break it up." If they persist, the parent punishes all the siblings, not usually bothering to find out which was at fault because of the blanket taboo. The assumption is that it takes two parties to make a conflict, victim as well as aggressor.

Parents report little antiparental aggression in the home, and in the few cases where it is evident, it is mostly boys. But when this happens, all mothers and most fathers are almost completely intolerant of it. On a scale of permissiveness for antiparental aggression, with 5.0 denoting high permission, the medians for both parents toward offspring of both sexes are 1.0. Mintz (1951:VI) reports that boys' tantrums are often tolerated and even encouraged so as to develop a strong *machismo*. My observations in Valle Caña agree with this, with qualifications. Boys are given more freedom of action than girls, but in the rather strictly circumscribed area of respect for parents, few boys are allowed to transgress the limits. A boyish tantrum is occasionally tolerated (though never in my experience was a girl's), but in these cases it was not considered aggression unless it became obviously so. The boy would have to direct verbal or physical abuse against the parents, in which case he would be reprimanded or punished. Negativism, whining, and so on, are not always considered antiparental aggression, although I have often interpreted and judged it as such.

Antiparental aggression is more of a problem for mothers (Table 20) because they are more easily aggressed against. This may be explained by (1) greater "respect" for the father; (2) the mother's lesser ability to enforce respect and other demands (while she will always insist that the children respect their father, the latter may not reciprocate); (3) the mother sometimes being herself the object of verbal and physical aggression by the father, which further reinforces respect-fear for him and his position but only opens the mother to attack by the children, even if only when the father is not present. It may be posited that mothers punish boys more heavily than girls for antiparental assaults (Table 21) because (1) boys' attacks against them are more violent and frequent than girls'; (2) this is a legitimate and husband-approved situation for punishing the more troublesome boys; (3) girls are in general held to be more *delicada* (delicate, fragile) and less deserving of punishment, though they are occasionally spanked by angry mothers. No father punishes his little girl physically, and only one by scolding, for antiparental aggression.

Obviously the foregoing adds up to a source of tremendous conflict and frustration for the child. Wherever it is apparent in socialization that the child's actions have been blocked or inhibited, we may assume that frustration has occurred. The result of frustration is not only the instigation to aggression but conflict over the possibility of aggression, which in turn increases frustration, which increases the instigation to aggression, and so on. Patently, all these self-reinforcing tensions must be released in some manner.

Neatness and Cleanliness

Vallecañese mothers, in spite of primitive living conditions, manage to keep their offspring clean to a surprising degree when poverty, inaccessibility of water, expense of soap (a luxury seldom purchased), and lack of clothes are considered. Keeping one's person clean and clothes neat is taught to many children at a relatively early age. As might be expected, standards are somewhat higher for girls than for boys. Scaling maternal standards for neatness and cleanliness yields a median of 3.0 for boys and 4.0 for girls, where 5.0 indicates extremely high standards. As mothers frequently put it: "You can let a boy go around any old way but you have to keep a girl looking nice all the time." But boys get dirtier and are subject to more pressure on this score (median pressure for cleanliness 4.5 for boys, 3.0 for girls on a 5-point scale). While violations of cleanliness and neatness taboos are often severely punished, most mothers realize that their children must get soiled when they play and do not keep after them with the same kind of desperate anxiety that I have observed in middle-class and upper-class families on the island.[4] This mother's practices are rather typical:

I expect Luis to be neat and clean. Of course, . . . he plays and gets dirty because he is always outside or playing on the floor. . . . But once I bathe and change him, he tries to keep himself clean and if he goes to play he puts on his dirty clothes. . . . I have told him, "You are big enough now [seven] so that you will take care of your clothes and stay clean." And if I change him and he gets dirty I scold him and sometimes I have even spanked him. In this way he has learned to take care of his body and his clothes.

Care of Property

There is little in these homes which can be called "property" and even less of intrinsic value. But what there is—the crude, unpainted homemade table and bench, perhaps a dish or two—is held in high regard by the parents. The play of most children indoors is rather restricted, therefore, and unnecessary pounding on "furniture" is not usually countenanced. Maternal restrictiveness on household effects and others' property produce medians for boys and girls of 4.0, where 5.0 indicates very high restriction. Some mothers make exceptions in the case of toys and food and insist children share them. But none make exceptions in the case of parents' personal property. Literally they must not be touched. Several of the more compulsive mothers would seldom let their children even play with their own toys. A new doll or other toy would be placed out of reach, but tantalizingly in

---

4. While observations of middle-class and upper-class practices were not systematic, I can state tentatively that they appear extremely compulsive about personal cleanliness and neatness. The middle-class child is a kind of "hothouse flower" that must always look scrubbed and pressed, and any deviation sends parents, siblings, and servants into a storm of worry, anxiety, and frenetic cleaning activity.

sight, on a high rafter, and the child forbidden to get it except with permission, usually given only when the mother can watch the child and protect the toy. Children's "Sunday clothes" are similarly handled and the result is that they quickly outgrow them (and especially their shoes, which nearly always seem to be squeezing their feet) without having worn them more than a few times.

Noise Restrictions

Vallecañese mothers are not very tolerant of noise and usually do not permit their children to be noisy. The majority feel that: (1) noise makes parents nervous; (2) it could make the children nervous also; (3) other people will say they do not have a well-behaved family; (4) noise bothers the father, perhaps the worst offense of all; (5) noise indicates that their child has been badly trained; (6) at night it may keep early sleepers awake. Boys are somewhat less restricted than girls, scaling a median of 3.0 compared with 4.5 for girls, where 5.0 is extreme noise restriction. A few mothers are relatively permissive about noise, however, feeling that the child should be allowed to make noise and enjoy himself or that noise by children is inevitable and their efforts to stop it in the past have failed. Strangely enough, these mothers were among the most restrictive in other areas, a seeming paradox for which I am unable to account.

As for adults, one does not notice so much noise in open-country houses. They are far apart, for one thing, and there is no electricity for radios. But in the houses along the road, if there is a phonograph or radio present, it will always be playing at top volume, even when a visitor attempts to speak with the occupants. Jukeboxes in *cafetíns* play day and night at top volume. At meetings, during and between school classes, and in and around the Evangelical church and the town Catholic church, there is always a lot of talking, moving about, and general activity. When people get together there is a kind of nervous anxiety about making oneself heard as often and as loudly as possible. How is this explained in view of noise restrictions in childhood? Noise is an adult prerogative; children are best neither seen nor heard.

Bedtime Restrictions

Only two mothers are at all strict about seeing that their child gets to bed at a certain hour. The others do not have a specific bedtime. Whenever little Juanito or Juanita gets sleepy they tumble into bed or hammock. Sometimes they stay up later than their parents though generally they are in bed sooner. None go to bed much past eight o'clock, but this is because this is the bedtime for adults also, especially in open country where there are no lights or outside attractions and especially during the cane season when the father gets up at daybreak or sooner. Those with any kind of restriction feel the child should retire early because he is a child, not because of what staying up late might do to his health.

When affairs are going on, particularly fiestas, children are permitted to stay up until they fall asleep on their feet or in their mother's arms. Even with children of nine or ten, the mother or father often will carry the sleeping child home in his arms. "Baby-sitting" is rare.

Obedience

In a culture in which the fundamental concept of the child is that of a helpless bit of humanity which must be constantly guided, directed, pushed, and pulled into desired behavior channels, it may be anticipated that (1) the child, thought of as dependent and always treated with this in mind, will indeed develop a large degree of dependence, and (2) since the child cannot be expected to act for himself and is born "bad," the most common mediating mechanism between parent and child will be obedience, and this will be considered by parents as one of the most important aspects of child training.

The good child in Valle Caña is first of all the obedient child, and parents are generally insistent and vehement about it:

Yes, I believe that children should obey immediately, although there are children that when you order them they "think about it," and then in a while they realize what one has said, and *then* they do it. I have a bit of patience and I wait awhile, but, if they do not do it, I take the strap and then they fly. A child should obey immediately. This way he respects [his parents] and one does not lose one's patience.

Fathers often are more tolerant than mothers about other restrictions but are just as stubbornly demanding about obedience. The father of a rather sensitive little four-year-old boy says:

I think that the child who is obedient is loved by everybody. One teaches them that they obey the things they are ordered to do. ["What do you do if he does not obey?"] ... I take a small switch and I spank him or I slap him easily on the hand so that he will go where he is sent. I ask him two or three times and if he doesn't go, then I spank him or scold him so that he will do it.

While mothers are more extremely strict about obedience than fathers (Table 22), fairly high standards are expected and enforced by

TABLE 22
Obedience Standards

	Mothers	Fathers	Fathers (as seen by wives)
1. Does not expect; child too young; no right to demand	–	–	–
2.	2	1	3
3.	6	6	–
4.	5	11	9
5. Expects instant obedience; no toleration; strict punishment	5	–	6
Total Cases	18	18	18

both parents. Both are generally more strict with boys than with girls. This must be understood in the light of differential role expectations of the sexes and conflicts set up in male and female as a result. Because he is given more freedom of movement and action, the boy will find more areas in which to challenge parental authority and therefore is subject to more rigorous obedience demands than the girl. It is the boy who is always being sent on errands and outside chores. No matter how disagreeable the girl's chores, she can do them in and around the home. Furthermore, in the everlasting test of his *machismo* the boy will feel constrained to prove himself against authority. This of course runs into direct conflict with the cultural and familial values that demand a "good, obedient, respectful" boy. The essence of maleness is inherent aggressiveness. The boy is born, so to speak, with all the urges of the man, which must be curbed. The girl is conceived of as a submissive, defenseless, delicate creature, who, while respect and obedience are demanded, must not be subjected to the same rigorous treatment as the boy. It is easier for her to adjust to submissiveness-passivity, which is not difficult to carry out, than for the boy to adjust to dominance-aggressivity, in a culture in which there are few opportunities to become dominant-aggressive except within the family.

The mother's conception of the father's obedience demands shows him as a much sterner, more authoritarian kind of figure than his image of himself (compare responses in Table 22). Fathers seem to be less strict and more tolerant than their wives, both in interview responses and actual conduct. The reason is not that they value obedience less, expect it less, or are less strict in its enforcement. It is rather that the mother has built up a fearful image of the father in her own mind, from the viewpoint of her own successive roles as daughter and then as wife, and passed it on to her children. The father is viewed as stern and imperious from the time the child is small. His commands are not to be violated on penalty of swift and terrible punishment. Obviously, then, the mother's image of the father and the image she conveys to her offspring function so well that it is not as necessary usually for the father to have to reinforce his demands as for the mother. Furthermore, he actually is the supreme arbiter, and when the mother's harshest measures fail, she turns the problem over to the father or threatens to do so—which is often enough.

It follows that mothers would have more trouble in exacting obedience. For this variable, mothers of boys yield a median scale value of 3.0 and of girls 2.0, compared with fathers with a median of 1.5 for boys and girls, where 5.0 indicates many obedience problems. Thus mothers have less trouble on this score with girls than with boys. Most mothers feel they do not brook delay once an order has been given. "No, I don't forget it, ever. Oh, no. I always see to it and I make her do it." "I always see to it that he does the things. After I order him, I do not forget it—ever. And I am after him until he does it." However, as we shall note later, they are not as consistent as this.

The observance of obedience is considered as a matter of course, like other "good" behavior, for which punishment is meted out if the child disobeys and little attention or praise is given if the child carries out commands. Even when praise for obedience is rendered, with girls receiving somewhat more than boys, it is matter-of-fact: "You see, that is the way you do things—fast. When one sends you, you obey immediately." The child is not so much thanked for correct performance as instructed that this is the way to avoid punishment. A few mothers praise their children when they obey at once, sometimes hugging and caressing them, and several of the more noncommittal mothers said that they were made happy by the child's obedience but did nothing to indicate their pleasure to the child.

Rewards and Praise

Not only is obedience usually unrewarded, but the use of reward generally is infrequent and unsystematic. These caneworker families, seasonally unemployed, seldom have material things to give their children. The rewards most appreciated by the children are: bread,[5] *lindberghs* (frozen, flavored ice-cubes), candy, fruit, or new toys. Says one mother:

Sometimes [I reward her] but not most of the time. When I want her to sweep or when I see that she is behaving well and not bothering me, I offer her a penny. And if I go to town and have promised her some little plaything, I bring it to her.... A child that is "hired" [paid] always does things for me. When I have money she says she is going to do something for me for a penny or for some kind of *dulce* [sweet] or food. And if I have it I give it to her. But when I do not have anything, she has to do the chore [anyway].

Boys and girls are about equally favored with rewards by parents, each with a median of 3.0, where high use of reward is signified by 5.0. Mothers feel that if they promise the child something they should try to keep their promise, though they would not mention the promised reward if they could not, or neglected to, obtain it. They do not deem this wrong; the main objective is to get chores done and obedience exacted, rather than to please the child (see note 1, p. 101).

5. Bread is a luxury and not part of the regular diet. These children have such a craving for bread that it is preferred over sweets. When school children are given two pennies sometimes for lunch, usually they will buy a *lindbergh* with one and a small hunk of *pan de agua* (bread with a water and flour base) with the other and eat the two together. Children frequently ate at the writer's house, and whether we put out a part or a whole loaf (sometimes two) it was always cleaned up before other food was touched. Soda crackers are similarly relished.

The general feeling of these mothers is that a child should not be praised, as a rule. When they are commendatory in response to specific good behaviors, they consider it not so much praise as instruction. That praise may be itself a means of instruction does not seem to enter into their reasoning. Perhaps these women are giving utterance to an unconscious conflict as to how desired responses by their child should be handled by them. As one mother expresses it:

However good a child is, I do not think they should be praised in front of themselves. Because they will "become too familiar" . . . so that they lose their respect for one. They will change for the worse, because then they will think they are so good. . . .

I consider it praise [when asked how, in view of past statements to the contrary, she could maintain that she did not believe in it], and I tell her so . . . to please her and so that she will do well for me next time. [realizes contradiction, long pause] Well, the truth is, I believe that one should not praise, and the truth is that I do praise. But I do it to encourage her, and I do it on the [spur of the] moment, but I realize afterward that when she repeats the things she does not do them as well. It is that sometimes one thinks one way and does another, but I maintain that a child should not be praised much. It may be that it is all right to tell her once that she has done it well so that she will feel well. But that business of telling her much—no. The more you tell, the worse they do things.

Fathers' use of praise is somewhat more free and more often given. A scale to measure the use of praise, with 7.0 being very high use of praise, finds mothers with a median of 3.0 for boys and 4.0 for girls, whereas fathers have a median of 5.0 for boys and 6.0 for girls.

It is apparent that girls are praised more than boys by both parents, in keeping with a general show of more considerateness toward little girls, particularly by fathers. A parental dilemma seems to exist. Mothers feel that nice things said to their child should not necessarily be construed as praise and do not intend them to have the "bad effects" of praise. They want to show gratitude for good behavior without the child becoming "swelled up with his own pride" or "too big for his britches." Praise, they think, will result in increased familiarity, "uppitiness," decreased respect, and tend to bridge the span of differences in generation, physical size, and authority. However, there is an unconscious tendency to overcome traditional devaluation of praise, due perhaps to the infiltration of new ideas.

Conscious Role-Modeling

Role-modeling—setting examples of the sex, occupational, and other status-functions—is of course always taking place whenever the adult behaves in the presence of the child. When it is done without intent or awareness, we may refer to it as unconscious role-modeling. In this section, however, we are concerned with the deliberate inculcation of status responsibilities and prerogatives, or conscious role-modeling.

Most mothers use models for desirable and undesirable behavior, but we do not know how frequently they are used. Two mothers do not point to themselves as examples, either because they do not think of it or because they believe role-modeling is undesirable. Two girls and one boy are given no models of good or bad behavior, one girl is given good but no bad models, and one boy is given bad but no good ones.

Desirable role models in rank order of their use by mothers are: Parents, neighbor children, older siblings, grandparents, cousins, godparents, uncles, aunts, younger siblings. Undesirable models are: Neighbor children, older siblings, cousins.

Reasons for using good models center on "getting things done around the house," "obedience," and acting *con humildad* (with humility) and *con vergüenza* (with shame). Reasons for bad models center mostly on avoiding "acting bad" and "getting into trouble." Most mothers who use good models point to themselves or their husbands as examples of how to be "humble," "treat everybody well," "return home in time," and to enforce standards around household tasks, fighting, and cleanliness.

Deprivation of Privileges

Privileges for Vallecañese children are extremely limited. Parents do not often depend on them as a means of getting things done nor often withhold them as a disciplinary measure. Boys are deprived of privileges somewhat less than girls by their mothers (scale medians, where 4.0 signifies high use of this technique: boys 2.0, girls 2.5), while fathers tend to favor the girls (median 1.0) greatly over boys (2.5). Mothers use deprivation only temporarily and often shortly thereafter give the child that which had been withheld. This procedure would seem to destroy whatever effectiveness this technique might otherwise possess and marks another of the many inconsistencies in Vallecañese child-rearing techniques. This mother is typical: "Many times—most of the time—I tell him that if he behaves badly I am not going to take him to his grandmother's house or to town. Or if he did such a thing, I won't give him money. This is mostly threats because I do not carry them out. I just threaten him to see if he will pay attention to me."

Mothers who do not use the technique at all feel it would be ineffective. Both parents feel that depriving their child of privileges is more cruel than more direct punishment. Mothers who use the technique withdraw things such as food, clothes, school, celebration on Three Kings Day, toys, sweets, money, and trips to town.

Ridicule

Observations and interview responses differ somewhat on the extent to which parents use ridicule with their children. I seemed to observe more than they report,[6] premising my judgments on ridicule as: "Those symbolic acts whose intent is to place the child in an undesirable category . . . includes derogation, ego-deflation, name-calling, teasing, sarcasm, negative role-modeling—" (Analysis Schedule, n.d.). Ego-deflation is commonplace, the obverse side of a coin whose one side is the quiet, meek, humble, respectful child. Name-calling and ego-deflation have the effect of reinforcing the basic concept of the child as *sin capacidad* and, therefore, of making him more amenable to parental discipline.

Now this is the behavior parents expect and encourage in most conscious and unconscious training. If the child acted differently, they would say he is *malcriado* (naughty, badly brought up). But in some situations, withdrawing behavior becomes embarrassing even for the parent, in which event he will say deprecatingly to the child and to the stranger, "Ah, Juanito is just a *jibarito*,[7] he is frightened of his

---

6. Their reported use of ridicule to censure children's behavior revealed a median scale value for mothers of boys of 2.0 and of girls 2.0; fathers of boys of 3.0 and of girls 2.0, where 4.0 denotes high use of ridicule. Thus girls get about same treatment from the mother, lighter treatment from the father.

7. *Jibarito* means little *jíbaro* ("hill-billy") with which city people commonly refer to rustics and carries with it a connotation of contempt and superiority. A term of more dignity, which rural dwellers themselves prefer, is *campesino* (countryman or farmer). They have, however, picked up the term occasionally to describe deprecatingly one of their own number, or a shy child, or even themselves.

shadow." Or when parents get together to talk about their children, particularly mothers, often they make quite derogatory remarks about their children, directly before them if they happen to be present, as if the children were not there or too insignificant to be considered.

Isolation

Mothers give scant indication that they use this technique, though they did not say it is not used. There is literally no place to hide if a parent wished to isolate a child from others. Not only are households small, but interior rooms seldom have doors or locks. Furthermore, the objective is to get maximum ventilation, which means always keeping shutters and doors wide open. Therefore, even if these parents felt that isolation was effective, they could use it only in a limited manner, if at all.

Here is a demonstrable effect of climate on culture and behavior. With no privacy, everyone's business is everyone else's. Vallecañeses of all classes live in "glass" houses. Activities are known to the household and the outside world as well. This engenders a conflict with the counter-tendency toward individualism. Yet the Vallecañese highly values this very set of affairs, for if he cannot hide, neither can his neighbors. The over-all effect on adults and children probably leads to constant tension, which is somewhat reduced by enjoying the sights and sounds of others in the social milieu.

Our account of Vallecañese patterns of indoctrination and training children is concluded in the next chapter.

CHAPTER 6

Bringing up the Child—II

Introduction

IN THE previous chapter we described the channeling and control
of behavior in the infant and several areas of inculcation with
regard to the growing child. These included caretaking agents; feeding
and weaning disciplines; control of sphincter release; modesty and sex
training and education; control of aggressive impulses; restrictions on
neatness and cleanliness; care of household effects, noise, bedtime;
obedience demands and expectations; use of role models for eliciting
desired behavior; and use of techniques like deprivation of privileges,
ridicule, and isolation.

In the present chapter we conclude this description of the bringing
up of the child in the Vallecañese family by investigation of the ways
in which mothers use threats to the child of environmental dangers;
use of techniques like reasoning, withdrawal of love, and physical punishment; degree of freedom and mobility permitted to the child; demands of the parent for the child to socialize with others; affection
and nurturance of the mothers; ways in which they respond to dependent and nurturant-seeking behaviors of the child; training for
independence; the process of identification and sex-typing in the child;
relationships between the child and his father; comparison of maternal
and paternal strictness; parental achievement standards; and the impact
of tradition and culture change on parent-child relations.

Threats of Dangers from the Environment

Parents use threats of environmental dangers much more often than most other modes of warning and nonphysical punishment, and more often with their sons than with their daughters (Table 23). The inimically perceived environment which structures the context of life for

TABLE 23

Use of Threats of Dangers from the Environment

	Mothers		Fathers	
	Boys	Girls	Boys	Girls
1. Does not use	2	1	—	2
2. Uses, with reservations	—	1	1	1
3. Uses, no reservations, but no indication of emphasis	6	3	7	4
4. Uses with emphasis; warns frequently; environment defined for child as fearful	2	3	2	1
Total Cases	10	8	10	8

Vallecañeses (see note 2, p. 78) begins quite early in life and often receives strong reinforcement, whether through realistic threats like being taken by the policeman or unrealistic ones that happen to coincide with real events, as in the case of the disease syndrome known as *mososuelo* (see pp. 39-40). The following threats are most often mentioned:

The policeman will catch you (jail you, take you away, etc.).
A madman will come and put you in a sack.
An outlaw (or spastic) will throw you in a sack.
A dog (frog, lizard, *ardilla* [wild squirrel]) will bite (devour) you.
Your urine (feces) will stop.
You'll get hanged with a rope.
No one will buy you clothes.
A man (father) will come and cut out your testicles.
The Enchanted One will take you to a place under the sea.
You will make the Virgin cry.
Don't bathe in the stream—Death will take you.
The *cuco* [bogey-man] is going to eat you up (take you away).
I'll leave you on a mountain with lots of ugly black people.

An old man will come and take you away.

Don't go outside and get *sereno* [malady carried by night air].

San Expedito [pointing to image of the saint] and La Virgen del Carmen will come down out of the sky and talk to you.

In heaven there is a saint called Jesus the Nazarene and he is going to eat you if you don't behave well.

God will punish you.

I will send you far away from here forever.

God has prepared a fire in heaven for children who lie.

These categories are included in such threats: Disapproval of deities; death; castration; isolation; desertion; kidnapping; illness and injury; and miscellaneous terrors.

Besides open threats, there are also disguised threats in songs which occasionally are sung to put little children to sleep, especially *coplas*, *décimas*, *bombas*, and *boleros*. The threats probably are not consciously intended as mothers croon these lullabies.[1]

A dormir, a dormir, que es tarde;	To sleep, to sleep, for now it is late;
A dormir, a dormir, que es tarde.	To sleep, to sleep, for now it is late.
Duérmete, chiquito, que viene el cuco	Sleep, little one, for the *cuco* comes
Pa' sacarte las tripas con un bejuco.	To pull out your intestines with a vine.
Y el cuco viene a comerse los niños que lloran mucho.	And the *cuco* comes to eat children who cry much.

Some songs contain forebodings of the traditionally arduous life of *los pobres* (the poor), such as:

Las heridas me duele, el pecho me arde	My wounds hurt me, my chest burns me,
De comer calambrenas en tiempo de hambre.	From eating *calambrenas* in time of hunger.

or

Caballero', la cosa no esta plomo,	Gentlemen, things are not well,

1. My analysis of songs, stories, myths, and other folklore they were exposed to, or that parents exposed their children to, led to the conclusion that songs are generally not often sung by parents to children. When songs are sung or stories told, it is more often by the mother. The songs herein presented are from many recorded from parents who used them and may not coincide with whatever "correct" formal versions may exist. Like most folklore, they are largely orally communicated from generation to generation.

Cada dija poniéndose peor;	Each day becoming worse;
Las mujeres muriéndose de hambre,	The women dying of hunger, and
Y los hombres hartándose de ron.	The men filling themselves with rum.[2]

Reasoning

Reasoning is rarely used by mothers (median scale value, where 4.0 marks high use, 1.0 for boys and girls) in dealing with a child but is used somewhat more frequently by fathers (boys median 3.0, girls 2.5). Since the former are generally more impatient this is understandable. If we recall the child as being held to be unable to reason for himself and unwilling to listen to reason and the tendency of these parents to rely on force, verbal and physical, as a means of implementing their injunctions, this becomes even clearer. In view of the father's and mother's roles, the former would probably find reasoning somewhat more efficacious than the more harassed, status-inferior mother.

When reasoning is employed, it is usually in warning of consequences ("if you do this, thus-and-so will happen"). Practically never is there an attempt to give children a fair trial, in the event of quarrels, fights, etc. Listening to the child's side and reasoning out a reply which would consider the child's testimony as possibly valid rarely occur.

Withdrawal of Love

There is a moderate use of withdrawal of love, but not as much as other mechanisms like physical punishment or warnings of environmental dangers. A scale of extent of use of this technique, with 5.0 indicating high use, shows mothers with a median of 3.0 for boys, 2.5 for girls; fathers with a median of 3.0 for boys, 2.0 for girls. (Table 24.)

2. I do not mean to convey the impression that such threatening or tragic ballads are the only ones sung. Just as often Vallecañese mothers who do sing may croon some touchingly sentimental and maternally tender lullaby:

Sueñito, vente; sueñito, vente;	Come, little sleep; come, little sleep;
A cerrarle los ojitos de este inocente.	To close the little eyes of this innocent one.
Duerme que duerme, duerme que duerme,	Sleep and sleep, sleep and sleep,
Boquita de azucena, labios de nieve.	Little mouth of lily, lips of snow.

TABLE 24

Frequency of Direct or Implied Threats of Withdrawal of Love

	Mothers			Fathers		
	Never	Some-times	Often	Never	Some-times	Often
1. Mama (papa) will think you don't love her (him)	8[a]	8	2	12	4	2
2. You're hurting mama's (papa's) feelings, or, You're going to make me cry	8	7	3	12	6	—
3. I'm not going to talk (listen) to you until you behave well	3	13	2	10	7	—
4. Go away; I don't want to see you until you smile (be good)	1	9	8	9	8	1
5. You're not my child; surely my child would not act like that	10	7	1	17	1	—
6. Mama (papa) does not like children who act like that	2	13	3	3	13	2
7. I'm going to send you away if you keep acting like that	5	9	4	7	8	3

a. Total cases for each of the two columns in each item is 18.

Physical Punishment

The purpose of all punishment is to censure for wrong-doing or the infraction of codes and rules of proper conduct and inculcate acceptable forms of socialized response. The net result of all punishment is to produce in the child a set of anxieties and anticipations of pain (or painful situations) which will result in his avoiding "wrong" responses and performing "right" responses and thus achieving the cultural and familial goal of socialized behavior (Davis 1947). Ideally, these anxieties should lead the child to seek the statuses most rewarding in the culture. These are the functions of punishment as parents see them, and to some extent as the anthropologist and psychologist see them, though the latter are aware that punishment does not invariably succeed in achieving the desired ends of parents and society.

There are other functions of punishment which the present writer feels are usually neglected by social scientists or seem to be considered only in the cases of psychoneurotic adults who also happen to be parents. Punishment, I feel, also serves to (1) relieve the need tensions of the parent himself; (2) arouse the parent's own anxiety level, on the other hand, because of pangs of remorse and conscience with having punished what, in sober retrospect, seems to be a helpless child; (3) relieve the parent of some of the burden of socialization that would be necessitated in more "rational" techniques like reasoning; (4) satisfy the punitive needs of the sadistic parent. While we cannot deal adequately with all these in this research, it should already have been apparent, and will continue to be throughout the study, how the various modes of discipline involving punishment do indeed serve these functions as well.

When the panel children were infants of about two years they were not spanked as often as now. But three mothers spanked their children even at this tender age at least once a week, three about twice a week, and two almost every day. Seven mothers rarely or never spanked their children as infants. Since the infant until the age of two or three is given more affectionate treatment than at later stages, it is surprising that even this many mothers reported infant spankings. This is another index of the inconsistency and uncertainty that enter the child's development from the earliest stage.

As the child leaves infancy, frequency of physical punishment increases, both parents utilizing it considerably, though mothers depend upon it more. On a summary scale of use of physical punishment over the child's lifetime, using 7.0 to indicate very frequent punishment, mothers have a median for boys of 6.0 and girls 5.0, while fathers have a median for boys of 4.0 and girls 3.5. The seeming paradox of the boy receiving both more punishment and more indulgence will be clarified when one considers the total socialization process with respect to sex differentials (see Chapters 7, 8).

There are many things for which a child can be punished. As one mother says,

Sometimes when she wants to eat lots of candy and she cries and bothers me, I spank her. Or when she wants to be in the street and does not come after I call twice—on the third time I spank her because she did not pay attention to me. When she plays in dirty water and wets herself I scold her and if she does not pay attention to me I hit her. And another reason I hit her is when she says a bad word. And if she takes off her clothes I hit her.

Another mother explains,

Two or three times a week when she cries much without any reason or because I don't please her and she keeps on crying, I spank her. If she quarrels or fights with the others or when she doesn't pay attention to me quickly, I spank her. If she says bad words I hit her. If she is disrespectful toward me I also hit her. . . .

We have seen that some parents punish or threaten punishment for practically all infractions of rules.

Mothers punish with hands, switches, sticks, and straps. Of all instruments the last is probably the most effective because it is the symbol of paternal authority. Most men have two belts, one to wear and one to leave home. The one at home hangs on a nail in plain view of the children and the mother is authorized to use it whenever she feels the need. Strap spankings are done as much in the name of the father as the mother who does the punishing, thus symbolically reinforcing his authority and prestige.

In addition to cuffs, blows, pinches, and outright spankings,[3] other types of punishment, though not frequently resorted to, include:

Making the child kneel (in a corner; in the next room; in the middle of the floor) and not move for a long time. (One variety was a father's making his child kneel on a metal grater while holding two stones in each hand.)
Tying the child's hands.
Making the child lie in bed (perhaps a kind of isolation).
Keeping the child indoors when he wants to go out.
Making the child sit down without moving.
Tying the child to the leg of a bed or some other furniture.
Pulling the child's hair, ears, arms.
Rapping the child's head with knuckles.

Thrashings do not usually involve the solemn ceremonialism of the classical American hairbrush. They are usually administered with the first handy object and may land on any part of the child's body. Their frequency, when scaled, yields medians for mothers of boys 4.0 and

3. Presumably the most effective type of punishment would be spanking, as differentiated from casual, spasmodic blows, since it is premeditated, lasts longer, and involves a kind of deliberate ceremony that conceivably would have more lasting effects than irregular blows or threats. As we have seen above, however, it is not highly ritualized in Valle Caña.

girls 3.0, and for fathers 3.0 for both sexes, where 4.0 is very high frequency of spankings.

Threats of physical punishment include:

I tell him I'm going to hang him from the mango tree.

I'll give you the kind of spanking you'll never forget.

If you don't stop quarreling, I'm going to hit all of you.

I'll tell him I'm going to cut off his *huevos* [testicles].

You damned boy, aren't you going to respect me? I'm going to cut your face into twenty pieces.

If you wet your bed I'll wake you up with the strap . . . and put you to sleep on the floor.

I spank him with a rope, and I scare him. I tell him I am going to hang him with this rope and start burning him at the legs.

Look, boy, I'm going to take you and mash your head against a stone so you'll pay attention.

Threats of punishment are not the same as punishment itself, of course, but the effects, especially if reinforced with some actual violence, may have equivalent or greater anxiety-inducing effects. However, half of the mothers prefer physical punishment above all other disciplinary techniques, in every case for their sons and in half the cases for their daughters. The other half prefer scolding their daughters. Fathers, on the other hand, prefer scolding to physical punishment for boys and girls.

Nearly all mothers are convinced that spanking performs a useful function and is effective in extracting desired behavior. Only two feel that whippings do no good and one has some reservations. They put the child "in his place," "humble him," and "make him respect." "To teach, a parent has to hit," says one mother. And another says: "The only thing I have done—well, their respect is the strap [pointing to strap on the wall]. And the only thing that I have to do is look at them and they know if they do not do as I want they have the strap for sure."

For punishment to be effective, it must be applied consistently and repeatedly or the undesired practice will reappear, especially if it was originally a strong one, although the recovery of the habit may be weak (Whiting and Mowrer 1943). Despite the claim of parents for the effectiveness of physical punishment, some contradiction is apparent in their complaints that their children are still troublesome, and some even say that the more they spank the child the more he misbehaves! Parents, especially mothers, are irregular and capricious in their administration of punishment. It is to be expected, of course, that fathers, being less involved in punishment situations, will also have a somewhat lower frequency of neglecting to carry out their threats, though no father is completely free of this inconsistency. A scale of the frequency of following through with threatened punishment, where 1.0 indicates consistent following through, yields a median for mothers of boys of 4.0 and girls 3.5, and for fathers 3.0 for both sexes.

Despite their high regard for public opinion, Vallecañeses do not allow the fact that others might see them prevent execution of punishment. The most common reasons for hesitating or not following through are that their pity for the child is aroused, he shows respect or affection, or flees from them.

MOTHER: When I feel sorry for him [I don't carry out my threats]. Because since he is the one that takes care of the house for me and the one I send to do things for me. . . . If I beat him much he will die on me. Or— when he goes running away I cannot catch him.

FATHER: Once in a while I am prevented by my conscience. The affection I feel for her also prevents me.

FATHER: Frequently I say to her, "Look, I'm going to punish you." Then she hides under the bed and I don't punish her. . . . Because if I punish her I pity her.

Dependency

Many antecedents of dependency have been discussed and inferred in preceding pages. The purpose of the next several sections is to deal explicitly with some additional variables in this specific behavior complex. As in all processes, the development of dependency implies a complementary (and oppositional) process, that of the development of independency. Both are basic to socialization and begin to be learned and unlearned in childhood.

Physical Mobility

Vallecañese children are quite restricted in their physical mobility. The girl is confined to a smaller "life-space" than the boy. On a scale to measure restrictiveness of this variable, where 4.0 is extreme restriction, median for boys is 2.5 and girls 3.0. One boy of seven is given a great deal of freedom, but his mother is also permissive in many other spheres where other mothers are restrictive. Children in El Camino are just as restricted as mountain children but have less room to play in.

Just as mothers do not permit their children to stray very far from the home, neither do they permit them to be alone for long without checking. Keeping track of the child when scaled yields a median of 3.0 for boys and 3.5 for girls, where 4.0 is a very high degree of checking. All except one boy are frequently checked. As one anxious mother said, "from moment to moment (I check on her)—every fifteen minutes, if she is not beside me I go and see where she is." Mothers believe that because of the child's potential for instigating mischief as well as learning bad things from other children, it is safest to check constantly on his activities.

Maternal Demands for Child's Sociability

Restricted living space and much checking on the child are only two aspects of the demands of parents generally fearful of the outside world and anxious to protect the child from its dangers and contamination. Not only is there a generally low demand for sociability (median of 4.0 for boys, 3.0 for girls, where 4.0 indicates very low demands), but most mothers prefer that the child not associate with other children at all. Strangely enough, boys seem subject to fewer sociability demands than girls. This may be explained by the greater fear mothers have that boys will "get into trouble" and the fact that the *machito* already possesses more freedom and does not have to be urged. As with preceding variables, road and open-country families show little difference.

Affection and Nurturance

We have seen that most of these mothers were fairly affectionate with the children as infants but there is a decided drop of overt affection for the preschool-age child. A scale of the amount of affectional demonstrativeness of parent to child, where 5.0 is high demonstrativeness, produces the following medians: mothers and fathers toward sons 2.5, toward daughters 3.0.

Affection instigated by the child is not heavily weighted on this scale. An observer often sees touching and sentimental scenes of affection between parent and child but they are mostly instigated by the child. The parent, while not always rejecting the demonstration, may merely tolerate it. Only a few children are literally "smothered" with affection. In statements of relatively demonstrative and relatively undemonstrative mothers, even in the former instance the child is responsible for at least half of the nurturance-seeking actions:

[Boy, age 6]. Yes, always [I show him affection], I as much as he to me. During the day several times he throws himself on me and hugs me and says, "*Mamita, yo te quiero mucho*" [little mother, I love you very much]. And every once in a while he asks me for the *bendición* and during the day I often hug and kiss him.

[Boy, age 6]. When I have some time—*de año en ciento una vez* [once in a hundred years] I sit down and kiss and play with him. In general I do not have time for these things, I am always very busy.

Fathers often show affection, although in some of their responses a note of caution and sternness manifests itself. And there is also a certain anxiety about insuring the love of the child in return:

They must be shown affection, seeing how they are—that although one arrives wet [with perspiration, from work] they come close to one. . . . The best way is to bring them small things, small presents and things like that, not to hurt them nor spank them viciously, not to teach them bad words. Other parents spank their child for anything but not I.

Naturally. Our father also showed affection to us. I think that it is not necessary to be punishing children always, but you must show them sternness and rigor when they say bad words—to correct them. But always showing them affection. . . . The best way is to win them over, taking them walking and giving them what they wish. When he invites one to a certain place, and one sees that it is convenient, one takes him there.

Perhaps of more importance than the amount of parental demonstrativeness is the nature of the parent's affectional relationship to the child. When scaled on this variable, mothers of boys have a median of 3.0 and of girls 2.0, where 5.0 indicates very little time spent playing with the child. This is a function of available time and the differential degrees to which mothers are attached to either sex. Vallecañese women seemed to us to be attached to their sons to a greater extent than indicated in Table 25. On the other hand, it cannot be asserted that the tabulated data are distortive of the real state of affairs. It is rather reflective of the inability of the interview to elicit information that will give a completely rounded picture of an extremely complex

TABLE 25

Nature of Affectional Relationship, Parent to Child

	Mothers		Fathers (as wives see them)		Fathers (as they see themselves)	
	Boys	Girls	Boys	Girls	Boys	Girls
1. Extremely warm, loving; enjoys child; proud	4	—	—	1	1	1
2.	4	4	2	2	1	3
3.	—	—	5	1	4	2
4.	1	2	—	1	—	—
5.	1	1	3	3	3	—
6.	3	1	—	1	—	—
7. Predominantly hostile, cold	1	—	—	—	—	2
Total Cases	10	8	10	8	10	8

emotional area. Values and behavior toward the boy are apt to be more laden with emotional content for both parents, but particularly the mother. Emphasis laid on the penis and facts of anatomical structure (the male's protrusive and therefore easily handled sex organ) may account for some of this. Her sons cause a mother trouble, are "evil and lustful by nature," may be and are more neglected, and for these very reasons the mother will also find them more attractive. The boy is a more manipulatable object to either parent, but the writer suggests that at least some of the mother's repressed sexual tensions seek release in play with her son (see pp. 107-13, 145-46). But even mothers who play in a sexual manner with their male offspring express a horror of the male organ and of any kind of masturbatory or sexual practices by the boy.

Not only in bodily contact, but in play in general, the boy is permitted greater freedom than the girl. Girls are permitted little physical expression. They must appear to act like "little virgins" while boys are allowed to play as hard as they like, so long as it does not end in antisocial aggression or some other disapproved activity.

A few generalizations may be inferred of the influence of family composition on affection and treatment of the sexes: (1) If children are relatively equally distributed according to sex, either boys or girls may receive preferential treatment, or they may receive more or less equal treatment, but the boy will be more highly valued. (2) If there are more males than females, girls will receive preferential treatment and perhaps greater affection from both parents. (3) If there are more females than males, the latter will be shown preference and definitely greater affection. After the age of six or seven, little demonstrativeness is shown to either sex. Then the concept of the "latency period" may be applied to not only the child's practices with other children but his parents' practices toward him.

Fathers rate themselves somewhat warmer toward their children than their behavior is reported by their wives (Table 25). In view of the wife's father-husband image this is not unexpected. On the other hand there is surprisingly close agreement regarding the father-son relationship as seen by the father and by the mother. Fathers are seen as warmer both by their own estimates and that of their wives.

Response to Dependency

There is no significant relationship between degree of parental response to dependency and dependency behavior. Thus there are four cases of high dependency–low responsiveness; five of low dependency–high responsiveness; five of low dependency–low responsiveness and four high dependency–high responsiveness—a result that is just about at the chance level. There seems to be, however, an expectable trend toward less responsiveness with increasing age.

Mothers express less responsiveness to dependency behavior than fathers and seem generally to be more negatively inclined toward a responsive attitude toward such behavior. When scaled, with 7.0 indicating very low responsiveness, we find medians for mothers of boys 6.0 and girls 4.0; fathers of boys 3.0 and girls 5.5. This is understood in terms of the mother's child-rearing and domestic responsibilities as compared with the father's generally more carefree role in the family.

Stycos (1952a) has characterized Puerto Rican boys as "over-valued and under-attended" and girls as "under-valued and over-attended." While in general our data bear out such a generalization, it is evident also that this is much truer of mothers, while fathers tend to respond, on the occasions when they are home, in a somewhat reverse manner, giving more attention to boys. It is possible Stycos' conclusions are based on reports of mothers only or heavily weighted with mothers' feelings; in any event his data are probably more applicable to a past generation of children, since no direct child-rearing data were obtained, but rather the recalled socialization experiences of his adult respondents when they were children.

Vallecañese mothers' relatively low responsiveness is a seeming contradiction which may in part be explained thus: Even though these mothers do most things in a manner to engender very early the strongest kind of dependency relationship, many resultant behaviors of the child are irritating to them, and they do not always respond directly, especially if they occur when the mother is very busy. But by the time this occurs dependency responses have become ingrained in the child and additionally receive buttressing from what Sears (1950:25-26) calls "associated acts": those acts which have no obvious dependency-inculcating function but which are the result of dependency habit systems and the performance of which effects reinforcement of these systems, such as thumb-sucking, snuggling, baby talk, drooling, etc. Many are observed among Vallecañese children (see Chapter 7).

Furthermore a case can be made for the point of view that this lack of providing positive gratifications for dependency, if we wish to employ psychoanalytic rather than learning-theory dynamics, will leave the dependency needs unfulfilled and thus prolong, rather than stem, the development of such behavior. Certainly, as we have pointed out earlier in many places, and as will occur in this study again, the whole atmosphere in Vallecañese family and culture and the whole philosophy of child training would seem to reinforce the image of dependency in the child. That these children behave with all the characteristics of dependency seems apparent not only from the testimony of their mothers, but from all my observational recordings. In this instance of low dependency responsiveness by mothers toward obviously dependent children, we have demonstrated again a weakness inherent in both psychoanalytic and learning theory: the same phenomenon may be explained in opposite ways. Both theories need to be modified in order to define explicit and specific conditions under which varying dependent or independent behaviors originate and develop.

Independence Training

More than half of the children are not given regular tasks to perform. Scaling assignment and encouragement of regular tasks, with 5.0

denoting a high degree, yields a median for mothers of boys of 2.5 and girls 2.0. Fathers very seldom assign duties to either.

Most prominently mentioned tasks assigned by mothers in order of frequency and seeming importance are:

For Boys: Getting water and wood, running errands, caring for domestic animals, taking care of baby or smaller siblings, carrying lunch to father, putting on water to heat, sweeping, dusting, lighting stove, taking care of house in mother's absence.

For Girls: Getting water, making beds, cleaning and dusting, sweeping, washing dishes and pots, taking care of siblings, rocking baby, bringing in clothes, feeding domestic animals, washing small clothes.

It must be remembered that these children are fairly young—four to seven years of age. After that period tasks and duties increase sharply and for some children tend to become an harassing burden. The writer has observed boys of eight or nine run up and down La Hoja, a rough climb for robust adults, several times a day, and then be assigned other chores as soon as they returned home. Many boys between seven and fifteen bring their fathers' lunches to them in the canefields, sometimes a distance of several miles. But children under seven are largely spared this fate; even when he is the oldest of a group of small siblings a boy will only be sent on an occasional errand or to put the hog in the shade.[4] Small girls are seldom given chores more difficult than shelling peas or throwing out an occasional bucket of slop for the hogs and chickens. As they grow older, their chores increase but never reach the point of relieving the mother of more than a part of her burden. It is assumed that the girl's own burden will begin with marriage, from which point it becomes as heavy as her mother's.

But even when chores get heavy, they are assigned as duties, not with the objective of engendering initiative and independence in the child but because of the practical necessity of work needs in the household. The Protestant value of work for its own sake is neither believed, practiced, nor preached by Vallecañeses, and their offspring therefore do not learn it. Quite the contrary, the person who can get along with as little work as possible is considered fortunate and is an object of

---

4. Livestock is never penned. Hogs are leashed to a housepost or a tree and must be moved as the sun shifts. Chickens run loose and roost in trees at night. The more prosperous families (not in our panel) who own a cow or two try to pen them, however, since they must be pastured for grazing and are very valuable.

envy. Labor is only the means to the immediate ends of everyday existence. The future is a matter of fate and luck; little the individual can do will alter it. The important end-in-view in cultural transmission is that mothers do believe that such training will fit sons and daughters for their proper and traditional roles as future husbands and wives. Vallecañeses would like to have economic independence and the rare few who attain it enjoy it to the hilt; but why work extra hard for what is at best the result of a whimsical throw of the supernatural dice?

Extent of maternal preschool teaching is divided into three categories: nine no teaching, seven some teaching, two considerable teaching. Academic subjects like reading, writing, counting, telling time, etc., are seldom taught at home. A handful of parents are themselves literate, and not much value is placed on teaching such skills to children, assumptions being that youngsters are *sin capacidad* anyway; if they go to school they will be taught, and if they do not it will not benefit them. There is the tendency of a minority of mothers to teach practical chores but, as we have said, with the goal of fitting the child into his traditional sex role rather than helping the child become independent. Practical task teaching increases with age but is always limited in range.

Folk skills or folk art scarcely remain except for a few herbal compounds and crude techniques for constructing houses or cultivating. Little is left by way of a handicraft tradition; storytelling and singing have given way in large measure to the jukebox and radio. A few men cling to the guitars, *güiros* (elongated gourds, serrated and scratched with a wired bow), *maracas* (gourd rattles), and *cuatros* (stringed instruments with from four to ten strings) which are traditionally part of the Puerto Rican scene, but their number decreases each year. Singers of *décimas* (verses made up from an impromptu cue and subject, having ten or more lines; sometimes sung by two singers who compete to see who can keep the verses going the longest), *aguinaldos* (Christmas and Three Kings songs), *boleros* (from Spain and Latin America), and other musical forms the people love are becoming rarer each year. Much of the uniqueness of Puerto Rican cultural forms which made life more enjoyable is being erased in the volcanic transitions which now penetrate to every corner of the island.

The dependency of the people on imported commodities and ideas, fostered in the colonial situation, still exists. The cultural lag in the new idea of self-help, except by urban and middle-class professional and business people, is still tremendous. Dependency impressed from the outside and above has become deeply carved into the socialization process, which in turn continues to reinforce the prevalent response modes.

Identification

Like Sears (1950:3) we are interested in two types of identification actions (or reactions): sex-typing or sex role differentiation and the internalization of values. The study of the process of identification is basic to the fundamental question in socialization analysis—how does the member of a society acquire its culture (Stoke 1950; Parsons 1952)? Sears (1950:7-8) says

The present hypothesis is that a secondary drive of identification produces the behavior that is replicative of the parents' qualities, roles and demands. In this sense it is a process or mechanism. It has the effect of transmitting the values of the culture from one generation to the next, and of providing for continuity, in a society of persons appropriately trained for the roles of which the society is composed.

Since dependency presages the development of identification, it will become apparent why we have ordered these variables in the present manner.

Sex Role Differentiation, Sex-Typing, Desirable Behavior Traits

Identification takes place in the earliest instance in relation to the parents. Differential familial values regarding the sexes and corresponding modes of action and interaction with children will depend upon how training agents conceive the sex roles. Parental conceptions of sex and sex-typing will color every phase of child rearing. In turn, introjection of parental behaviors and values will result in identification which produces a double-faceted role, one side of it being the behavior of the parents as they actually are and the other the kind of behavior they would like to see in their child.

Vallecañese parents have sharp and rigid ideas of what should constitute the roles and actions of their children. Parental sex role differentiation of their children, where 7.0 indicates a very high degree of differentiation, scaled as follows: 16 mothers and 14 fathers scored 5.0, one mother and two fathers scored 6.0, two fathers scored 5.0, one mother scored 2.0. This area, when mentioned, caused a good deal of shock and uncertainty, but responses tend to approximate "reality" as experienced by the external observer. Not only must "boys act like boys" and "girls like girls" but usually they must not associate with each other, once latency is reached, even though they be siblings.

[Girl, age 4]. It is very important that she act like a *mujercita* because she is very different. Girls have their games of dolls and are more homebodies, and a girl is more humble—that is, quieter and calmer, but the boy likes to play hard and play "tops" and run and is stronger. A girl should be like a girl, because this way when she is small she will know how to behave. She should play games calmly so that she will not get hurt. She goes to pick flowers and she does not even like to play ball; when the males play, she looks at them, but does not play with them. . . . I have told her that the main thing is that when the males are changing their clothes she should not observe them. Not to watch them through the cracks in the wall—she, ah, should not see the males nude. . . . She rarely plays with her brothers but I watch her, because she can be hurt. She plays most with the smallest one [an infant] and that is all right because he is smaller. She should make the boys respect her and behave well in front of them.

[Boy, age 6]. It is very important that Chico act like a *machito*. The *niñas mujeres* are more delicate than the males. You have to dress them more and have them with shoes and dresses and attend to them more. But a boy can go around any old way. And if he goes to school, it does not look so bad if he is without shoes. He should know how males act, so in the future he will know how to act like the male that he is. . . . It is not good for him to play with girls' toys. I do not let him. He has his male games, like tops and little cars. But if he plays with girls' things he will get used to this, and then they will make fun of him when they see him. . . . For males it is not so bad that they be nude and they spend their time outside . . . it is all right. But girls always have to be dressed and more delicate and you have to take care of them, and they are more *de la casa*. I have told him he should not play with *niñas mujeres*. He should always try to play with males . . . they have their own games. And he should become accustomed to this with males and not with girls. I have told him to respect girls.

A few parents find it difficult to resolve their confusion and inner conflicts as to what their position toward the sex roles should be, and these are reflected in apparently contradictory child behavior.

It is important, yes [hesitates, not knowing how to proceed] . . . Because behaving like a boy—. Ramonito is old enough to know he is a boy, but he does not behave like one. No, I would not let a girl go nude. People would criticize it. That's the difference. A girl—you have to cover her flesh always . . . Well, you've seen in *Imparcial* [Puerto Rican tabloid] the cases of what men have done to girls. Because it is bad and that gives them temptations, and they rape them. Because—it is bad—I don't know. [Laughs] . . . I let him play with dolls. They all go under the bed and they all play [male and female siblings]. It isn't worthwhile to tell him now not to do it, because he does not pay attention to me, because he is small. When he is about eight years old, I will teach him to do boys' things. If he plays with dolls he will grow up lazy. You have to teach him to do male things, like taking care of the animals and things like that. . . . He does not act like a boy. . . . No—he does not act like a girl—Because he does not pay attention to me, and he would rather put on a dress than a pair of pants. Yet, there is a difference, because I would not let a girl walk around without clothes and Ramonito—even though I don't like it, I don't think it is too bad. Because—girls have to cover up . . . a boy—nothing happens to him.

Thus is revealed a recurring streak of high parental sexual anxiety, which to some extent presumably will be passed on to their children through identification. Strangely enough, the boy in the quotation from the confused mother seemed to the researcher to be among the most *macho*-like of all the panel boys and his play did not seem to reflect that his mother's anxiety had been passed down to him, though this does not imply that such role confusion may not exist.

There is little agreement among mothers and fathers as to which of them their child resembles. If we can accept these parental estimates, some of the confusion about sex-typing seems to have directly influenced identification. Another possibility is that the strong feelings of most of the group about sex roles has *not* come through but has itself resulted in a confusion of sex identification on the part of the child. Observations indicate that identification is stronger than parents realize but that at the same time there is uncertainty and confusion among many children regarding sex roles.

Keeping in mind the possibilities we have raised, and our observations of children and parents, it seems reasonable to conclude that identification is (1) moderately strong, (2) perhaps has not yet had time at this age (four to seven years) to develop deeply, and (3) is not always sharp and clear-cut.

Parents are quite emphatic about resemblances, when they do not confuse behavior with phenotypical traits. They frequently refer to character, temperament, and way of doing things. Personality mannerisms also receive some attention: walking and talking (which were asked specifically), laughing, smiling, anger, seriousness, gaiety, sobriety, love of play, love of a good time; and one mother even noted that her daughter "talks stuttering, like her father." Stress is placed on the desirability of a calm temperament (*tranquilidad*) and being nice in an understanding way (*simpático*), as against the undesirability of being easily angered or quickly excited (*temperamental, mal genio*). Approved traits also include respectfulness, obedience, liking people, pleasantness, being nice to people. Disapproved traits include lack of respectfulness, disobedience, stubbornness, sourness, timidity. The anthropologist was continually struck by the feeling that parental behavior would often seem to discourage approved qualities and viceversa.

Father-Child Relationships

From the point of view of the mother, the boy's relationship with his father is moderately affectionate, friendly and close, and the girl's somewhat more so. Fathers tend to see themselves as about the same with boys, but colder with the girls. As a whole, however, by either parent's estimate, father-child relationships are neither especially warm nor especially frigid. Both parents are generally sterner and at the same time more demonstrative with the boy than with his sister. The *mujercita* is adored by her father when very young but in a protective rather than emotional way. This adoration of the little girl by the father is particularly evident either if there are no other children or if most of the other children are males. If there is a family of predominantly female children, the father will lavish little affection on them, and if they are all on the distaff side, he may be called a *chancletero*, a characterization which is status-debilitating both in the eyes of the community and in his own self-image.[5] In addition, while fathers gen-

5. See the case of Anselmo, p. 64. People say the father of a preponderantly female brood can only make *chancletas* (slippers), which they synonymize with females. Therefore he is dubbed a *chancletero*. The symbolic significance of the slipper as feminine and sexual has been noted in psychoanalytic dream theory. *Chancletero* is also used commonly in contemptuous reference to a vulgar person.

erally contribute little to the child-rearing and caretaking constellation, they spend rather more time with their sons than their daughters.

Maternal and Paternal Strictness

Though both parents tend to rate the father as generally more strict, objective judgments of their entire interviews reveal that the mother is actually the more strict. Strictness is operationally defined as the insistence on discipline and standards as it actually occurs in parental practices, not as perceived in the parent-image.

Strictness, then, is the degree to which demands are enforced. By objectively evaluating what each parent thinks, we found that fathers are expectably less restrictive than mothers.[6] This evaluation seems to bear out our observations, just as interview judgments of strictness did. The mother is both more restrictive and more strict in demands and their execution.

Nevertheless she still acts as mediator between father and child. As if in compensation for the severity of her discipline, her high demands, and her insistence, at least some of the time, that they be carried out, she is often the refuge to which the child scurries for shelter in a paternal gale. The difference between the father-child and mother-child strictness situations is that between the enforcement of immutable laws by a god who only descends his throne to execute measures in "serious offenses" and disciplinary measures by his aide for run-of-the-mill offenses. The wife, being removed from the seat of ultimate power and therefore closer to the subjects, may be more amenable to childish pleas for mercy or forgiveness. The father, in his own eyes, appears to be quite indulgent at times, like a benevolent despot, since

> His sceptre shows the force of temporal power,
> The attribute to awe and majesty,
> Wherein doth sit the dread and fear of kings;
> But mercy is above this sceptred sway. . . .

6. A "superscale" was erected for this purpose based on all previous specific scales of restrictive demands in all areas covered in the interviews: eating habits, toilet training, aggression, physical mobility, sex play and modesty, etc. All these were expanded or contracted to five-point scales and their means were used in the construction of the superscale (high 5). Median for mothers of boys is 4.5 and of girls 5.0; for fathers of boys 4.0 and of girls 3.5. There are at least three times as many areas covered in the mother interview and therefore her restrictiveness is broader-based. In the actual situation this is about the way it would be. The father is simply not involved in many crucial areas of child rearing.

The paternal sceptre is the strap on the wall, his subject the child, his prime minister (who must assuage him as well as administer his kingdom) the wife-mother. The ruler is superhuman and above the populace, farther away and therefore more awe-inspiring. But his prime minister always has an ear tuned to the crowd.

There is one fly in this overliterary ointment: The father, it is true, is kingpin in his own household. He is not, however, kingpin in the outside world; being a caneworker he has a low social status. Thus a father powerful at home may be ordered around in a very imperious manner by a middle-class woman and sometimes even a child. And to middle- or upper-class men he is "*el jíbaro*," a hill-billy, a creature not ordinarily respected. To his own lower-class world he must appear constantly *macho*, and his *machismo* must from time to time be reaffirmed by some kind of actions: sexual powers, fertility, aggression, etc. But there are strong cultural punishments and lack of opportunity for all the ways in which he might prove his *machismo*, and so the lower-class male is impaled on the horns of an insoluble dilemma. Perhaps the easiest way is to maintain his superior position in his own home. But it appears inevitable that his children will know of his status on the outside and tend to devaluate him to some degree.

Parental Achievement Standards

Parental demands for achievement will directly affect the development and operation of the child's superego. If these demands are high the child will want to conform as much as possible in order to be assured of achievement, since it is usually conforming behavior which is rewarded. It may be argued that if demands for achievement are extremely high, the child may utilize illegal means to satisfy them, but even this is working toward the rewards of conformity by circumventing the usual means; the attempt will always be made to appear legitimate in the eyes of the society. Conversely, with low achievement demands, it may be expected that the need will not be great for conforming behavior beyond that of fulfillment of traditional roles, and this should negatively affect superego operation.

An over-all scale for parental pressure for conformity to their demands, using 7.0 for very high pressure, produces a median for mothers of boys of 5.0, of girls 5.5, for fathers of boys 5.0, of girls 4.0. Thus while restrictive demands are high, pressure for conformity is only moderately high.

But positive demands for achievement are even lower. With the highest scale value at 7.0, we obtain medians for mothers of boys of 3.0, of girls 4.0, for fathers of boys and girls 3.0. Why are achievement demands relatively low?

The environment has been deadening and frustrating of even minimum ambitions for so long that Valle Caña parents have culturally inherited little in the way of traditional aspirations. Most parents feel little reason to instill high levels of aspiration in their children. They frequently say that while they would *like* the child to get an easy job (the height of ambition for most adult Vallecañeses) they are convinced their son will end up working in the cane and their daughter will proceed along the traditional lines of domesticity and drudgery. It is not unexpected, then, that they have made small aspirational demands on their children. It is considered fortunate if a way can be found to send the child to school, for example, but this is as far as they feel they can be expected to go.

Mothers have a high level of aspiration ideally as to the importance of their child's success in school, but this is only in terms of a desirable goal, not a desired or realistic one. Most of them say they want their child to do well in school but do little to encourage this and oftentimes many things to discourage it. Doing well carries with it a broad connotation not so much of scholastic excellence as being well-behaved, not causing the teacher any trouble, etc. There is little understanding or appreciation of education as a real task; the child's physical presence in the schoolroom will somehow miraculously effect his education. The dynamics and requirements of the formal educational process are understandably mysterious and remote. Absences are tolerated and, in the case of bad weather, insisted upon. If a child is needed to help either parent, he must stay home, and if the need persists, he is unceremoniously removed from school for a long time or permanently. Even with free schools and free lunches it is a sacrifice for these parents to send a child to school, and if results are not thought to be commensurate with material costs, it is better that the child at least contribute to the family work load.

Few parents venture to suggest that their child might go to a university, but they realize little likelihood exists for such an accomplishment. A few, somewhat more realistically, think they might manage to send their child to junior high or high school, but most picked elementary school, often as low as the second or third grade (see pp. 58-62).

So achievement demands are low and pressures for conformity to parental demands are not especially high. It is enough that the child, to show the marks of good training, be obedient, respectful, silent, etc., and special skills, hard work to achieve high goals, and finely delineated appropriate social behaviors need not be sought.

According to Sears (1950:13-14) the strength of identification varies positively with the amount of affectionate nurturance, severity of demands, degree to which nurturance and punishment are contingent on successful accomplishment of or failure to meet the demands, degree to which maternal demands are successfully accomplished, and amount of absence of the person with whom the child identifies. We would expect, on the basis of restrictive demands, a relatively high degree of identification and subsequent superego development. However, the inconsistency with which many of the demands are put forth and accomplished, the lesser insistence on conformity to them, and low achievement standards make such a prediction uncertain. This assumption will be further examined in Chapter 8.

Tradition, Culture Change, and Parent-Child Relationships

The parents of the great majority of these mothers and fathers were much stricter than the latter are with their own children, according to our mothers, fathers, and other informants. Not only was discipline harsher on the part of both parents, but there was also a stricter division of discipline in the household. While the father reigned supreme as far as authority was concerned, punishment was meted out along sex lines, the father taking care of the boys, the mother of the girls. For example, boys often received delayed punishment, if their transgression was committed in their father's absence, upon his return home, whereas today a much larger share of the burden of punishing both sexes is taken care of in the immediate situation by the mother. Fathers in former times seemed more inclined to follow through with punishment unsparingly and to hunt up the culprit if he ran away. The following story was told by a man who was raised as a country lad but is now working in the city:

My father was the harshest and most serious man I have ever known. We all respected him very much. We respected him so much we would hardly dare even to speak when he was around. I remember once that I got into a quarrel with my brother and my mother tried to separate us and we ended up fighting. My mother said she was going to tell my father and I was so frightened my knees shook. So I stayed outside when he came home that evening. I hid out in the yard. In a few minutes I heard him call out to me, but instead of answering him, I ran away, as fast as my legs would run. I ran into the woods and my father ran after me. Then he lost me— I don't know how far I ran. But he ran back and got a lantern and came looking for me again, calling out and warning me that I had better come back. . . . Then, I don't know how, somehow he caught me by the arm. When he got me home he called everyone around to watch. "This is what happens to a boy who does not obey," he shouted. He was terribly angry. He tied me to the leg of the table and began to beat me with a stick. My mother screamed out for him not to hit me so hard, but he kept on and finally I managed to get loose from the ropes and started to run, crying. He caught me and pushed my head between his legs and held me there so tight I almost choked, and started beating me with his fists on my back. *Ave Maria!* Finally my mother held his hands off and I ran into the bedroom.

He often beat me with a stick or a rope or just his fists, and he would hit me on any place he happened to land the blows. Oh, he was good to us sometimes, too, and sometimes he would bring us things, but if we were disrespectful his anger was worse than the wrath of God.

As harsh as these times were for children, most of them today, in Valle Caña at least, admire their parents for "knowing how to raise children." Nearly all agree things are different now, but most mothers tend to blame the difference on the inherent evil in present day off-spring:

Well, it was different. Because before, mother would put us on house chores from the time we were small. She always had us busy. But now mine do not do half what I did. Girls were more serious and went out less from the home. And parents were more respected. Now a child is freer.

Before it was different. Before children were obedient—very obedient. And now they are not. In other times children treated their parents of *papa* and *mama* and *usted*. But now children call one by one's [first] name and are disrespectful. Before the sons were good and did not gamble or drink. Now from the time they are born they gamble and drink [!]. And girls, before they are ten years old, they take themselves and fall in love [!].

Before it was better. Because of the humility and respect it would have been better to bring up children.

. . . Before, by just looking at a child, they would pay attention and if a visitor would come, we would not dare even come out until the visitor had gone. Before there was more respect and less of the child being an *averigüado* [busybody]. Today a child wants to know more than an older person.

Compared with contemporary parents, thirteen of the older generation were more strict, two about equally strict, and three less strict. There was insufficient data to judge one case. The foregoing sentiments are very probably instances of a universal tendency to regard olden days as golden days. But evidences of real change will be apparent throughout this study.

Some mothers, however, are willing to weigh the pros and cons though they are in the minority:

Before one was brought up with more respect and was punished more strongly. Many spankings were given. Mother used to run after me many times with a rope. The children were forced to obey their parents. We were put to bed very early and we could not hear the conversation of older people. . . . I think that one was reared better because the parents educated the children more in respecting and caring for them. Today when a son does not like his parents or what they say, he leaves the house and does not care about the parents any more. Today children are badly raised because one does not give them the training or the punishment that was given in those times. . . . But now there are better times, too. Because they would tell me before that one could not have a party or a dance—that it would always end in a fight—but not now. Now people behave much better at parties. I don't know why—[perhaps because] some were brought up better and some were not.

A third of our panel of eighteen mothers said they are trying to bring up their children in the same way as their parents. Only two are consciously trying to bring up their children differently; the remainder feel they need to effect a compromise and bring up their children like their parents did in some ways and differently in other ways. Thus tradition plays a strong role in Valle Caña but some cracks have been pried into the rigid cultural mold by indigenous and acculturative changes. Whatever their precise nature, these changes are having an effect. At least in part Vallecañeses are cognizant of new levels of aspiration and new appetites. "That time was a very good time for bringing up children. Today there is more pride—more luxury; luxury is used much more. Shoes, 'permanents'—today is more demanding in work and money. In those times people did not demand so much out of life. People were simple and lived better. One could attend to one's needs."

Probably no family on the island is free of these changes. Undoubtedly their effects on mothers and fathers and the resultant confusion in deciding how to handle their children in the face of newly acquired values help to explain broad areas of disagreement concerning socialization, since presumably such uncertainty will itself be transmitted in identification.

One of the most disastrous consequences is that while these changes are being impressed from within and without at a varying but accelerating rate, they seldom take place within the frame of reference of the old ways, and little is done by the society to take up the cultural slack. The result is a kind of aimless social disorganization approaching what Durkheim and Merton call *anomie*. While the family has always been the bulwark of the social structure and individuals caught in the contradictions of social and cultural change naturally tend to fall back on the family, even its foundations are beginning to show signs of wear. That the family and social structure no longer fulfill their traditional functions is graphically illustrated in rising rates of crime, increasing tempo of emigration to cities and to the United States, artificial kinship inventions like the institution of *compadres de voluntad* (see pp. 52-53). The family is still the most important primary group in Valle Caña, but it has reached a crucial impasse with the demands of the times and the realities of a sub-subsistence level economy. This is not by way of predicting "disintegration" of the Vallecañese family. What the observer witnessed was the throes of transition through which the family was passing as it evolves, as in all culture change, to a new synthesis.

CHAPTER 7

Coming of Age—I

Introduction

LET, US move now from cultural and familial socialization practices and values to the early experiences of the Vallecañese child and some of his reactions to these cultural and familial conditions.

Data are drawn from observations, parent interviews, informants, and free projective doll play, four sessions of which were administered to one child between four and seven years from each of the eighteen families in our sample (see pp. 13-22 and Appendix D). The doll play was partially successful in eliciting the kinds of material we were looking for (see Landy 1959a). Three boys and one girl are categorized as nonparticipators, since after several trials they could scarcely be induced to enter the doll play situation. Of the remaining fourteen, about three produced sparse protocols and at the other extreme three yielded very rich productions. The ones in between exhibited little originality but were satisfactory. The nonparticipators were accorded extra observation and attention to make up what was lost by their refusal or fear to participate. In Chapter 9, for cross-cultural perspective, the doll play results of Vallecañese children are compared with those for two social class groups in the continental United States.

Infancy

Until recently, the Vallecañese child was born at home and delivered by a midwife. But in recent years, mothers increasingly have gone into the town or district hospital to have their babies delivered by doctors and to spend about three days obtaining a much-needed rest. However, the day of the midwife has not completely passed and some babies still see the light of day through their offices, which now are regulated by government training and inspection.

Occasionally there is no time to get the mother to the hospital or call in a midwife. One day we discovered that

. . . Teresa had given birth seven days ago. Labor pains started about four in the morning and by six she had given birth. When the pains began her husband called in a neighbor. Teresa says she is not the type to stay in bed, so she walked around and started to make coffee for the children but could not finish it. Her husband was readying a hammock with which to take her into town, but by the time he got back, Teresa had already given birth with the neighbor's help. Then her husband went down the road and got the *comadrona* (midwife) to cut the cord.

Most of the children were asleep but the oldest awoke so they placed her in a corner. Now Teresa's mother comes in to wash the baby's clothes and look after her. By the third day Teresa was up cooking for the children. She said she would like to keep the *cuarentena* (traditional forty-day postnatal confinement of the mother to the house, with tabooed bathing), but there is too much to do, though she will stay around the house most of the time anyway.

When a baby is born at home, it is often a public event, though the midwife more and more insists that curious onlookers stay out and only the husband or a female relative remain around to help. As one midwife says,

When there are several persons present, everyone wants to tell you how to do things and they only get you confused and it is worse on the mother. If anyone is there I try to keep them in the kitchen to help me boil my things, so that I can be alone in the room with the mother. There was a case where when I arrived at the house there were several of the mother's sisters there. They belonged to a religion [probably a nearby Pentecostal sect] that caused them to pray and scream and tell the mother that the devil was hanging from the wall and looking at her—when the child would be born, the devil would strangle it. The mother was of the same religion and she was so frightened she did not want to bear down, so I went quietly to her husband and told him to prepare a hammock, that we had to take her to the hospital. . . .

However, soon after the delivery, at home or hospital, the neighbors come in anyway, peeking at *el nacido reciente* (the new-born), gazing over at the exhausted mother, congratulating the father (especially if it is a boy), and carrying on friendly conversation. Birth, like the rest of the life cycle, including death, is not an isolated occurrence. Few experiences in the child's life will be unknown to his family and community. Far from resenting this lack of privacy, he will come to delight in it and to expect likewise to share the experiences of others.

Whether boy or girl, the infant is usually dressed in a tiny sacklike gown, swathed in receiving blankets or old clothes, and placed in the tiny hammock called the *coy*, which is near the mother's bed. She may reach out and rock the child at a moment's notice. Siblings often pass by and do the same, although at times with what may seem excessive vigor for the tiny being. When only a few months old, siblings who themselves are only a few years old may be permitted to hold the infant, sitting or sometimes even walking about. I have never seen one dropped, though the handling is often far from gentle. Baths are not usually given daily, but at intervals of several days, and during cool spells, sometimes several weeks. Especially during the first few months the infant may see little sunshine and is never out at night, since mothers fear the *sereno*, the night air which is thought to carry many maladies.

Feeding and Weaning

We have seen how the infant is fed and weaned (pp. 102-4). According to the mothers, nearly two-thirds of the infants in the panel families who were weaned (two were not weaned at seven years) experienced only mild reactions. Since weaning often is a capricious decision, it would seem that where removal of sucking [1] is sudden, the long preparation which most babies enjoy may cushion the shock. The transition may also be softened by the fact that, though after weaning the infant no longer takes food via sucking, many of them continue to suck. This may be evidence of oral frustration in those who are weaned early. Most infants after weaning become addicted to the rubber nipples which are stuck into their mouths as pacifiers. A common sight is one or more children sucking small nipples. Several siblings in a family, ranging in age from a year to seven or eight, may

1. This analysis makes no assumptions about whether sucking is instinctual or learned but only that, once activated, it seems generally to focus the child's infant-like responses and reinforce and typify infantile behaviors.

take turns serially sucking one or two nipples, a steady drool down their chins, and this will go on through all the activities of the day. Frequently there are fights for these pacifiers, and one child will torment others by stealing or hiding their nipples. This prolonged infantilism helps fixate early dependency systems. A mother who may be annoyed that her child craves attention when she is busy will often stick a nipple into his mouth, so that while there is nonreward or punishment for one kind of dependency response, there is unintended reinforcement of it through associated acts of dependency like prolonged sucking and drooling. Thumb sucking also is evidenced by small children, but not nearly as much as nipple sucking.

Nearly half the mothers feel that the subject children, when babies, cried relatively little and were quite good. Only two say their babies cried a great deal; however, half could not recollect to what extent their babies cried. Contemporary babies seem to cry somewhat more than indicated for these children. I do not know whether this discrepancy between mother interviews and observations is due to hazy memory, a wish by the mothers to have had such good babies, my own tendency to distort observations, or to a real difference between the two generations of infants. Another likely factor is the difference in the mothers' and ethnologist's conception of "much."

Reactions to Sphincter Training

The severity of the child's reaction to maternal attempts at sphincter control is high; when scaled according to the mother's testimony, girls show greater traumata with a median of 4.5, compared with boys at 3.5, where 5.0 is a severe reaction. Since it tends to last longer, bedwetting, as we saw in Chapter 5 (pp. 106-7), brings a harsh response. Child reaction is given in this mother's description when a bedwetting occurs:

I wake him up with a *correaso limpio* [a "clean" whipping, with a strap]. He has not yet learned to get up to urinate [five years]. The other day I gave him a beating in the middle of the night. He made believe he was sleeping so I would not continue to hit him [at this point mother parodied how child cried, how she beat him, etc.]. He doesn't dare call me because he knows I am going to hit him. I give him a tremendous spanking and scolding. When he did it last I spanked him and then in the morning I hit him in the face with a blanket. For a few days now he has not done it.

Eleven of the children stopped wetting the bed at a median age of 15 months (range 6-30 months). Of the six still wetting their bed, two are seven years old. Eneuresis in some children lasts even to puberty.

Differential reaction of the sexes, a reflection of earlier and severer training for the girl, is manifested not only in the latter's reaction to training, as just noted, but also in doll play. In routine behavior, girls show several times more toileting activities (7.3 percent) than boys (1.5 percent) but for both it was the third most important routine category. Mintz (1951:VI/41) also finds this true in Cañamelar and suggests that this is a manifestation of the early cultural differentiation of the sexes. It is worth noting that the toy *letrina* in the doll set was used fairly often by both sexes as a lethal weapon (throwing the baby down the hole, stuffing in the father doll), but this was recorded as aggression, not toileting. This may be a possible symbolic acting out of anal aggression, but many other objects were also used as weapons, the trunk (a favorite), table, benches, etc.

It should be emphasized that once the child has learned not to soil his clothes or the house floor, he is free to use almost any area of the outdoors, and outside of the immediate house area there were few restrictions.

Sex

Whether the child is a girl or boy oftentimes makes a sharp difference in how the infant is received into the world and how he or she is handled throughout life, as was pointed out previously. The male child will be handled by both parents a good deal more than his sister and by siblings and relatives as well. While there is some handling of the female child in the early years by mother and siblings, one senses that almost from birth the hands-off policy, based ultimately on incest-fear and differential attitudes toward the sexes, is in effect.

From the beginning the boy usually goes around without pants, and his sexual organ is in much prominence and not infrequently manipulated by others and by himself. While before middle-class visitors the mother may become self-conscious about the boy's nude lower quarters, her admonitions do not conceal a note of amusement and admiration, very unlike her high anxiety toward female nudity:

The mother asked the three-year-old boy why he did not have clothes on. "*Mire, fresco, como se atreve a andar por ahí con los huevos al aire, y esa muchacha mirándote?*" [Look, fresh, how dare you walk around here with your eggs (testicles) in the air and this girl (ethnologist's assistant) looking at you?] This was said in a laughing tone. The boy laughed and ran into the other room. Later she called the boy's attention to this fact again, telling him to put on some pants and "stop running around with that long thing," but again this was said good-naturedly and the boy still paid no attention.

In spite of parental denials and prohibitions, both sexes, but especially the boy, were observed to masturbate, sometimes directly, as when one sees a small boy pull his penis to erection or playfully grab at the penis of a sibling or playmate, sometimes indirectly, as when he plays *vaqueros* (cowboys) and runs about with a stick between his naked legs. The latter method absolves him from blame in the eyes of his sexually anxious parents.

Again, despite parental claims to the contrary, group sex play is not rare. On two occasions I came upon mixed groups of children playing together near a *letrina*. They withdrew into the outhouse, giggling among themselves while closing the door as though caught in an embarrassing act. These may not have been instances of mutual sex play, but the writer finds it difficult to explain the children's reactions in any other way. At this time I was already well-known to them.

From the first, the child learns that sex is not only forbidden but dirty and dangerous. He observes how anxious his mother will become if such a thing is mentioned, and he hears stories of young women who are "ruined" by men. He learns that even as a boy he is capable of such evil, and he learns from older boys and men that this evil is also a pleasure to be sought after and one with which he may establish his worth as a male. The girl learns that she will probably be able to do little to defend herself if put into a compromising position with a boy, that fearful things may happen to her and she will have to bear the weight of responsibility for unwanted children. Later as she grows older, she finds that the mother usually will avoid the subject, but here from a widowed aunt, there from an older girl who "knows," she picks up bits of information. Boy and girl may hear the sounds of intercourse in the tiny cabin at night, and both may observe domestic animals and conclude that sex may be more aggression than mutual pleasure. It may not be accidental that the object of aggressive acts by both boy and girl in doll play most frequently is the mother, though of course there are many other implications of nurturance, dependency, and aggression, as we shall see.

Sex is hardly manifested in most children's fantasy play, and among the few who did make a sexual allusion toward the dolls, the mean percentage for the group as a whole was less than one percent for either sex, with boys slightly higher (o.5) than girls (o.2). As we have shown, parents spend a good deal of energy suppressing even verbal references to sex and are especially suppressive of girls. We are forced to infer that at this age sex has been successfully suppressed for these children in a doll play situation, where they may have been reluctant to express feelings before even permissive, albeit alien, adults, yet autoerotic and mutual sex play actually do take place. As one might suppose in a predominantly "other-oriented" or "other-directed" or, more properly perhaps for Valle Caña, "opinion-directed" culture, the important thing is not to mention a forbidden act. If one does not get caught and thus lose face, the consequences are not so bad, since internal pangs of conscience are not strong. This seems also true of another tabooed activity, interpersonal aggression, which, however, as in life, receives somewhat more expression in doll play than sex.

Aggression

Most parents, particularly fathers, feel their children get along pretty well with each other. A scale to measure the amount of quarreling among siblings, with 5.0 representing a large amount of quarreling, reveals a median of 3.0 for boys and girls, as seen by mothers, and 3.0 for boys and 2.0 for girls as seen by fathers. This moderate aggressivity, within the range of parental perception, is probably due to the high restrictiveness (Tables 17-21) placed on aggression of all kinds. Since my observational data include more aggression than parents imply, it may also be due to the parent, especially the mother, being too busy to notice much and not considering a good deal of bickering and quarreling as aggression. Sibling play frequently is characterized by rivalry and hostility. The following situation illustrates direct, "playful," and verbal forms of aggression.

The boy, two, was very active and aggressive toward all the siblings, and in general his aggression was more tolerated. Siblings and mother frequently referred to the six-year-old girl, who is a midget, by that name,

usually contemptuously. Their shyness toward me soon wore off and the
two-year-old began to swat at me until his mother admonished him to
cease. The midget girl played a game of teasing the boys with a rag, causing
much shouting and tussling. The girl played a lone game, the two younger
boys ganging up on her. Occasionally the seven-year-old boy would join
the struggle, taking sides alternately with each one, hitting a good deal and
desisting only temporarily when his mother rebuked him. The four-year-
old boy and six-year-old girl began to hit each other very hard, and
finally the boy ran crying to his mother who patted his head absently,
not looking at him. He soon got back into the fray. They were now hitting
each other with fists, sticks, and small stones. Once the oldest boy took a
stick from the youngest and tried to throw it out the door, but it rico-
cheted and struck him on the head. Everyone laughed while he rubbed
his head ruefully. The newborn baby lay across the bed, and the girl
caressed it roughly, sometimes throwing herself across the infant. Once
she picked up the baby and jumped off the bed. The mother stopped her
several times but she went back to it. Frequently the oldest boy would
grab the genitals of the younger ones and laugh as they whined and tried
to get away. For over an hour the two-year-old tried to sleep, but the
older one would not let him until the mother made him stop.

Boys, as in Mintz' Cañamelar, are allowed relatively more aggression by mothers and relatively less by fathers. Since the mother's
supervision is most prevalent, the boy actually does aggress more than
the girl. However, a chip-on-the-shoulder attitude is largely missing,
even on the part of the boys. The good child is one who is docile with
his elders and plays without fuss. There may be some pride in the
aggressive prowess of the *machito,* but it seldom reaches the bullying
proportions of the *guapo* (see p. 116) with non-relatives, since this
is socially punishing. When a parent comes upon a fight (apparently the above instance was interpreted purely as "play" by this
mother), as we have shown, if the children persist after two or three
warnings, they are usually punished, and this throws a burden of fear
regarding persistent aggression onto the child, for all share the blame
equally. What then is a child to do, especially if he feels a genuine
stake in the outcome? He may aggress verbally, and often does. Or
he may tell the parent and often does. There are so many recrimina-
tions to parents about other siblings and so much tattling that the
observer begins to wonder if any child feels safe for long in openly
flouting parental taboos.

One sibling, usually the oldest, is given control over the destinies of the others in the parent's absence. This sibling is charged with keeping order and is usually given full powers of punishment. Therefore an offending child may be punished by his older sibling who will settle a quarrel then and there. If the older child cannot make peace, he or she then fetches the parent, who quickly puts an end to it. Older siblings also use their position of power to extract favors from the younger ones and sometimes to aggress against their subordinates on the pretext of controlling aggression. But they are usually considerate of them; mothers often say they "spoil" the youngsters by doing things for them, carrying them about (often when there is scant difference in physical size), and above all protecting them faithfully against harm from other children, animals, and the general environment.

Boys tend to exhibit more aggression than girls in the home, especially against parents. On a scale to measure this activity, with 5.0 as high aggression, mothers of boys report a median of 3.0 and of girls, 2.0, while fathers report 3.0 for boys and 1.5 for girls. This may well be because male aggression is somewhat more tolerated, though boys' tantrums, while sometimes tolerated if limited to negativism and whining, seldom are if the aggression is openly directed against parents (see p. 116). A good deal of whining, nagging, and negativistic behavior was observed in both sexes.

In doll play boys had a more uniform pattern of aggression (24.5 percent) than girls (17.6 percent). But one extreme feminine case had 69.1 percent aggression, higher than any boy, and if we omit her case, the girls' percentage would be reduced to 10.3 percent. Her diffuse fantasy aggression was matched by her actual behavior vis-à-vis the ethnologist and his assistant.

In this fantasy behavior, the self was the agent of aggression most utilized. Of the doll agents, the boys used the father most, and the mother second; the girls the mother most and the father third, with the boy as the second agent of aggression. We have seen that the mother actually is less punitive against the boy. Also, in real life, the boy appears to aggress, in the eyes of others, more than the girl.

The most used objects of aggressive acts, in rank order, are: BOYS: mother, father, girl, boy, baby, self; GIRLS: mother, girl, father, boy, baby. The mother is a more frustrating and presumably aggression-inducing object for the girls, with both sexes also seeing the girl receiving more aggression than the boy. She also finds siblings of the same sex among the dolls more frustrating, perhaps because the older girls are most often parent surrogates. On the other hand, girls regard the baby more tenderly, aggressing against it only half as much as boys, which reflects reality as I perceived it.

Compared with a group of American preschool children (Hollenberg and Sperry 1951) with a mean for aggressive acts in doll play of 48.3 percent, Vallecañese children have a mean aggression in doll play of less than half of this (21.1 percent). Since, in an absolute sense, most of our children are highly frustrated and punished for aggression at home and, relative to the continentals, do not express high aggression in doll play, what happens to their frustration needs? Presumably they are expressed in some other way—"displaced" or "projected," in the idiom of learning theory and psychoanalysis.

Observation leads us to conclude that the Vallecañese child does vent aggression, but upon permissible objects, or out of sight of punishing parents and older siblings. We have seen above how older sibling caretakers aggress, often by whim, against their younger charges. Other permissible objects are open to all children and are attacked freely. Thus the infant lying in the *coy* is open to an occasional surrepetitious blow by a passing sibling, or an "accidental" bumping. And "playful" (in parental eyes) aggression, as we have seen, may be routine.

Perhaps the most universal objects of aggression for children and even for adults are animals, especially dogs and cats (despised by almost everyone), cows, pigs, horses (though sleek horses are admired as mounts), goats, and lizards (all varieties of which are harmless in Puerto Rico). A horse on a farm where the ethnologist lived had one eye knocked out by a rock at the hands of a man who said the horse "almost bit me." Children frequently injure domestic animals with rocks and sticks and otherwise torture the beasts while they laugh amusedly at their squeals of pain. One afternoon in the *batey* (yard) of one mountain family,

The older boys constantly threw stones and mud clods at the animals, especially the starved, miserable-looking dogs, with much laughter. The little girl continued to hit the hog on the rump with rocks while he tried to eat, pulled the legs of the sucklings to trip them, pounded the dogs with rocks and sticks, and pelted the chickens. The boys caught a small tarantula and impaled it on a sharp stick; then they captured a small lizard and placed it on the struggling spider. The lizard sank its fang into the spider and the spider clutched the lizard in its trembling limbs and bit it. Both animals finally died while the boys shrieked with delight. Then they caught a larger lizard and tried to make it eat the dead spider, but the lizard escaped, to their disappointment. They turned to the farm animals again. . . .

Very often a child will simply take out his hostility needs on the natural environment, pulling up young plants, hacking at trees, etc., in a reckless, abandoned way. Also there is a good deal of verbal aggression against other children, although little was expressed in doll play, and this seems to intensify with age and mastery of language. In such ways the Vallecañese youngster relieves frustrated tension; since there are few toys and other means of entertainment, and therefore displacement, these ways must succeed fairly well. Furthermore, unlike his mainland contemporaries, the Vallecañese child is not used to displacing his aggression on objects like dolls. Actually these are relatively rare, highly valued, and not to be treated roughly.

Adults displace their aggressive needs through their own projective systems, some of which were discussed in earlier chapters: for example, the widespread beliefs in the evil eye, in witchcraft, in Spiritism, and even some belief in sympathetic magic. And a common vicarious release is found in gossiping and tale-bearing.

Reactions to Punishment

How do these children react when punished? Eleven mothers (six girls, five boys) say that when they are spanked the children act as though their feelings were hurt. Six mothers (two girls, four boys) say the child becomes angry and cross. Several also say their child, when hurt or angry, goes to bed or otherwise attempts to withdraw from the situation. A few parents say the child, after hiding for awhile, becomes repentant, perhaps even sending in siblings to act as go-betweens with the parents. One or two report that their child sometimes after a spanking throws a tantrum in which he aggresses against objects and people in the environment. One child threatens to tell her father when her mother spanks her! One little boy refuses to take food when his mother spanks him and runs off to his grand-mother's house in anger. Nevertheless, most mothers are proud that their children's affection continues even after a spanking. As one put it: "His feelings get very hurt and after he cries awhile he comes to me and throws his arms around me and then I tell him to behave well and I will not have to punish him any more. That boy is very attached to me, more than the others. At night before he goes to bed he asks me for the *bendición* [blessing] and kisses me."

A consequent of the parental tendency to inconsistency in administering punishment and other negative sanctions seems to be that the child never quite knows when to expect to be punished, nor consistently for which transgressions of familial rules and taboos. One result is that he often tries to get away with as much as he can before he is caught. With so little at stake except the pain involved and so few things to do or external stimuli to titillate him, the child often runs the risk of being punished in order to do something which has become a strong need. This field observation is quite typical:

Susa tells the child to put on clothes instead of running around nude. The boy does not listen to her but continues to play. She repeats this several times. Still no response. Finally she goes over and slaps him and forces him to put on a little shirt (which still exposes his genitals, incidentally). He plays awhile with his siblings and then goes outside, takes off the shirt and throws it away, glancing around slyly at his mother, who is busy. For awhile she does nothing and he thinks she has forgotten, but suddenly she grabs a strap and flies toward him. He sees her coming and dashes away down a steep hill below the house. In a rage Susa picks up sticks and stones and flings them at the fleeing child. She curses loudly, but she cannot chase; there are other children and so many chores to do. After perhaps an hour the boy returns. The mother is preoccupied and quite placid, speaking with a visitor.... The boy edges into the house and finally goes quietly over and sits beside his mother. She glances at him but continues speaking to her guest. Suddenly she grabs for him and snatching the strap off the nail begins to whack him. The boy flees again.

Physical and verbal punishment by a small minority of mothers are sometimes carried to vindictive extremes, and the product is not so much an obedient and docile child but one who is surly and counter-abusive.

Lydia said, "I have nothing but *candela* [fire; trouble] with Carlito, he is so bad. Today I gave him a terrible beating. There is an old lady he likes very much and he is always inviting her to come home with him and drink coffee; and she comes, he even calls her grandmother. Today that woman was very nasty to Carlito, she insulted him. When I was told about this I beat up Carlito. First, I pinched him so hard that I almost took a piece out—it was on his vaccination so it would hurt more. Then I pulled his hair hard, I felt like pulling it out; and I hit his head against the floor. This way he will learn not to do such things so nobody will bother him. After I beat him I felt sorry and I almost cried."

Carlito was present, listening intently but saying nothing. Arturo's wife tried to signal Lydia but the latter did not heed. Finally Arturo's wife said, "Children know much more than people think they do."

Lydia's little girl, Pita, went indoors [everyone was sitting outdoors since it was a warm evening]. Lydia called her back, but she only screamed out, "*Mielda!*" [shit]. Lydia repeated it as a joke and the others laughed too.

Arturo's daughter began to counsel Carlito, telling him not to be a bad boy and to behave well with his mother. He replied, "That *pipona* [big belly; Lydia was pregnant] is good for nothing, that's what my *pai* [papa] says; the only thing she's good for is to cook rice with too much salt in it." Lydia became irritated and told him to be quiet and to leave but he did not go. After a while Carlito remarked, "The policeman is a *pendejo* [fool; literally, pubic hair]," and repeated it several times but everyone ignored him.

Lydia said that she was sending her younger boy to school, but Carlito was "so stupid he can't even learn to write his name." At this point an adolescent boy came over and began to pull Carlito's hair. When Carlito objected, the older boy remarked loudly how bad Carlito was. Lydia nodded her head in agreement. When Carlito complained to his mother, she told him very harshly to go home to bed.

At the other extreme are permissive parents like Anita and Cruz. Combined with Anita's permissiveness, however, one finds extreme casualness and sometimes outright unresponsiveness and rejection.

When I [field assistant speaking] got to the house Anita was in the patch picking *gandules* [peas] and the boy was alone in the house. I told him I was going out to help his mother, but though he came along, he made no attempt to help. He repeatedly told his mother that he owned the trees and everything planted there, and his mother laughed that he was very possessive and frequently would say everything in the house belonged to him. Josito asked his mother for water several times but she ignored him. Later in the house Josito began to play with her purse, emptying the contents on the floor. Anita told him mildly to stop, but he continued. He asked for water again and she finally gave it to him, commenting that he was very bothersome sometimes.

Josito went under the house and started singing very loudly. Anita said the neighbors liked the boy's singing but she was irritated by it and did not want him to sing so loudly. Josito came in and asked for the keys to the trunk, got them, opened the trunk, took out a book and began to "read." The father said with amusement that he had many books at one time, but the child had torn them up. The boy then changed his clothes and ran off to a neighbor's house, without a word to either parent.

Action and Interaction in the Small Child

Not only is the child's physical mobility limited, but, as we have seen, so is the psychological *lebensraum* within which he may interact with others, especially of opposite sex, older generation, and class superordination. One measure of this in doll play is to divide all acts into two categories, interaction and noninteraction (solitary behavior with no object), and compare the proportions. The ratio of interaction to noninteraction is two to three, the proportions being 40.2 percent to 59.8 percent.

Even more interesting is that when broken down by sex, the proportions for boys are 34.7 per cent to 65.3 per cent, while for girls they are more evenly divided, 45.7 per cent to 54.3 percent. In actual physical mobility we have shown that the girl is more circumscribed. However, in fantasy, as in her actual observed behavior, the play of the girl tends toward more original, elaborate, and logical themes. As we have pointed out, while both sexes are cloistered to some extent, the girl is much more so, but at the same time she finds it easier to act out her role, since the home is more conducive to feminine activity, while the society tends to punish the very actions which it expects of the boy. Relative permissiveness results in turning the boy loose to fulfill his needs in an unrewarding society and therefore works to his detriment, while the relative restriction of the girl forces her to remain close to the very environment through which she may fulfill her role. The female ego thus becomes more self-sustaining, less dependent, and better equipped for adult responsibilities. The boy's lesser adaptability tends to have a deadening effect on his ego development.

The result is a more frustrated, aggressive, and lonelier person in the male. And when he meets other males contending with the same personal-social conflicts, he reaches out to them, yet he is unable effectually to respond, even should a relationship be attempted. This

constant reaching out toward other males is sharply exemplified in
the adult male. The anthropologist found in his association with
Vallecañese men and older youths that almost invariably, if there was
any rapport, and often when there was not, men would beseech
him to form a *confianza* (trust) relationship. "With each other," they
would say, "We shall have *confianza*, you to me and I to you, so we
can be close, like brothers." And to assure me of their sincerity, they
would insist on buying many rounds of rum, even though they could
ill afford to. Often these were married as well as single men. If after
several hours of incessantly reiterating their *confianza* I suggested that
we certainly had become friends but it was growing late and perhaps
we should be getting home, they would become discomfited and
sometimes appear hurt. Admittedly, the anthropologist found long
hours in strictly male company somewhat cloying, and he began to
wonder if Vallecañeses did too. At any rate heterosexual relationships
were so restricted, they usually had little choice.

Miscellaneous Activities

In the previous chapter much of the usual behavior surrounding
eating has been described. In doll play the second most frequent type
of routine activity was concerned with eating and cooking, with the
girls having more (21.0 compared with 7.5 percent for boys) because
they are more concerned with cooking as a sex role activity. In real
life these children have a primary concern with food (see pp. 104-6),
a point also noted by Mintz (1951:VI). They eat much when it is
available and long for food when it is absent, which is quite often.
There are references to food and *tiempo de hambre* (time of hunger)
in the folklore (see pp. 129-31).

The most important single category of routine activity in doll play
was that concerned with sleeping and resting. This is understandable
when we think of factors like these: (1) Due to the layout of the
doll set, it was inevitable that the hammock, *coy*, and bed be among
the most obvious pieces of equipment. This might have made them
more attractive though they were in about the same proportions and
prominence as in the Valle Caña household. (2) In real life, an important part of the day is taken up with sleeping and resting since
(a) there is not much to do anyway and life is often unexciting;
(b) inadequate diet of these children, and their parents, undoubtedly

results in a good deal of energy insufficiency and the need constantly to recuperate strength; (c) the year-round mild climate is conducive at all times to sleeping and resting; and (d) as was mentioned earlier, lack of privacy makes sleeping in the case of the punished child one of the few ways of withdrawing from the outer, all-seeing world. It should be noted that boys resort to this behavior (42 percent) more than girls (33.3 percent), which might be a reflection of the boy's being punished more and needing to withdraw more and to the greater general dependency of the boy. It also demonstrates another fact of life, that boys and men spend more time, especially during the long dead season, resting and loafing about, while women and older girls work as usual.

Girls are more concerned with cleanliness activities (5.9 percent) than boys (1.0 percent) (a result, no doubt, of stronger parental demands for them to be neat and clean) and with the acting out of their household role as cleaner, an activity barely mentioned by boys.

All other routine acts were thrown into a "wastebasket" category called "miscellaneous" and came to 47.5 percent for the boys, and 31.4 percent for the girls. These were mostly of the type of "The boy goes for a walk," "The father sits down," "The father stands up," and so on, and for some children was the most frequent type of behavior utilized.

The Nonparticipators: Variants or Deviants?

Of the eighteen children with whom doll play was attempted, four could not be induced into the situation after repeated attempts or produced too infrequently to be included with the participators. These cases were allotted additional intensive observation. Herewith are presented brief summaries of each case extracted from field notes and doll play work records. Ratings of high and low are based on medians as the splitting points of scaled variables.

TONIO

Male, six. Youngest of a large family, mostly males. Constantly hung around doll play sessions (we were using his grandmother's house, near his own). Would tell mother and grandmother he wanted to come, then could hardly be lured inside. After two attempts on our part, finally entered, but in five sessions produced such thin protocols (a single, rigid, routine theme), they could not be used. Was never as timid or frightened as other nonparticipators, but once in the situation he did little more than stare from experimenter to scorer to his toes with a characteristic grin. Not even promise of increase in his reward of candy and small toys could persuade him to leave the security of his monotonic theme.

Behavior at home: At home is not at all shy, at least not with friends and siblings, but seemed never to be willing to speak a word to me, though we had known each other for six months and he knew I was a frequent source of candy or chewing gum. Play was usually of the tail-following variety, waiting until someone else initiated an activity before he participated but then wanting to hog the show. Frequently aggressive, especially against smaller children and farm animals. One morning he and two other boys about his age tortured a chicken, which he was supposedly "minding," for more than an hour, pulling out its feathers, almost breaking its limbs, etc. His mother is out several days a week, only sample mother who works nearly full-time, but when she is home he often whines and otherwise nags at her. She accepts this with good grace, at least in my presence, but she will often promise him candy or something if he will go away (a promise she tells me she does not usually keep).[2] Generally, however, she seems solicitous of many of his needs.

Ratings: According to mother's interview, he is high in dependency behavior, and mother's response to his dependency needs is also high. Her nurturance in his infancy is rated low, but the effect of this variable on current dependency has not been established. Mother also low in frustration of interpersonal relationships. Maternal restriction and punishment of aggression, general maternal frustration, and maternal punitiveness are all low, and since his observed behavior is often aggressive, these variables probably relate directly to each other.

BLANQUITO

Male, four (approximately; mother uncertain). A shy, soft little child, with blond hair and baby-like skin and large green eyes, most effeminate in appearance, especially when wearing his *cota* (dress-like garment). On first two attempts he would not even come to house where doll play was taking place. On third attempt would not come with us, but later came alone (the house was near his). In first session, could scarcely be induced

2. This practice of bribery is part of a general pattern. In Chapter 5 it was shown that reward is not a usual concomitant of good behavior in Valle Caña. The bribery pattern is a kind of negative reward, usually, as in this case, to remove the presence of the child when it becomes annoying to the parent or to elicit desired behavior in certain social situations.

to pick up dolls and after a few minutes burst into tears. After this would come into sessions, but produced very little. Next to youngest of small family (four boys). Mother has had several other children who died in childbirth or within a few years—all girls. Now wants a girl very badly and has allowed the hair of youngest boy (between one and a half and two) to grow long, a practice seldom done with males in Valle Caña.

Behavior at home: In spite of effeminate appearance, Blanquito is very much a *machito* when he plays, taking his sex role quite seriously. Seems to get along well with siblings and peers, but seldom plays with anyone outside family except neighbor Chico, also a nonparticipator. Seems to have warm relationship with both parents and they like him very much. Obviously before the advent of Blanquito's younger sibling he was the apple of their eye. Occasionally he shows some resentment against the younger child, but plays pretty well with him, though not often. Has shown a modicum of aggression in play, mostly against the environment, against younger brother, and against older boys who tolerate it with amusement; but his aggression is by no means as marked as that of Tonio, Chico, or most other boys in panel. Exhibits much dependency behavior, especially desire to stick close to mother, but again this is not as marked as Chico's, though about the same as Tonio's with less of the latter's whining. His security with his parents, however, seems more apparent, and more taken for granted by him, than with many other children. Frequently initiates own play, which is often complex and original, by contrast with either Tonio's or Chico's.

Ratings: Mother's response to dependency is high and so is his dependency rating, taken from mother's interview. Her nurturance in infancy is also high, and her current frustration of interpersonal relationships low. Mother's restriction and punishment of aggression, total frustration, and punitiveness are low but his behavior is only mildly aggressive.

CHICO

Male, four. Second youngest of large family of boys and girls. Dark, extremely shy little child, with strong, well-built body. Very much withdrawn from adult world and occasionally even from peers. Older siblings and mother report that sometimes he seems to "go into trances." What they meant was withdrawal in which he refuses to speak to anyone for several hours, even mother. Often "trances" take the form of going to bed, sometimes to sleep, something he did after first attempt to get him into doll play.

Of two complete refusals even to go to scene, and six attempts, all unsuccessful, to draw him into situation, Chico produced partially in three sessions, but only with urging for each movement, and once only when in a "group session" with friend Blanquito.[3] On first three sessions, even when persuaded to approach the house (around which ordinarily he played very often), he stayed outside and cried, and derision of other children at his crying did not help. When finally induced to pick up a doll and do something inside, he would function for two or three minutes, then stop and become so uncomfortable that the session had to be stopped when tears welled in his eyes.

Behavior at home: Chico exhibited dependency behavior with mother, sometimes whining around her, sitting near her as soon as she would rest from her work, jabbing and nudging into her ribs and breasts, and moaning. She responded to dependency demands sometimes, but often ignored him, or bribed him with food to keep him quiet, or sent him outside to play. Played with sisters and other neighbor girls mostly, and sometimes with close friend Blanquito. Since latter defended himself, Chico did not often aggress against him, but frequently aggressed against girls, younger and older, and none dared return blows and taunts. Also extremely aggressive against environment and animals. Once I saw him attack a tree with father's hatchet (children in Valle Caña are usually permitted to play with machetes, hatchets, and knives). Cut at the tree in cold fury for half an hour until exhausted, and part of tree was eaten away. Play seems rather aimless and themeless, much less intelligent that Blanquito's. For instance would often throw stones against very close objects. When they glanced off and hit him, he would cry, but in a little while repeat the performance, usually with the same results. Most introverted of all males in panel; yet among peers, especially girls, asserts himself in overt aggressiveness. In all the time we knew Chico he never spoke a word directly to me, although I would be around him for hours at a stretch. After several months, did bring himself to shout *adiós* to me as I walked up mountain past his house, laughing excitedly to his peers as though this were a real piece of daring.

Ratings: Present dependency behavior, as reported by mother's interview, is low. Mother's response to dependency, as well as nurturance in infancy, also low. Current frustration of interpersonal relationships by the mother, maternal restriction and punishment for aggression, total frustration and punitiveness are all high.

DOLORES

Female, four. One complete refusal to come to doll play, five attempts, all unsuccessful. Only time she responded to doll play situation was when we left her with brother who had accompanied her, writer remaining

---

3. Group sessions were tried experimentally as warming-up periods for nonparticipators but did not stimulate fuller participation. (See Appendix D, and Landy 1959a.)

hidden behind a wall and watching through a crack. Then did respond, although mostly on brother's initiative. Enjoyed play until brother discovered my presence, and the assistant reappeared, at which point she froze and refused further play or communication. Later remarked to brother, "I'll play for you but not for her." Next to youngest of large family. Most siblings are boys. Cried, or came close to tears, at every session. I found out afterward that mother had forced her to come, threatened her with punishment if she did not come or did not play. So each time child came home, she lied to mother by saying she had played, and built up a fantasy of what the doll play was like.

Behavior at home: Extremely lonely child, isolated in family of male siblings, so that she plays alone, almost never with them, not even with the younger one when her mother permits, except without enthusiasm. When all children are playing outdoors, for example, Dolores will withdraw and play alone. This is usual pattern of female vis-à-vis male siblings and has been demanded by parents as part of rigid segregation of the sexes. Most introverted of all female children, but once in a while, when girl her age comes to her house, seems to play willingly, even eagerly. Mother is reputedly one of harshest on La Hoja; people say she beats children severely. Mother does not respond much to dependency appeals except in offhand or cold manner, yet at times shows tender solicitude for the child.[4] While dependency may be perceived in Dolores in many ways, mother's general coldness seems to have resulted in child's dependence being to the home as such rather than to person of the mother. While Dolores will occasionally pelt pigs and dogs with stones, in imitation of her brothers, she is for the most part nonaggressive, and I never saw her strike even her smaller sibling for whom she does not show affection. Older brothers are kind and tolerant, care for her, accompany her on rare excursions away from home, and protect her from the environment. I have never seen aggression among them overtly, although once there was a brief quarrel.

Ratings: While mother is high in maternal nurturance in infancy, rates low in current response to dependency behavior and child's dependency behavior rating is correspondingly low. Maternal frustration of interpersonal relationships rates high, which is not expected with low dependency rating for child but may perhaps be explained by the remark regarding dependency on home in above paragraph. Maternal restriction and punishment for aggression, total frustration, and punitiveness all rate high.

---

4. The judges remarked of this mother's interview that the responses seemed to indicate possible personality disorganization. This same implication is made independently in the remarks of the writer's field assistant, who was most intimate with the mothers.

Are the nonparticipating children variants or deviants? [5] Do they exhibit behavior which, while it does not strictly conform to the culturally defined norm, still lies within its outer limits, or is their activity expressed in ways which are not culturally acceptable? Using these operational definitions of "variant" and "deviant" our conclusion is that, as a group, their behavior has aspects of both characteristics. While their introversion, withdrawal, timidity, and negativism may seem exaggerated to a continental observer, the first three are demanded by the society of all children in Valle Caña and the latter is expected but universally deplored by parents and other adults. On the other hand, when carried to the lengths to which the nonparticipators went in their relationships with the ethnologist and his assistant, these characteristics no longer are pleasing to Vallecañese parents, but irritating.

It is important to note that all nonparticipators are mountain children and therefore have fewer contacts and less social stimulation than El Camino children. Generally most of the least imaginative children were from La Hoja.

It may be worth speculating, also, about the fact that, while all these nonparticipators were among the youngest of large series of siblings, in every case they had themselves been displaced by later arrivals. Such displacement in the family, plus the possibly overwhelming numbers of older siblings, may combine to engender excessive insecurity in these children. And their displaced position may also stimulate them to acts of passive aggression against adults who, insofar as they may be identified as parent figures, may be seen as somehow having contributed to their present uncomfortable status.

It is doubtful, however, that any of these children are considered deviants, or even that necessarily they will be deviants in the adult culture when they grow up. When she is older Dolores' timidity and withdrawal will more probably be considered as desirable traits by her parents, adults, and potential admirers and husbands, in a day when some girls are showing a desire for more independence and self-assertiveness. The timidity and withdrawal of the three boys will

5. The same question may be asked of the three children who produced the richest protocols. And a similar conclusion might be reached—that they possess aspects of both characteristics. A more definitive conclusion would depend on a larger sample than we used. Given a change in some of the test conditions (see Landy 1959a), it is possible that the middle group would have produced somewhat more original and less routine-like projections.

probably be submerged, first by their negativism, then by an aggressive asserting of their *machismo*. Submerged, however, they will not disappear but remain the basis of the contradictions which plague the male in Valle Caña and, as Stycos (1951a, b) has indicated, in other parts of Puerto Rico as well.[6] But to understand better the behavior of all these children, participators and nonparticipators, a brief consideration in the following chapter of some of the outstanding variables in their climate of socialization will be in order.

6. Such behavior resultants and familial-cultural situations make it difficult to define such terms as deviant, variant, and abnormal. Eager to point up the obvious fallacies in ethnocentric definitions of the abnormal, anthropologists like Benedict (1934, 1949), while performing an invaluable service in creating a climate of cultural relativity, undoubtedly reified the concept as a catch-all causal category for observed behavior which could not otherwise be easily explained. A needed warning and a more precise attempt to define these concepts cross-culturally will be found in Wegrocki (1939).

CHAPTER 8

Coming of Age–II

Introduction

WE HAVE discussed previously some of the behaviors of the child who grows up in the culture of Valle Caña. We have seen how the infant comes into the world in this rural Puerto Rican village and how later he reacts to attempts of his family to influence and modify his behavior. These have included his reactions to parental attempts to control his sexual and aggressive impulses and the ways in which he takes in food and gets rid of his body wastes. We have seen how the Vallecañese child reacts to punishment by his parents and the extent to which he is a lone actor and interactor with others. And we reviewed at length the cases of the four children who were nonparticipators in the free doll play which was attempted by the anthropologist with the eighteen selected children, and we have discussed whether their behavior could be seen as deviant or variant departure from village norms.

In this chapter our discussion of the coming of age in Valle Caña is concluded with a descriptive analysis of the manifestations of dependency in Vallecañese children, the relation of dependent behavior to expressions of negativism and aggression, the identification process from the viewpoint of the child, and the development of his ego and superego systems.

Dependency

It has been noted that because of the basic view of the child, it was almost inevitable that these mothers and fathers would encourage dependent behavior in their children. This is just what they report and what we experienced so characteristically in the field. The world view, built on an environment perceived as predominantly hostile, or at least unhelpful, would also influence fearful parents to bind the ties of dependency tightly. Not only is physical mobility sharply curbed, but on the occasions when children are permitted to go out, they are admonished to stick closely to their friends or siblings, and this injunction is literally interpreted by the children. For the mountain children there is, of course, the very real menace of a dangerous terrain, and for the road children there is the threat of the paved road, over which cars and busses careen at breakneck speeds. For both there are the actual dangers of insect pests like hookworm, of colds and pneumonia because of inadequate housing and clothing during sudden chills, infection, etc. There are thus some realistic bases for maternal fears which tend to reinforce them and in turn to strengthen the child's fears and dependency needs.

Their degree of sociability is reported by their mothers as being higher than I observed it to be. Boys and girls both rated a median of 3.0 where 4.0 is very high sociability, which seems somewhat deceptive in the light of my impressions. I have seen that when they are together with children who are not siblings or close acquaintances, most children find themselves at a loss as to what to do and are shy, awkward, and inclined to wait for actions to be initiated. And if on first meeting other children they do not give way to such diffidence, the encounters often end in conflict. These maternal responses would lead one to believe they feel their low and partially restrictive sociability demands are pretty unsuccessful. As far as siblings and close friends are concerned this is true. But it has been my experience that the Valle Caña child feels at home only at home. When he goes off, accompanied by mother or older child, he will tend to cling closely to them. Away from home he is under the double handicap of not knowing how to initiate action and fear in the presence of parent or older child that he will do wrong, especially since children who are too outgoing are suspected of being *presentado* (fresh; too big for his britches).

As infants, these children exhibited a strong tendency to cling closely to their mothers. For example, a "... small girl had been sick with an earache the night before and was lying in her mother's lap wanting to be caressed. She sucked her finger and with the other hand rubbed her mother's breasts, sometimes putting her hand inside the woman's dress. The mother did not seem to mind. She would caress and kiss the child as she talked to her guest."

As older children between four and seven, the tendency is almost as strong. Fathers are more irritated by clinging behavior than mothers, but this may be because the mothers are more accustomed to it and have more patience with it. Nevertheless, mothers frequently refer to their child as one who "*Mí siempre pega'o*" (always sticks close to me). Says a typical mother:

She asks for much attention. *Ella no me pierde ni pie ni pisada* [She does not lose me, neither my foot nor footprint]. Like chicks and a mother hen, she is always following me, and on top of me to give her this and that. She follows me around much. Wherever I go out I have to take her. That one will not stay [home when I go out]. In the morning if I go to the stream [to wash clothes] and she is still in bed, she wakes up and sees that I am not here, and she goes running to the creek. I have to come back and give her coffee.[1] So I wait for her and take her, because she is always going to come with me.

Like many conflicts, this dilemma is both the product and producer of happiness and unhappiness. The mother encourages dependency and usually insists that the child remain close at hand. She takes much pride in the fact that her child follows her like a shadow, and the closer the child clings the better mother she considers herself and is considered by others.

The child who is good is the one who knows its proper place and is shy and clingy. But at the same time the mother pays for this gratification by having to take her "shadow-child" wherever she goes, and even the most dependency-encouraging mother can tire of this in its extreme form, which is common in Valle Caña. But once the motivational system of dependency is learned, dependency begets dependency; it becomes self-satisfying and therefore an end in itself. These children have learned their lesson well. The mother reaps the bittersweet fruit of being dogged by the child, which she encourages, but is frequently assailed by demands for attention, which she does not usually promote or enjoy. Boys are more demanding of attention

---

1. Coffee is the universal beverage, even for babies and children. When milk is afforded it is diluted half-and-half. Bottle-fed babies are given a bit of coffee in their bottles. The huge amount of sugar used per cup suggests that coffee satisfies the craving for sweets as well as a warm beverage.

than girls, according to scaled mothers' reports, having a median of 4.0 to 3.0 (where 5.0 denotes very high demands), a fact which previously we noted through observation.

One result is that the mother will often say ruefully that her child is spoiled but continue to tolerate the harassment, since in addition to marking her as a good mother, "I think it is that he loves me much. That [holding on to her skirts] does not bother me. Sometimes I tell him not to pull my dress, but I know that he does it because he loves me."

Benedict (1949:421) has pointed out that in every society the individual is expected to behave differently at different stages of life. When these changes are not recognized through "rites of passage," there are discontinuities in what she calls "cultural conditioning" which result in strain and conflict, but

Many societies, however, minimize strain by the techniques they employ; and some techniques are more successful than others in ensuring the individual's functioning without conflict. It is from this point of view that age-grade societies reveal their fundamental significance. Age-graded cultures characteristically demand different behavior in the individual at different times in his life and persons of a like age-grade are grouped into a society whose activities are all oriented toward the behavior desired at that age. Individuals "graduate" publicly and with honor from one of these groups to another.

Vallecañeses do not have such an age-graded society. The passage of the child from one stage to the next, except for school graduation and baptism (the latter is not strictly an age-grade phenomenon, especially with the Protestant minority), is not marked by ceremonies. Little recognition is given the various changes which the society nevertheless expects. Time is such a fluid concept that the ages of children often are not remembered by parents, even in infancy and early childhood. But while time flows continuously and smoothly, cultural conditioning and development of the child do not. These discontinuities are especially crucial for the boy and they begin early in life. The earliest one comes at a time when ordinarily the infant would still be enclosed in the first warm blankets of security. Because the foundations of personal security in the individual are usually laid down in the earliest life stages, I call this break the "preschool security gap." A second discontinuity occurs when the child begins school, but this is not a sharp break since the school is within the community and the child already knows, by sight or reputation, school staff and classmates.

Whether or not the child is wanted, and we have previously shown that sometimes it is not, once it comes into the world it is usually handled with nurturance and affection by the mother. In the first few months of life the husband often may pay little attention to the very tiny babe. But after a few months he and the mother and older siblings and relatives handle it affectionately and frequently. The child is fondled and caressed by all until about two to three years of age.

At this point intimate physical manipulation begins to taper off, quite rapidly in the case of the girl, although the boy may still be fondled at times until five or six. However, in many families, when the youngest child is about the age of two or three, another child is born. Then almost at once this source of physical contact and emotional security is dropped while the bulk of attention is lavished on the neonate. The older child will suddenly seem too large for corporal handling, and this awkwardness is in turn reflected in the child himself, who is now uncertain about his role. If he throws a jealous tantrum, he may be laughed at or punished. If he attacks the apparent cause of his plight, the younger one, he may be disciplined if caught.

Since the parent-daughter relationship never quite reaches the emotional pitch of the parent-son relationship, the break is not quite as abrupt for her. Additionally, she seems to be integrated earlier into some of her sex role functions than the boy. Neither is considered a really useful adjunct to the domestic labor force until after six or seven years, but the small boy, who is considered too young to bring his father lunch in the field or run errands, is especially lost. Being a male, he is expected even at that tender age to be less vulnerable than the girl to the rigors of life, and less attention is paid to his needs. "Affect hunger" (Levy 1943), which to some degree characterizes both sexes, is especially evident in the boy.

For the boy, also, the *machismo* expectations of the culture are, as we have seen, difficult to fulfill with the many restrictions hedging aggression. He becomes frustrated, especially in relation to the adult world. In the few cases where he can, he tries to take out this frustration in some kind of indirect aggression against adults. Negativism, as we shall see, is a frequent mode of response in this connection, and it will become very exaggerated in the rare case where an adult is wholly permissive with him.

But the formative first five or six years should be not only a security-building period, but an ego-forming one as well. At the very time that the child could be launching the hull of his ego-structure upon the cultural waters, he finds not only that the skids have been insufficiently greased by family and society but that the blocks on the runway have not been removed. Later he becomes more useful, of course, in his own and his family's eyes, but his ego, instead of having a firm foundation, is characterized more by formlessness than by well-directed behaviors. In all his years the boy is never fully able to bridge the security gap, which opened up so widely in this very early era, as we have pointed out in the endless and often fruitless search for *confianza* relationships by the Vallecañese adult male.

Such antecedent conditions lead expectably to deep dependency. However, just as mothers could not always see how sharply dependent on them their children were to the same degree that I observed it, on some of the attributes of dependency they seem also to report less than I perceived. Thus, according to their interviews, in scaling reactions of the children to being separated from the mother, however briefly, we find that boys have a median of 2.5 and girls of 3.0, where 5.0 signifies a severe reaction.

Mothers are not generally happy to see their child begin school, and only one of our group felt happiness that the child was now to achieve a bit of independence. One mother subsequently withdrew her child as "too young," though well past six years. This little girl's father happened to be working on a job, during the dead season, just outside the school, and all day long the child could not resist running to the window and shouting at her parent who, chagrined but proud, would always come to see what the matter was. The matter was that the child wanted to see him more than her teacher and classmates and was unhappy away from home. Frequent reactions to being left at home are crying and anger. "She remains home angry, and cries, almost always. Even if she stays with her father, she always cries; so he takes her for a walk so she will get over her anger."

One mother of a large family claims a degree of independence for her child in her absence, accompanied by a bribe, but even as she speaks she contradicts herself.

She remains happily and tells me, "*Mamí*, leave me a *'chavo* [penny] and go, but come back early." She does not cry, she does not say anything. And she helps the others that stay at home. If I go someplace near, I have to take her with me, because she will not leave me alone until I bring her with me; if not she goes and looks for me. It's terrible. If I go to the settlement I have to take her with me, because I always buy her candy. But I do not get her used to being taken far because there is nothing worse, because afterwards you cannot move without them.

A negative index of dependency is its opposite, striving for independency, e.g., the extent to which the preschool child demands teaching at home. Growing up in an impoverished environment, the child is not stimulated to demand much in the way of preschool teaching. Only four children are reported by their mothers as demanding such training, and two of these to a very limited degree. Two mothers say that not only did their children not demand such inculcation, but they show little interest in being taught at all. Certainly one observes little striving toward independency, and when it does occur, it receives scant reinforcement, and at times even punishment, by parents and others.

Little indication of dependency appears in doll play, and one may wonder whether it is because it is so well reinforced in everyday life and there is little need to project it into the doll situation, or whether this technique just did not succeed in capturing this important aspect of child behavior. The total dependency acts (based on both succorant and nurturant responses) is only 7.1 percent. We might conclude from such a result that the more the child's attempts at independence are thwarted at home, the more he will revert to real dependent behavior, and the less he will display such behavior in a fantasy situation. The answer in part to the implied question is that frustration of all kinds becomes additive, so that in the permissive doll play situation, aggression or some other type of response is much more likely than nurturant-succorant acts. If such a hypothesis is true, it adds to other evidence that the boy is more dependent, since he exhibits fewer nurturant-succorant acts in doll play (2.1 percent to 12.1 percent for girls).

It would be expected that the most used agent of nurturant behavior in doll play would be the mother doll. This is true for girls but not boys. The most used agents are ranked in this order: Boys: self, mother, father, boy, girl. Girls: mother, self, father, boy, girl.

As with aggression the self seems used by the boy as agent of behavior more than doll intermediaries. In part this is because boys are generally less original and expressive in doll play and probably could not identify with the doll agents as readily as the more imaginative girls. From a realistic point of view, since the mother does not in fact nurture the boy as much as the girl (although she strengthens his dependency in other ways), he is less apt to perceive her as a nurturant agent. And conversely the girls should perceive the mother as most nurturant, which is the case.

The girl uses the father doll less than the mother, just as the boy does, but she uses it proportionately more, which also seems logically to follow from the father-girl relationships shown earlier.

The objects of nurturance in rank order are: Boys: boy, baby, father, mother, girl; Girls: baby, girl, boy, mother, father. The boy, characterized so often by "affect hunger," sees himself in fantasy as the most frequent object of nurturance. The girl, as previously noted, is also affect-hungry, but not nearly to the same extent as the boy, and this is reflected in her yielding first place to the baby as object of nurturance. This also corresponds with her sex role as *mujercita* (little woman). Incidentally, girls are alluded to frequently by Vallecañeses as "little women," with several synonyms, though boys seldom receive the appellation of "little man" (*hombrecito*), but rather "little male" (*machito*), more in keeping with his sex role. The girl's order of nurturance objects seems more accurately to reflect the actual situation, while the boy seems to project his wishes into the fantasy arrangement. The girl regards the mother as receiving somewhat more nurturance than the father, while the boy reverses the order. This seems to accord with the differential adaptation of the boy and girl to their sex roles as we have discussed this throughout the study. Girls more likely would perceive themselves as agents of nurturance.

Dependency, Negativism, and Aggression

Permissiveness, as it is commonly used, seems in general to be that type of behavior on the part of parents or parent-surrogates which permits maximum expression and minimum restriction of the child's needs. The antithesis would be restrictiveness. In any culture it may be expected that the two will to a large extent complement each other as conditioners of the socialization process.

Eggan (1949:225) characterizes a markedly permissive cultural milieu for Hopi socialization:

While the infant was small he was bound to a cradle-board where his movements were restricted, except when he was removed for bathing. But Dennis was unable to discover any measurable effects of this on modern Hopi children. The child was released from the board as soon as he became restless in his bonds, and from then on had few restraints. A cry brought the breast or whatever attention seemed desired. There was no slapping of fingers, no mechanisms to prevent thumb-sucking or masturbation, no objects labeled in one way or another "mustn't touch." Toddlers even learned that a hot stove was "taboo" by being allowed to touch it rather than from restrictions enforced by parents.

To the reader the question arises: If there were no objects marked "mustn't touch," how did the child learn about highly prized sacred objects in each matrilineal Hopi family, like prayer sticks? Does this mean that the child could never profit from the experiences of elders? Or does this also mean that the adults themselves were not aware of the consequences of some things and permitted the child to test the danger potential? How much of all this was permissiveness, how much casualness based on indifference toward consequences?

Permissiveness as we have defined it has often been confounded or synonymized by anthropologists with parental casualness verging on neglect, perhaps in their unconscious need to demonstrate an idyllic parent-child relationship in nonliterate societies. Certainly the cultural climate for socialization in Valle Caña does not appear to be merely permissive, nor, as we have seen, merely restrictive. Much of its apparent permissiveness on closer examination reveals the kind of casualness just referred to (see also pp. 36-39). Thus, looked at from one point of view, when a Vallecañese mother tells us she does not fix her child's pus-ridden sores because the child objects, it may be permissive insofar as not restraining the child's wishes are concerned, but scarcely that as far as the child's health is involved. This is so even though culturally the mother does not anticipate the consequences. I suspect that there are many classes of "mustn't touch" objects in every culture, due to the necessities of survival for child and adult.

What is perhaps more relevant for an understanding of socialization in a culture is the way in which, and the degree to which, permissiveness and restrictiveness take place, and how they intermesh with each other to help mold the child's behavior. The reader will recall that in Valle Caña the two techniques are imperfectly meshed, so that there is a good deal of capriciousness in the way in which permissions and proscriptions are administered to the child. The result is heavy anxiety about proper fulfillment of sex and other roles.

One consequence of this kind of situation for the child is a gnawing uncertainty about how to act when the rare situations arise in which adults expect genuine reciprocity from them in social interaction and the milieu created by the adults is, intentionally or otherwise, almost completely permissive. As demonstrated in real social situations, and in the experiences of the anthropologist in doll play, a very frequent response is a kind of negativism on the child's part, again particularly evident in the male. Why?

It was noted that while sometimes this negativism dissipated itself after the first or second doll play session, it often continued and even increased through the third and fourth periods, as the nonparticipators demonstrated. The same effect was also noted in real situations. This is so analogous to the manifestations of doll play aggression, both in our own doll sessions and in those of other experimenters (Hollenberg and Sperry, 1951) that the writer suggests the following hypothesis:

In a child-rearing environment which is more restrictive than permissive, in which punishments and rewards are capriciously distributed, and in which child-adult relationships are invariably marked by submission-dominance and sharp limitations on child-adult interaction, negativistic behavior will be a frequent response of the child to a situation with adults in which reciprocity is expected and permissiveness is granted. This negativism will result in part from anxiety and uncertainty, but its function for the child will be a form of aggression against the permissive adults.

It is the writer's contention that the child's interaction with adults is so limited and child rearing in Valle Caña so unevenly balanced with unpredictable swings back and forth between permission and restriction that his reaction to a permissive situation with adults, as in free doll play, is negativism, the intent of which is to irritate and therefore injure the adults. Even in such a permissive situation the inhibitions against direct aggression aimed at adults do not completely crumble, but this negativism (manifested by apparent unwillingness to do something of which he is capable but, sensing the desires of the permissive adults, he will not do) serves his aggressive needs, and in a more adaptive (less punishing) way than overt hostility.

Another effect for Vallecañese children is to "get away with" as much as they can, since neither rewards nor punishment are certain, but the latter is more probable.

The degree to which the child becomes dependent seems to depend not merely on a permissive or restrictive situation alone. A child, as our data have shown, may be more or less dependent with either or both influences present, if dependent behavior is also responded to with nurturance and affection (i.e., rewarded), and if some of the other variables already mentioned in previous sections are present—or absent. The same should also hold for the complement of dependence, independence. Merely permitting a child to do things for himself will not necessarily bring on independence, any more than restricting his movements necessarily will hamper the growth of independence. More important are the rewards and punishments associated with the permissiveness or restrictiveness, their consistency and timing, the attitudes of parents, realistic dangers, etc.

Another, perhaps unintended, consequence of this constellation of child training patterns is the probability that the dependent child will be a dependent adult. If we combine this trait in adulthood with the concern for public opinion and the emphasis on face, we find a kind of "bandwagon" mentality in which the individual, often no matter how much he wants to do something, will not attempt it until it has first been attempted by others, but once the latter event occurs, he will be eager to duplicate the action. Such behavior is manifest in many areas of Vallecañese life. When we were trying to get children to come to doll play sessions, most of the mothers were adamant and a bit suspicious at first. But once they saw that one mother, bolder than the rest, was sending her child, they were so eager to have their own child participate that they frequently felt incensed and slighted if we did not take their child along, whether or not we wanted to use him (see Landy 1959a). For this reason many mothers, as we later discovered, made their children go to doll play whether or not the latter desired to. The influence of this forcing factor on doll play results cannot be measured, but it must have been felt in some ways which were not conducive to ideal conditions for projective testing.

Identification

The overt manifestations of identification, that is, the degree to which the child's behavior resembles that of his parents,[2] are a difficult variable to measure. One way is to ask the parents, but this is highly unsatisfactory and self-contradictory. Five mothers feel their sons resemble themselves, four that they resemble their fathers, and one both parents. Four fathers think their sons resemble themselves, one their mother, five both parents. Three mothers feel their daughters resemble themselves, three their fathers, one both, and one a relative. Four fathers feel their daughters resemble themselves, three their mothers, one both parents. Even if we discount the "both" ratings, the picture from the parents' point of view is clouded.

Another possible measure is to gauge the frequency with which each sex used the various family members in doll play. Sears (1951) hypothesizes that there may be a "dimension of degree of identification comparable to a dimension of stimulus similarity" so that "the principles of generalization should operate with respect to identification also." This is borne out in doll play so that the frequency of the use of dolls was roughly in this order for both sexes: parent doll same sex, parent doll other sex, child doll same sex, child doll other sex. However, the difference between use of the mother and father dolls by the girl (12.3 percent) is greater than the difference between their use by the boy (3.4 percent). It has already been suggested that the boy finds it more difficult to adjust to his role than the girl, and that while identification does not seem very strongly developed in either at this age, the boy did not seem to be as closely identified

2. Stoke (1950) distinguishes usefully between emotional identification and behavioral identification. Most of his evidence on the former derives from case studies of parents and children, on the latter from doll play and observation. Much of his evidence on emotional identification is largely inferred and unfortunately he does not provide operational definitions of his concepts, though differences between the two are apparent in context. But his main point, that Freud confused the two and used them indistinguishably and that Freudian discussions of identification are incomplete, seems well taken. "A practical fault with Freud's etiology of identification is that it leaves no place in it for guidance or control" (*ibid.*:229) or for the temperament and self-action of the child apart from biologically determined impulses. See Parsons (1952) also on these and other factors in identification and superego development and the crucial role of the superego in articulating the individual with the cultural and social systems. In the present study we are dealing almost completely with behavioral identification because of the nature of our data.

with the father as the girl with the mother. This receives some confirmation from the above doll play data.

Observation-wise it is extremely difficult to get valid data on
identification. Such data are so complex and subtle the observer is
apt to miss their manifestations completely or be tempted to make
assumptions which are more impressionistic than accurate. It is possible
for a boy to be exhibiting behavior which seems very much like his
father's and yet this may be no more than what is thought of in the
culture as *male* behavior. The child may pick up this sex-typed behavior not only from his father but by instruction from his mother,
relatives, and friends and by imitation of all categories of males in
his environment besides his father. The same could be stated for female
behavior. Kroeber (1948) feels imitation is probably more important
than inculcation in the process of socialization, though of course this
does not gainsay the Freudian hypothesis about identification with the
same-sex parent as a means of learning sex role and laying the basis
for superego development. Impressionistically, I could say that little
boys in Valle Caña often seem to have identified with their father
and girls with their mother. Certainly by the time they are grown,
most men act in a "masculine way" and women in a "feminine way,"
but it is not clear to me how much this derives from identification
with same-sex parent and how much from imitation, or which plays
the greater role.

Supporting data for confused and weak identification with parents
are seen in the generally high dependency of both sexes, with the
boy more dependent, and in the low superego development noted in
the next section. One would expect all three: weak identification, high
dependency, and low superego in the predominantly tradition-directed
and opinion-directed culture which seems to exist in Valle Caña.

Superego Development

According to Margaret Mead (1949:513-514), the process of identification or "cultural transmission" takes place at a very early age,
when the child,

> ... soon after learning to talk, begins to take as its model the parent of
> the same sex. The child accepts the standards of that parent, as stated *to*
> the child, as its own until, in the absence of the parent, the child learns
> to act as if the parent were still there, and to choose and reject courses

of action as it conceives the parent would have done. Failure to conform to these standards induces in the individual a retrospective discomfort, which is technically called "guilt" (traditionally referred to as the idea of "conscience"), which is independent of actual discovery by the parent, or any other member of the society.

We are using superego, rather than conscience, to describe the censoring mechanism which is formed as a result of identification. The term is more broadly cross-cultural and implies not only a censoring function to insure proper behavior but an emancipating function to free the child to some degree from dependence on his parents. "Conscience" has specific linkage with the idea of sin, as conceived in Western Christianity. Of course, Valle Caña practices a culture which is a variation and derivation of a European culture, yet the bulk of evidence in this study points to it as being based more on external sanctions, or "shame," than on internal sanctions, or "guilt."

To a large degree superego formation will be as successful as identification with the parents has been. But the role of the agents of religion, formal education, government, etc., should not be underestimated. True, the parents are "primary" in the sense that they are first in time, close (at least physically) to the child, and are in most societies allocated primary socializing roles whether or not it pleases them. But as the child grows older, the so-called secondary institutions exert an increasingly stronger influence in most societies, competing for, and often supplanting, loyalties and identifications with the family. The primary parental or parental-surrogate identifications are probably never completely erased, however. Another facet of child training to consider here is the nature of parental demands, which seem qualitatively and quantitatively to differ from those we have come to associate with American "middle-class" socialization.

As we shall see in Chapter 9, Vallecañese parents may be more harshly restrictive in such areas as obedience, respect, aggression, and female sexuality, and carry out their standards more forcefully in these areas with less resort to "reasonable appeals." But eating practices are commonly restrictive only in the limited sense of mannerisms rather than manners, bedtime restrictiveness is almost nil, and so on. They are qualitatively different in that the very conditions of Vallecañese life make it impossible, for example, to be restrictive about nonexistent furniture and furniture finishes or to differentiate among a wide range of properties which are to be handled and not handled, since most properties are in general nonexistent.

In addition, as we have said, demands are different in that it is not so much the community which is being wronged by disapproved behavior, but the parents themselves. Thus respect and obedience are usually exacted through punishment on the personal parent-child basis. The high regard for public opinion of the child's behavior is not so much what the public will think of the child—others may speak ill of the child but parents may take comfort in its inherent "innocence"—but as the child's behavior may cast the parents pejoratively in the public eye. The behavior code toward others, a foundation stone of the superego, is therefore simplified for the child: "Don't fight, don't aggress in any way, don't initiate activities, don't steal, don't curse, don't play with the other sex." That is largely, though not completely, the extent of the child-other, and therefore child-community, ethic. Parents take few risks in the preschool years, especially, with potential violations of even these simple negative commandments. To obviate against most possibilities, the child is simply removed from contact with most children.

Furthermore, the child is removed from much adult-child interaction, even to a large extent with his own parents. And because of the paucity of stimuli in the way of folklore, myths, etc., there are few people known to the child in fact or in fantasy and relatively few therefore to identify with. Since there are not many potential adult identificants, the child should presumably identify primarily with the parents. But even this source is not particularly inspiring, for while parents hold up themselves as models of approved behavior, for instance, they do not encourage imitation of their behavior. Mimicry of adult behavior is generally frowned upon. The child is felt rather to be *gracioso* (cute) when he acts like a child, and the period of dependency and closeness of mother and child is prolonged for a relatively long time (in a psychological sense, it practically never ceases for many males), so that strong identification becomes unnecessary and perhaps even undesirable.

Another possible clue to the nature of Vallecañese superego development is the occurrence of withdrawal of love, not as a disciplinary technique, but as a sudden decision of the parents, either when a new baby arrives or when the parents feel too burdened with other chores to respond with the nurturance and affection which were rather freely given in infancy. For withdrawal of love to be successful as a technique for eliciting approved activities, the parent must first have given love freely in the child's infancy. By the time the child becomes used to it—dependent upon it—the parent begins to withdraw it when disapproved behavior occurs and to make the giving of love contingent upon approved behavior. When the child grasps the contingent nature of the bestowal of love, he begins to function in desirable ways so as to elicit the needed love. Thus he must identify with the parents' values, and so he internalizes them and they become, within the context of his own needs and limitations, his own values. When these values become strong enough, they begin to function autonomically, whether or not the parent is present. In such a socialization process, the groundwork is clearly laid for high superego formation.[3]

Such a series of events does not characterize Vallecañese child development. We have seen that nurturance and affection are usually accorded the infant. But we have also noted that after about two to five years love is suddenly withdrawn, not as a mode of discipline, but because the parents, especially the mother, find it necessary to focus attention on a succeeding child or on their household duties and responsibilities. I have called this the preschool security gap.[4] The contingency of love as a reward for good behavior is not evident however. Desirable actions will not elicit love, though undesirable ones will frequently elicit the various kinds of disapproval and punishment we have demonstrated in earlier sections. Nothing the child does will very much alter the situation. And so he becomes more interested in avoiding punishing situations than in creating rewarding ones by acting "right." Thus he has little need to internalize the positive values of the parent, and the superego will not have the strong identification with parental standards on which to develop. So in his early years, especially, the child (particularly the male) is characterized by strong "affect hunger." As he enters adolescence, the boy finds that he begins to receive deference and attention from mother and sisters. He is beginning to achieve the status of a man. But while this undoubtedly calls into play again the infantile con-

3. I am indebted to John W. M. Whiting for pointing out the dynamics underlying the reasoning in this paragraph and its suggested application to Vallecañese socialization in the next paragraph.

4. Wolf (1951) points out that often the mother can hardly wait for the child to *perder la falda* (literally, lose the skirt; leave the lap and demand less attention).

ception of his mother as a nurturant figure, the contingency is linked not to anything that lies within his own powers but upon the biological facts of his age and sex. The Vallecañese adult male pays frequent and sentimental tribute to his mother—in song and story. He verbalizes protestations of his love for, and dependence on, her. And he often ignores her material welfare completely. The female, on the other hand, does not proclaim her love for her mother as vigorously, but being generally the more stable and responsible, more often cares and provides materially for her.

Two primary reactions to violations of the mandates of the superego are thought in psychoanalytic theory to be guilt and an urge to admit transgressions, or "confession." These reactions may be thought of as mechanisms whereby the superego is manifested to the external world, which, by its demands for conformity, expects the individual to "feel" culpable and confess his guilt.

The superego of the preschool child in Valle Caña has been developed to a rather low degree, if outward manifestations of guilt and admission of wrongdoing are to be accepted as a barometer of it. Evidences of high superego are: confession of deviation from prescribed behavior; acting guilty and feeling badly over deviations; admitting rather than denying guilt; and reparations for wrongs. Hiding and other indications of fear are taken as low superego evidence; reparations for culturally-defined wrongs are taken as evidence of high superego.

According to their mothers these children almost never admit guilt when violating a familial or cultural tenet, by either voluntarily coming forward with a confession or confessing when asked by their mother. Rather their tendency seems to be to say nothing, to hide if suspected, to deny if asked. As we said in connection with another variable—the anticipation of uncertain punishment—these children tend to try to get away with as much as they can, since they are not sure of the consequences of being caught. And the implication in practically every mother's responses is that the child hid because he feared to be punished and that the only motive by which he could be brought to confession was the threat of punishment if he did not admit guilt when demanded. But superego, properly functioning, acts like the gyroscope set by the child's parents, "maintaining its axis in constant relation to a plane" (Reisman 1950; Murphy 1947), without parental demands or in the absence of the parents. It must become as reflexive as the blushing, sweating, trembling, and other physiological reactions which sometimes accompany it.

In addition to these factors in superego development, a few additional characteristics of the culture and social structure making for a weak superego, and which in turn are reinforced by the latter, may be mentioned:

1. The fragile sense of community solidarity, the lack of a strong sense of communal responsibility and duty, and, conversely, a highly developed sense of familism (now somewhat tattered and strained) and individualism in terms of face and *dignitad* rather than ego-ideals and ego-aspirations.

2. The tenuous hold of the church and religion on the people, one of the strongest of all reinforcements for superego maintenance and formation, and the dearth of compensatory symbols, beliefs, and ideals in a substitute belief system, in the name of which appeals to conscience could be instituted.

3. The absence of tangible rewards for hard work, saving, good behavior, etc., in the economic and occupational systems, rewards which characterize the Protestant ethic and its concomitant demands on conscience.

4. The regard for most secular authority as a substitute for the parent-image and therefore to be feared, respected, and to some extent obeyed, but without identifying that authority as the protector of the common good—a prime requisite of communal cooperation and motivator and maintainer of public morals and private conscience.

5. The outlook of Vallecañeses as a material and this-world oriented people. Virtue lies in material remuneration on earth rather than in the hereafter. Honesty and trust are highly valued, but the fact that men overstrive and frequently compete for *confianza* relationships with new acquaintances and strangers is an indication that this latter virtue is more sought after than found. It is a highly desired security mechanism in an inimical universe, but it is not deeply sculptured in the shield of the superego, although trust relationships, once established, are usually kept by all parties.

6. The social sessility of lower-class Vallecañeses. They are not highly motivated to demand that their children achieve the accoutrements of upward-climbing, and the superego is little constrained to insist on these.

CHAPTER 9

Child Training in Valle Caña
and New England

Introduction

ANTHROPOLOGISTS are interested in the study of particular modes of human adaptation to the requirements of group living and ecological situations for their own sake as they contribute to the ethnographic knowledge of a society, a region or culture area, or world ethnography as a whole. Our study so far adds another cultural case, with special reference to the primary cultural process of socialization, to our knowledge about Puerto Rico, about the Caribbean, and about culture as such. However, we are also interested in cultural process, in the way in which the people of Valle Caña transmit their traditions, values, and practices to succeeding generations. We have seen in part how this process seems to operate in this rural Caribbean village. But we are compelled further to ask comparative or cross-cultural questions. We would like to know how socialization in Valle Caña compares with the same process in other cultures.

For fairly strict comparisons, and because it will include examples of the powerful society of the United States with which the little island has been in continuous acculturative contact for six decades, we will use the data from a study of two class groups in a New England community. In addition to the general descriptive comparison we may perceive the glimmerings of an answer to the question of which of the Vallecañese practices and policies seem indigenous, which are class associated and seem to cut across cultural and national boundaries.[1] This will be discussed further in the concluding chapter.

Method

Maccoby, Gibbs, *et al.* (1954), using interview schedules and a set of rating scales[2] which were the same as those used in the present study, divided 372 urban mothers from a suburban-residential and a working-class residential area in Massachusetts into upper-middle (198) and upper-lower (174) class groups. Kindergarten children in selected public schools and their parents were chosen for the population. "Families were then excluded from the target group if either of the child's parents was foreign born, if the child was not living with both natural parents, or if the child was a twin or suffered from some physical handicap" (*ibid.*: 381).

Social class was determined by the Socioeconomic Status scale of Warner (1949), in which occupational status of the father is weighted twice as much as a score for family income. Some of the occupational categories in the upper reaches of the upper-lower group might be classified lower-middle in other classification systems, but for the present we shall accept the division as used by Maccoby, Gibbs, *et al.* (hereafter referred to simply as Maccoby). One may of course assume that each social class practices a culture of its own, by definition. But the assumption in Maccoby's study and the present one is that each represents a subcultural group sharing some attributes of the culture of the larger society of the United States.

Maccoby's test of the null hypothesis for each of the variables was the t-test. However, I would not be justified in making an assumption of normality for my data. Since this assumption underlies the t-test, it was necessary to use a nonparametric or distribution-free statistic, and it was felt that the median test (Moses 1952; Mosteller and Bush 1953; Walker and Lev 1953:435-436) would be suitable for our purposes.[3]

The median test is a variation of the chi square test. The procedure

1. Further consideration of this important anthropological problem is discussed by the author elsewhere (Landy 1959c).
2. Some examples from a total battery of 140 scales will be found in Chapters 4 and 5.
3. This decision precluded use of Maccoby's t-test data as such. Instead we were permitted by Maccoby and her associates to utilize the raw distributions as they were set up for IBM coding.

consists of obtaining a combined median for the samples being compared so as to derive a common splitting point. A contingency table
is then set up and a chi square, which makes no assumptions concerning the shape of the distributions, is computed.

For chi square we used the formula (Walker and Lev 1953:106):

$$\chi^2_y = \frac{(|\,ad - bc\,| - N/2)^2 N}{(a+b)\,(a+c)\,(b+d)\,(c+d)}$$

which includes a factor to take care of Yates's correction for continuity, and where the contingency table is set up as follows:

a	b	a+b
c	d	c+d

a+c b+d   N

In the tables that follow in this chapter, percentages above the median
only are reported for each pair of group comparisons (Puerto Rican
vs U.S. upper-lower and Puerto Rican vs U.S. upper-middle). Following each comparison the significance level, if any, appears. It was
decided that .05 would be the minimum confidence level below which
differences would be considered due to chance factors.

Some of the implications and limitations of using this test with
these kinds of data should be mentioned. According to Guilford
(1942:42-43) the mean should be used for greater reliability, i.e., it
is more sensitive to each score in the distribution, when we may assume
a normal distribution and when we want to find measures of variability. The median is suggested when distributions are badly skewed
(often the case with the Vallecañese data); when we are not as
interested in the way the scores cluster around the central point but
only in which half (upper or lower) they appear (which we did
wish to know); when only an incomplete distribution is given (which
is the case both for Valle Caña and the U.S. class groups data); and
when there is uncertainty about the equality of the units of measurement (which certainly seems true of a good many of the scales used).

Being less sensitive to the shape of the distribution and each score
therein, the median test is a cruder measure than the t-test, but because
of factors noted above, the wide difference in the sizes of the samples,
and the fact that our sample was selected and not randomized, it
seemed better to use a cruder test. For one thing, this means that we

must have a very sharp difference for the probability level to reach significance, and this should be insurance against certain otherwise close comparisons slipping through and being accepted as significantly different. It seems reasonable to assume that if our sample had been larger some of the differences which were not here significant might have become so, and vice-versa.

In a few cases the Vallecañese scores distributed themselves bi-modally. These are noted when they occur. In such instances neither the mean nor the median express the actual central tendency. We had to make a decision whether to obtain a combined median for all three groups for each scale or for each of the two groups in each paired comparison. While choosing the first method would have lent the appearance of more uniformity to the reporting of results (thus the reportings of the percentages of the Puerto Rican mothers above the median will be observed often to differ from each other as be-tween pairs of comparisons for the same scaled variable), we de-cided on the latter method of separate combined medians for each pair tested. Our decision was based upon the fact that since we wished to compare the Vallecañese data with each Massachusetts social class, to have used a combination of all three medians would have meant that the combined median would be affected by all three distributions although only two are used in any one test. If we were simply interested in a test for three or for k samples (Walker and Lev 1953:437) of the null hypothesis that all three or k samples came from the same population, a 3×2 or $k \times 2$ contingency table could be set up, and we would proceed to find our answer. However, such a contingency table yields nothing regarding the differences between any pair of groups, but only between the upper and lower halves of all the groups, with respect to the common median.

Another drawback of the median test is that since we cannot split the frequencies within an interval because we are dealing with scales, it is often necessary to throw several cases which lie in the interval containing the median one way or the other, tending in such instances to overweight one half of the distribution.

Since the median test does not always do justice to the U.S. data when comparing the two groups, we have often in the following pages referred to the Maccoby results, particularly when the t-test yielded significant differences.

Reliability of judgments of our data is discussed in Chapter 1.

Since ethnographic descriptions of behavior concerning each of the variables have already been presented earlier, only when necessary will such data be used to illustrate the findings of this chapter.

Infant Feeding

Sharp differences in feeding practices differentiate the two cultural groups (Table 26). The island mothers preponderantly breastfeed their babies: 89 percent compared with 37 percent of the U.S. lower-class and 43 percent of the U.S. middle-class mothers. They also keep

TABLE 26

Infant Feeding by Culture and Social Class
(percent above median)

	P. R. Rural-Lower	U. S. Urban-Lower	p	P. R. Rural-Lower	U. S. Urban-Middle	p
Median length of breastfeeding (1 = −1 mo., 8 = 15+ mos.)	88	34	.001	88	41	.005
Median age beginning weaning a (1 = −2 mos., 8 = 24+ mos.)	88	29	.001	88	32	.001
Median age completed weaning a (1 = −5 mos., 8 = 30+ mos.)	83	44	.01	83	32	.001
Time needed for weaning (1 = 1 day, 9 = 24+ mos.)	47	47	—	47	64	—
Severity of weaning (1 = mild, 9 = severe)	56	62	—	56	59	—
Scheduling of feeding (1 = self-demand, 9 = rigid schedule)	11	51	.005	11	52	.001

a. Change-of-mode weaning: from a sucking (breast or bottle) to a non-sucking (cup, can, glass) mode of liquid intake.

them on the breast significantly longer (12.3 months average compared with 2.1 months for U.S. lower class and 2.4 months for U.S. middle class). Furthermore the Puerto Rican mothers begin change-of-mode weaning (see note, Table 26) later (24.0 months compared with 8.2 months and 9.1 months for the U.S. lower and middle groups), and this likewise is true of the age of the child at completion of weaning (30.0 months compared with 12.6 months and 12.0 months respectively). Extreme examples of this lateness of weaning are seen in two of our eighteen children, who at seven years of age were still carrying nippled bottles of coffee mixed with milk to school.

However, once weaning begins, the difference in the amount of time used for the process does not differ significantly between the rural Puerto Ricans and the urban continentals, though upper-middle mothers tend to take somewhat longer than either of the two lower-class groups. In Valle Caña the acts associated with sucking dependency are apparent in many children; often until five or six years of age the child may be given a rubber nipple to suck, and much drooling and other infantile behaviors are associated with this.

There are also no significant differences in the severity of weaning between any of the groups. However, it should be noted that the Puerto Rican distribution is sharply bimodal, so that we have gradual or self-weaning bunching up in one half of the scale and abrupt weaning in the other half, whereas the distributions of both mainland groups tend to be smoother and roughly approach normality.

Overwhelmingly the island mothers feed according to the child's demands, while both class groups tend toward a more normal spread between the extremes of self-demand and rigid scheduling, and the differences are highly significant.

Toilet Training

While differences are not significant, there is a definite trend toward the Puerto Rican mothers beginning sphincter control training later (13.0 months compared with 9.9 and 9.6 months on the average for the U.S. lower class and middle class. See Table 27). They also take longer to complete this training (average age of child at completion of training 22.0 months compared with 16.4 months and 18.6 months for the U.S. class groups respectively), for which lack of plumbing may be no small factor. However, there is a highly significant difference between Vallecañeses and both class groups regarding the severity of sphincter control training, especially with respect to the upper-middle class mothers in New England, who train most mildly of all. It is apparent through observation and interview that Vallecañese lower-class mothers are relatively anxious and harsh in training for sphincter control and are more prone to use physical and verbal chastisement than the mainland mothers (subscales to measure punishment are included in the summary scale of severity in Table 27). But

TABLE 27

Toilet Training by Culture and Social Class
(percent above median)

	P. R. Rural- Lower	U. S. Urban- Lower	p	P. R. Rural- Lower	U. S. Urban- Middle	p
Median age beginning bowel training ($1 = -2$ mos., $9 = 40+$ mos.)	79	52	—	79	50	—
Median age completed bowel training ($1 = -4$ mos., $9 = 40+$ mos.)	67	58	—	67	45	—
Severity of toilet training ($1 = $ mild, $9 = $ severe)	100	53	.001	100	40	.001

there are extremes which, in terms of traumatic potential for the child, have not been reached, as Maccoby reports for her upper-lower mothers, two of whom "rubbed their children's faces in their soiled diapers in an effort to teach them how 'disgusting' accidents were." (Maccoby 1954:382).

Sex and Modesty Training

Generally Vallecañese rural lower-class mothers are much more anxious about sex and much more severe in handling sex and modesty training of their children than either mainland group, though their practices more closely resemble those of the New England lower-class families (Table 28). Maccoby (1954:382-384) also found that the upper-middle mothers were less restrictive in sex training practices and much less severe in enforcing modesty rules.

Vallecañese mothers exert significantly greater pressure for the child to keep on its clothes by comparison with both mainland groups, especially with respect to the lower-class mothers. Their general policies regarding nudity are also more restrictive than the mainland groups, especially the middle-class mothers. This is particularly emphasized with respect to their daughters, as we have seen in earlier chapters. They begin modesty training at a younger age (2.0 years on the average compared with 2.8 years for the New England lower-class and 3.4 years for the middle-class children), especially by comparison with the middle class.

TABLE 28

Sex and Modesty Training by Culture and Social Class
(percent above median)

	P. R. Rural-Lower	U. S. Urban-Lower	p	P. R. Rural-Lower	U. S. Urban-Middle	p
Nudity restrictiveness (1 = permissive, 9 = restrictive)	72	52	—	94	68	.05
Pressure for modesty rules (1 = very low, 9 = very high)	89	52	.01	94	49	.005
Median age beginning modesty training (1 = −2 years, 9 = 4+ years)	39	69	—	39	89	.001
Severity of pressure against masturbation (1 = none, 9 = heavy pressure)	94	62	.025	94	39	.001
Restrictiveness against masturbation (1 = permissive, 9 = restrictive)	89	43	.001	100	43	.001
Restrictiveness against mutual sex play (1 = permissive, 9 = restrictive)	83	50	.02	100	53	.001

These Puerto Rican mothers restrict and punish masturbation and mutual sex play among children significantly more than either continental class group, again in both respects differing most from the upper-middle class mothers.

Training for Aggression Control

Maccoby (384) found that her upper-middle class mothers in several respects were more permissive of aggressive behavior by their children than the upper-lower mothers (Table 29). Our data reveal that, in this respect, Vallecañese parents are much more restrictive of hostile behavior than either of the mainland classes, tending to be slightly closer to upper-lower than upper-middle norms. There are significant differences between the insular and continental mothers regarding aggression of the child toward siblings, other children, and parents, and the latter type of aggression is much more severely punished in the rural island community. Only with respect to encouraging the child to retaliate when he is the victim of aggression

TABLE 29

Training for Aggression Control by Culture and Social Class
(percent above median)

	P. R. Rural-Lower	U. S. Urban-Lower	p	P. R. Rural-Lower	U. S. Urban-Middle	p
Restrictiveness of aggression toward other children (1 = permissive, 9 = restrictive)	94	46	.001	94	33	.001
Parental encouragement of child to fight back if attacked (1 = none, 9 = very strong)	44	58	–	44	59	–
Restrictiveness of aggression toward siblings (1 = permissive, 9 = restrictive)	86	40	.001	86	34	.001
Restrictiveness of aggression toward parents (1 = permissive, 9 = restrictive)	100	51	.001	100	52	.001
Severity of punishment for aggression toward parents (1 = none, 9 = very severe)	100	51	.001	100	37	.001

are the differences not statistically significant, but the trend in the general direction is unmistakable.

Maccoby found significant differences at the .01 and .02 levels, with the upper-middle mothers being more permissive of aggression toward other children and toward parents and less severely punishing the latter. Except for severity of punishment for aggression toward parents, the same trend in the two mainland groups is reflected in our statistics, the smaller-appearing differences being an artifact of the cruder median test and the use of separate common medians, as compared with the more sensitive t-test used by Maccoby.

Restrictions and Achievement Demands

In their interviews the island mothers report themselves as slightly more restrictive of the child's wandering about during eating than the other two groups, although we observed in practice somewhat more wandering than they report (Table 30). There are few differences between any of the groups with regard to using the fingers for eating, though Maccoby (386-387) found a significant variation between upper-middle and upper-lower U.S. mothers, the latter being

TABLE 30

Restrictions and Achievement Demands by Culture and Social Class
(percent above median)

	P. R. Rural-Lower	U. S. Urban-Lower	p	P. R. Rural-Lower	U. S. Urban-Middle	p
Restrictions on child remaining seated during meal (1 = low, 9 = high)	50	36	—	50	38	—
Restrictions on use of fingers to eat (1 = low, 9 = high)	28	30	—	61	66	—
Restrictions on interrupting adults (1 = low, 9 = high)	100	65	.01	100	60	.005
Pressure to conform to eating rules (1 = low, 9 = high)	89	36	.001	94	62	.02
Restrictions on care of house and furniture (1 = low, 9 = high)	61	62	—	61	49	—
Pressure for neatness and orderliness (1 = low, 9 = high)	72	58	—	72	45	.05
Strictness regarding bedtime (1 = low, 9 = high)	6	60	.001	6	59	.001
Strictness regarding noise (1 = low, 9 = high)	50	38	—	67	78	—
Keeping track of child (1 = rarely checks, 9 = often checks)	89	53	.01	89	42	.001
Giving child regular jobs (1 = none given, 9 = many given)	28	53	—	28	52	—
Demands for instant obedience (1 = none, 9 = many)	83	30	.001	83	27	.001
How far child expected to go in school? (1 = grade school, 9 = college)	22	52	.05	0	63	.001
How important for child to do well in school? (1 = unimportant, 9 = very important)	89	45	.001	89	35	.001
Sex role differentiation of child by mother's expectations (1 = none, 9 = high)	94	46	.001	94	44	.001

more restrictive. On the other hand, where she found no differences between the groups regarding the interrupting of adult conversation, we obtain a highly significant difference between each New England class group and the rural island mothers, the latter restricting this behavior much more. This also holds true with respect to conforming to eating standards, though it should be borne in mind that Valle-cañeses have little conception of "table manners" in the middle-class U.S. sense and have few eating restrictions in number. As a whole Maccoby also found the lower-class U.S. mothers more restrictive. For the Puerto Ricans these restrictions are not so much a result of achievement-orientation as, to put it the way some mothers did, because "eating is like praying, a time for quiet." Food is scarce and eating is to be taken seriously. There are few cases of eating problems of children. And restricting the interrupting of adults while eating is part of the general demand that children maintain a status subordinate to adults.

Maccoby found the lower-class mothers in the United States more restrictive about house and furniture care, but our mothers differ little from the mainland mothers, being a bit closer to the lower-class group. The writer would have expected a somewhat greater difference here in the direction of the island mothers being much less stringent in demands for care of household effects. Maccoby indicates that upper-lower mothers are more demanding about neatness and orderliness; the Puerto Rican lower-class mothers are also more demanding than either group, particularly the middle class. This is strongly influenced by an emphasis on personal cleanliness rather than obsessive orderliness of surroundings, on which they place relatively little emphasis.

Maccoby also found the upper-lower class mothers significantly more restrictive about noise-making than middle-class mothers, while the island mothers are slightly less strict than either group. Both mainland groups are moderately restrictive about bedtime while the island mothers are extremely lax on this variable by contrast.

The more protective, even overprotective, island mothers keep closer track of their children, checking on their whereabouts much more frequently than either group of their mainland contemporaries. The middle-class U.S. group seems least concerned on this score. We have seen how closely the mothers in Valle Caña hedge the physical mobility and freedom of their young, who in turn learn to stick quite closely to their mother's skirts.

Vallecañese mothers are more constrained than either continental group to demand that their child obey orders instantly. This reflects, as do the findings which follow, the less egalitarian, less achievement-oriented society of the island, since on the mainland, presumably, the child is given somewhat greater freedom from parental control and encouraged to initiate independent activity, and obedience is therefore of less concern. The low level achievement expectations of Valle-cañese parents is further seen in the scale (Table 30) indicating that they give their child fewer regular tasks than either mainland group (at least at the preschool level) and teach few things to him before entering school (in a scale which does not appear in Table 30), not only with regard to reading, writing, and arithmetic, but even manual skills. We have seen in earlier parts of the book, however, that as the child gets older they do allocate quite a few tasks to both sexes, whereas probably, though we do not have specific evidence, neither mainland urban group does so to the same degree. Maccoby found scant differences in task assignation between her class groups.

Another mirror of the level of achievement expectations is seen in the comparative picture of educational aspirations of these parents for their children. Being both materialistic and realistic, Puerto Rican rural mothers realize their children are not likely to go far in school and have few expectations in this direction by comparison with either mainland group. The mainland lower-class group, in turn, did not have as high expectations as their class superiors. Paradoxically the island mothers score high on expectations for their children's school achievement. There is more here than meets the eye, however, as Maccoby found when comparing her lower-class and middle-class groups:

Although the upper-middle families take it for granted that their children will go to college, they do not seem so concerned about current school achievement as the lower families are. Possibly the upper-middle children adjust to school more easily; for the lower-class families current school achievement may be more of a problem, and more parental pressure may be required to keep the child performing up to even an average standard. In any case, our data do not show any tendency for the lower parents to devalue school achievement—on the contrary, they seem emphatically interested in having their child do well in school (Maccoby, 86).

Thus Maccoby finds that while her lower-class mothers thought it more important that the child do well in school, they did not actually expect the child to go as far in school as the middle-class mothers. This is precisely the picture when we compare our lower-class caneworkers' wives with the two mainland groups, the former varying from the latter at an even higher level of significance than the latter vary between themselves. At least as far as the Puerto Rican mothers are concerned, we feel this reflects the real situation. They would like their children to do well in school but realistically they realize that it is highly improbable that their child will even finish high school, much less enter college. And as we have mentioned above, they make little attempt to teach the child academic skills at home. Finally it should be added that, seen in context, their interview responses indicate, despite their high positions on the scale, that "doing well" in school contains a large component of "being good," "acting right," and "staying out of trouble," all of which are expectable lower-class ethics for children who must perform before a middle-class teacher.

While academic achievement thus has low motivational power for Vallecañeses, these mothers have high expectations with regard to another type of achievement, that of acting in accordance with cultural expectations for one's sex role. This can be seen in the significantly higher sex role differentiation of the island mothers by comparison with both U.S. class groups. Upper-middle and upper-lower New England mothers are less demanding and in fact less clear about this problem in definition of child-training expectations, as Parsons (1942) pointed out long ago.

Techniques of Discipline

A key to child-rearing philosophy as the underpinning of conscious culture transmission may be found in the ways in which discipline and mores are inculcated. Some of these techniques become apparent from an examination of Table 31. The rural island mothers resort to praise as a training technique significantly less than lower-class New England mothers, and almost so with respect to the middle-class mothers. The U.S. mothers are moderate dispensers of praise, considering it necessary as "positive" reinforcing of sanctioned behavior, whereas the rural island mothers feel it is actually harmful for the child, tending to spoil him and make him "fresh."

The three groups do not vary widely on the use of withdrawal of love. This is somewhat contrary to the suggestions of many writers on child development in the United States that many Americans,

TABLE 31

Techniques of Discipline by Culture and Social Class
(percent above median)

	P. R. Rural-Lower	U. S. Urban-Lower	p	P. R. Rural-Lower	U. S. Urban-Middle	p
Responses to expected table behavior (1 = never praises, 9 = always praises)	11	60	.001	39	49	—
Responses to children playing well together (1 = never praises, 9 = always praises)	6	57	.001	59	54	—
Use of praise (1 = never uses, 9 = often uses)	22	50	.05	22	46	—
Use of withdrawal of love (1 = never uses, 9 = often uses)	61	48	—	67	61	—
Use of reasoning (1 = never uses, 9 = often uses)	0	63	.001	0	71	.001
Use of reward (1 = never uses, 9 = often uses)	28	53	—	28	50	—
Use of money as reward for work or good behavior (1 = never uses, 9 = often uses)	28	49	—	28	50	—
Use of ridicule (1 = never uses, 9 = often uses)	22	47	—	22	31	—
Use of deprivation of privileges (1 = never uses, 9 = often uses)	11	62	.001	11	53	.005
Use of physical punishment (1 = never uses, 9 = often uses)	83	33	.001	94	47	.001
Consistency with which mother follows through obedience demands (1 = seldom does, 9 = always does)	78	32	.001	94	51	.001
Consistency with which mother follows through on punishment (1 = seldom does, 9 = always does)	28	54	—	22	55	.025

especially in the middle class, frequently utilize this mode of obtaining "proper" behavior from the child. However, neither Maccoby's data nor mine are very clear on this scale, due probably to the inadequacy of questions built around this variable in the interviews, and so caution should be exercised in interpreting this result.

Both stateside groups use reasoning significantly more than the insular mothers. This is understandable when we recall the Vallecañese conception of the child as *sin capacidad*, not capable of reasoning, whereas in the United States the child is considered early to be capable of reasoning and furthermore to be on a more equalitarian basis vis-à-vis adults. As a corollary of praise, rewards for approved behavior are also used less on the island than in either mainland group (this statistic was just short of significance). However, instead of rewarding "good" behavior, the island mothers punish "bad" behavior, very reliably more than the mainland mothers in either class group. Maccoby (*idem*), according to the t-test, found that the upper-lower mothers used physical punishment significantly more than upper-middle class mothers, so that the island mothers, while differing widely from either group, are relatively closer to the other lower-class group.

In line with the Protestant ethic the continental mothers tend to use withdrawal of privileges much more than the Vallecañese mothers who, while they may be more punitive of transgressions, do not believe in withholding the relatively meagre range of material dispensations which is the lot of the lower-class Puerto Rican child. In fact they value and practice giving gifts to the child, not in return for approved behavior, but because they want to give to their children, whom most of the island parents cherish, despite their ambivalence.

Our observations cast some doubt on the scale measuring extent of use of ridicule. Maccoby's (*idem*) data show that the upper-lower mothers use ridicule as well as deprivation of privileges significantly more than the upper-middle mothers, according to the t-test. Our data indicate that the Puerto Rican mothers use it less than either group, but our observational data strongly suggest that they use it a great deal more than reported in the interview.

One indication of the effectiveness of disciplinary methods is the consistency with which they are carried out. It will be seen in Table 31 that Vallecañese mothers are highly consistent as far as seeing to it that obedience demands are carried out, differing significantly from both mainland groups. Obedience is very high on the socialization list of values in Valle Caña. Punishment as a mode of discipline is also highly valued but these mothers do not consistently administer it and their testimony and performance indicate much ambivalence, uncertainty, and irregularity. In this they also differ from the continental mothers, especially the middle-class ones. Pressures of domestic

duties often interfere with consistent administration of behavior sanctions and by the time the mother gets around to it, the original cause
has been forgotten. The apparent contradiction in consistency of
obedience demands and punishment is another of the many inconsistencies that characterize the primary cultural process in Valle Caña.

Agents of Child Care and Discipline

In almost every culture and class group the mother does the bulk
of caretaking of the infant and later of the child (Table 32). But

TABLE 32

Agents of Child Care and Discipline by Culture and Social Class
(percent above median)

	P. R. Rural-Lower	U. S. Urban-Lower	p	P. R. Rural-Lower	U. S. Urban-Middle	p
Proportion infant caretaking by mother (1 = almost none, 9 = all)	72	46	.05	72	43	.05
Proportion infant caretaking by father (1 = almost none, 9 = all)	39	51	—	39	50	—
Caretaking of older child (4-7 years) by father (1 = none, 9 = great deal)	44	52	—	44	51	—
Proportion of caretaking by nonparental agents (1 = none, 9 = more than half)	89	39	.005	50	36	—
When other agents are involved, who are they? (in percent)						
a. older sibling	65	7			2	
b. maid, sitter, friend	6	12			58	
c. grandmother	12	61			35	
d. other relatives	17	20			5	
Total	100	100			100	
When both parents are present, who disciplines? (1 = husband, 9 = wife)	56	44	—	56	40	—
Responsibility for child-rearing policy (1 = father almost entirely, 9 = mother almost entirely)	44	60	—	44	58	—
Who is stricter with child? (1 = father, 9 = mother)	72	43	.05	72	54	

while Maccoby (389-390) found no differences between the main-land classes, Vallecañese mothers perform a significantly higher pro-portion of caretaking than either class group. While Maccoby found that upper-middle infants have reliably more caretaking by non-parental agents, most are maids and sitters whom upper-middle parents can better afford. Vallecañese infants have significantly more care by agents other than the parents than the upper-lower children and somewhat more than the upper-middle children, principally as regards the use of siblings. Interestingly, it seems that among the continental upper-lower group proportionately more of the nonparental surro-gates are grandmothers than even among the islanders. While this accords with our general observation that in Valle Caña the aged are rather neglected and left to themselves, it would seem that the older generation as represented by the grandmother exerts perhaps more influence on child training in the United States, at least in the lower class, than may have been suspected in the light of persistent statements by social scientists about the "isolation" of the American nuclear family. Perhaps such generalizations are more applicable to the Ameri-can middle-class family.

When both parents are present in the Vallecañese family it is the mother who disciplines more than the father, whereas to a slight degree just the opposite occurs in the U.S. families. Of the latter families Maccoby says, "In both classes the father is slightly stricter than the mother in terms of severity of discipline and his demands for obedience and self restraint." This tendency does not exist among the Valle-cañese fathers. It is obvious from Table 31 that it is the mother who is the stricter parent in Valle Caña, significantly so by comparison with the New England lower-class parents and almost to this degree when compared with the middle-class group. In both U.S. groups the mother has a slight edge over the father in assuming responsibility for child-rearing policy, while in Valle Caña the mother in theory leaves this more to the father. As we have seen in earlier accounts, the father in general actually tends to leave most matters concerning the raising of children to his wife, so one might anticipate that the mother would be stricter since she has more problems of child rearing and more areas about which to be strict. The Vallecañese father may rule the roost putatively, but it is his wife who must maintain the everyday busi-ness of running the family's affairs.

Affective Atmosphere in the Family

Vallecañese mothers have a warmer relationship and display more affection toward their infant and child than upper-lower mainland mothers, but while they also display more affection toward the infant than upper-middle mothers, they are slightly less demonstrative toward the child when older, and their affectional relationship with it differs very little (Table 33). None of these differences reaches significance. The Vallecañese father has a somewhat colder relationship with the child than the upper-middle class father, but differs only slightly in this respect from the upper-lower father. Maccoby (*ibid.*: 390-392) found that

The upper-middle mothers are slightly more demonstrative toward their five-year olds and seem to have a somewhat warmer relationship (significant at .01) with them than upper-lower mothers, although the majority of mothers in both classes are warm toward their children and display only minor elements of hostility toward them. . . . Those which did occur were found primarily among the upper-lower families.

By contrast the rural islanders display a good deal of hostility and are significantly more rejective than either group. This ambivalence on the part of these mothers is another of the many internal inconsistencies in the socialization climate for the child in Valle Caña. Actually the distribution of scaled values for the mother-child and father-child relationships is bimodal and not faithfully described by a measure of central tendency. That is, several parents of either sex were quite warm and several were quite cold, but as a group their tendencies must be expressed through the common medians.

Upper-middle and upper-lower class mainland mothers show general acceptance of their domestic and child-training roles, but these are more highly valued by the island mothers though this difference does not reach the .05 level of confidence. The latter are also somewhat more anxious about their training problems, especially by contrast with the upper-middle mothers, though again this does not quite reach our minimum significance level. This anxiety is particularly evident in the aggression and sexual spheres, as has been noted in Tables 28 and 29.

TABLE 33

Affective Atmosphere in the Family by Culture and Social Class
(percent above median)

	P. R. Rural-Lower	U. S. Urban-Lower	p	P. R. Rural-Lower	U. S. Urban-Middle	p
Warmth of affectional bond, mother to infant (1 = very cold, 9 = very warm)	61	55	—	61	54	—
Affectional demonstrativeness, mother to child (1 = none, 9 = great deal)	61	41	—	50	55	—
Affectional relationship, mother to child (1 = very cold, 9 = very warm)	57	37	—	56	51	—
Affectional relationship, father to child (1 = very cold, 9 = very warm)	44	47	—	44	53	—
Maternal rejection (1 = none, 9 = complete)	100	40	.005	100	24	.001
Mother's attitude toward mother role (1 = values highly, 9 = subordinates to other roles)	39	54	—	39	51	—
Mother's child-rearing anxiety (1 = none, 9 = extreme)	78	56	—	61	38	—
Mother's feelings about being pregnant (1 = delighted, 9 = displeased)	83	49	.005	89	51	.005
Father's feeling about wife being pregnant (1 = delighted, 9 = displeased)	94	50	.005	94	47	.005
Mother's evaluation of father (1 = critical, 9 = admiring)	0	63	.001	0	54	.001
Family balance of authority (1 = father, 9 = mother)	6	46	.005	6	32	.05
Wife thinks of husband's strictness (1 = too strict, 9 = not enough)	72	62	—	72	76	—
Husband thinks of wife's strictness (1 = too strict, 9 = not enough)	0	51	.05	0	41	—
Parental child-rearing agreement (1 = closely agree, 9 = sharply disagree)	17	44	.05	22	53	.05

For the subject child, the mainland mothers and their husbands were much happier about her being pregnant than the Vallecañese spouses. Maccoby (*idem*) found a slight but not significant tendency for upper-middle husbands and wives to be happier about the birth of the child than their subordinate class contemporaries. In Puerto Rico attitudes about having the child were closely connected to the particular economic situation at the time of pregnancy and somewhat related to the size of the family, smaller families generally being less concerned about "another mouth to feed" than larger families.

The balance of family authority is tipped heavily on the side of the Vallecañese father and in this he is reliably more in command than the mainland fathers. Maccoby (*idem*) also found that upper-lower fathers had significantly more family authority than upper-middle fathers. On the other hand they were much less admired than upper-middle fathers by their wives, and Vallecañese fathers are significantly more devaluated and disesteemed than either U.S. group.

There seems to be reliably greater agreement between the island marriage mates regarding child rearing than either group of their U.S. contemporaries, and this might be expected of a more tradition-minded family (see Table 33). Maccoby (*idem*) found a significant difference in favor of greater agreement about child rearing between the upper-middle mates. It should be emphasized that the close agreement among Vallecañese spouses is due not only to their mutual tacit acceptance of many of the folkways regarding the training of children, but also to the very wide communication gap between them, which is itself part of the tradition. Child-rearing practices and most other matters of policy are seldom discussed between them, each taking for granted that the other will act according to culturally defined modes.

By inspection of the raw distributions it is apparent that there is a very slight tendency for wives in all three groups to think of their husbands as being too strict, so the results on this scale in Table 33 are deceptive. It is also apparent by inspection that there is a slight tendency for husbands in all groups to think their wives are not strict enough, but again a peculiarity of the data makes the results of this scale comparison misleading also. In both cases it was necessary to push upward a large number of cases in order not to split a very large median interval. In both scales the effect was to cause the segment above the median to become excessively large and thus change the actual direction of the data. In the second scale, moreover, it seems absurd not to obtain significance with the very large differences between the groups until we realize that I had no information for more than half the sample on this question. In the first case, where there is something approaching a normal spread in Vallecañese data, the t-test might have produced a more logical statistic. However, since neither Maccoby nor I found significant differences with these two scales, and I have described the actual tendencies according to the raw data, no harm is done.

Education, Culture, and Social Class

Maccoby (392-393) wondered whether the upper-middle class mothers might not have been telling the interviewer what they felt were "right" answers rather than what they actually do and whether upper-lower mothers, "having had less exposure to modern child-rearing doctrine, would not know so well what was the 'proper' answer to the questions and would therefore be more frank." Since she did not find out the amount of child-training literature read by these mothers, she felt their responses might be indirectly checked by considering the degree of education within and between classes, her assumption being that more education would mean more reading, as well as more direct training in "modern" methods. Now it is my contention that any group of mothers from any culture, regardless of formal education, would have some idea of a "proper" answer, at least in terms of their own social standards, and this might not always coincide with actual practice. However, it is interesting to note the results of comparing the two mainland groups with respect to education, class, and certain child-training variables. In general Maccoby (393) found that: "... when education is held constant, significant differences between classes are still found on the major scales for which sizeable differences were reported earlier. This fact provides some grounds for confidence that the class differences which have been discovered are not simply a result of the mothers' telling us what they believe we would like to hear."

On the basis of further comparisons when the mothers were arranged according to ethnic origins and class, she concluded that "the differences in child-rearing practices between social classes ... cannot be traced to differences in the ethnic origins of the two classes" (*idem*).

For Vallecañese mothers we may regard formal education almost as a constant factor. Only two of the eighteen mothers had gone past the fifth grade, and nearly half had no schooling at all and admitted being illiterate. The mean and median of formal schooling are 2.5 years. So we may conclude that formal education of rural Puerto Rican mothers is not an important factor in their child-training practices.

As mentioned in an earlier chapter, Vallecañese mothers tend to train both according to tradition and whimsy, though of course certain ideas have begun to seep through, especially as their children achieve more schooling than they did and relay practices of the *Americanos* as they read of them in schoolbooks and see in an occasional movie. But, being more isolated, yet closer geographically to their mothers and other relatives, we would expect them to rely more strongly than continental mothers upon tradition. In Table 34 it is apparent that

TABLE 34

Child Training of Contemporary Mothers vs. Older Generation by Culture and Social Class
(percent above median)

	P. R. Rural-Lower	U. S. Urban-Lower	p	P. R. Rural-Lower	U. S. Urban-Lower	p
Contemporary mothers vs. older generation (1 = more lenient than own parents, 9 = stricter than own parents)	33	41	—	33	49	—
How much does mother try to pattern self after own mother? (1 = consciously tries same ways, 9 = consciously tries other ways)	38	63	—	13	42	.05

our rural island mothers much more consciously try to pattern themselves after their mothers' ways of raising children than either U.S. group, the difference being significant between them and the upper-middle class mothers and just short of significance between them and the upper-lower mothers. As was also pointed out earlier, most Vallecañese mothers feel they are more lenient than their mothers were, this being the biggest factor of divergence from the old ways. In this respect they also differ, though not significantly, from both mainland groups; they seem slightly closer to the upper-lower mothers. Undoubtedly to some extent with all the latter groups there occurs a kind of halo effect surrounding older ways of bringing up children.

In Chapter 11 the findings of this chapter will be summarized along with those for the rest of the study and their implications will be discussed further in Chapter 12.

CHAPTER 10

Child Behavior in Valle Caña and New England

Introduction

W E HAVE SEEN how our rural Puerto Rican mothers compare in their child-training techniques with lower-class and middle-class mothers in a New England community. These patterns of child rearing or ways of inculcating cultural values and norms of behavior into the inheritors of the society's traditions may be considered as antecedent factors in the socialization of the child. The consequents of these as well as other variables may be perceived in part as the characteristic behaviors expressed by the child. In an earlier chapter Vallecañese child behaviors were described. Now, as we have done with the practices and policies of their mothers, let us compare the behaviors of children in Valle Caña with the children of the New England families.

Here our data, while derived mainly and primarily from mother interviews, will also use some material from free doll play, which was administered to the child in each family in both cultures on which centered the parent interviews. Two doll play sessions were considered sufficient in the U.S. study, but because of a number of factors (see Chapter 1, Appendix D, and Landy, 1959a) we felt it necessary to use four sessions of doll play. However, it is the averages for each child for all sessions in which he participated which will be used, so it is doubtful whether, for our purposes, the difference in number of sessions will make important differences in the comparability of the two cultural groups.

Primarily in this chapter our doll play data will be compared for aggression, since, unfortunately, this is the only variable, aside from "neutral-positive" (which is defined by the U.S. researchers as all acts which were non-aggressive, but in my scoring is only one of several categories which are non-aggressive), for which computations are available. In Chapters 7 and 8 the reader will have noted the many other areas in which we have scored the Puerto Rican protocols.

As in Chapter 9, we have used the median test to decide significance in group comparisons, and in the tables we have reported the percentage above the median for each class and culture group on each scaled variable, as well as the level of significance if at .05 or greater. For the tests within the Puerto Rican sample, where the quantities in each cell of the contigency table are very small, we have applied Fisher's exact test (Siegel 1956).

Weaning

Though the differences between them are not significant, Valle Caña children as infants cried slightly more than either the upper-lower or upper-middle class children. All three groups show relatively mild reactions to weaning, with the U.S. upper-middle class tending toward easier reactions than either of the two lower-class groups, though this is not at a significant level (Table 35).

Sphincter Control

The Puerto Rican children had more severe reactions to bowel training than either of the Massachusetts groups though these differences do not quite reach a level greater than what might have been due to chance factors. Children in all three groups tend to stop wetting the bed around three years of age or earlier, but Puerto Rican children manage urination control significantly earlier than U.S. upper-middle class children and almost significantly so when compared with the U.S. upper-lower class. Since the common medians in both comparisons lie between 1 and 2, the percentage of 63 above the median reported in Table 35 for the upper-middle class children is somewhat deceptive; in all groups the scales are skewed toward the early extreme.

TABLE 35

Behavior of Child, According to Mother, by Culture and Social Class
(percent above median)

	P. R. Rural-Lower	U. S. Urban-Lower	p	P. R. Rural-Lower	U. S. Urban-Middle	p
Reaction to weaning (1 = mild, 9 = severe)	44	43	—	44	33	—
Crying by infant (1 = very little, 7 = very much)	67	50	—	67	51	—
When child stopped bedwetting (1 = 2 yrs old, 8 = still wets almost every night)	39	47	—	39	63	.05
Reaction to toilet training (1 = mild, 9 = severe)	71	53	—	71	56	—
Quarreling among siblings (1 = infrequent, mild, 9 = continual, severe)	25	43	—	75	66	—
Aggression against parents (1 = none, 9 = great deal)	56	74	—	56	74	—
Reaction to punishment (1 = feelings hurt, 9 = impassive, now behaves better)	44	24	—	44	27	—
Infant's tendency to cling (1 = almost never, 9 = very "clingy")	71	39	.05	71	36	.02
Child's tendency to cling (1 = very little, 9 = very much)	83	46	.001	83	48	.01
Child's attention demands (1 = few, 9 = great deal)	67	54	—	56	47	—
Child's sociability (1 = low, 5 = high)	72	69	—	72	70	—
Reactions to separation from mother (1 = none, 9 = strong, frequent)	78	38	.01	78	40	.005
Total dependency pattern (1 = very little, 9 = great deal)	72	50	—	72	49	—
Child's resemblance to each parent (1 = mostly mother, 9 = mostly father)	50	57	—	44	50	—
Child tells parents of deviations? (1 = seldom, 9 = never)	22	58	.01	22	60	—
Admits wrongdoings when asked? (1 = always admits, 5 = always denies)	61	33	.05	61	38	—
Total evidence of superego (1 = none, low, 9 = much, high)	11	55	.005	11	49	.005

Aggression

According to the amount of aggression in the home as reported by mothers (Table 35), somewhat less quarreling takes place between siblings for the Vallecañese children compared with the upper-lower class mainland children but somewhat more when compared with the upper-middle class. These are of course relative figures; the reason for the apparent discrepancy in the two columns for this variable is due to some bunching toward the middle of the scale on the part of all three groups, with nearly half of the small Puerto Rican sample in one scale point. Thus when compared with the upper-lower class, this group was included in the below-median group, but when compared with the upper-middle, it was included with the above-median group. This points to another shortcoming of the median test. But the differences noted above are merely in direction and none is significant. This is likewise true of the other aggression variable, aggression against parents. Here there are no discrepancies between columns. There is somewhat more aggression in each U.S. class group of children than among the Puerto Ricans, but again, this is not a significant difference.

Turning to the doll play results in Table 36, we find proportionately more fantasy aggression as a whole among the Puerto Rican children, but their differences from either mainland group are slight and not significant. However there are some suggestive differences in the differential uses of various members of the family in projective aggression as between the two cultures. Thus Vallecañese children use all of the doll agents less than the children of either U.S. class group, and these differences are all significant except in the case of the mother doll—and even here they are not far short of significance. However, the island children use themselves as agents of aggression significantly more than either group of continental children. Thus, despite the emphasis on punishment of aggression in their culture, these children find it easier to express aggression using themselves as agents than to displace this direct expression through use of doll agents.

As far as reaction to punishment (parental aggression against the children) is concerned, Vallecañese children tend to have their feelings hurt more, while children in both mainland groups tend rather to accept punishment more or less impassively and to behave better

TABLE 36

*Proportionate Use of Dolls and Child's Self as Agents
of Aggression in Doll Play by Culture and Social Class
(percent above median)*

	P. R. Rural-Lower	U. S. Urban-Lower	p	P. R. Rural-Lower	U. S. Urban-Middle	p
Father doll (1 = 0-3.9 percent, 12 = 44+ percent)	7	58	.001	7	47	.01
Mother doll (1 = 0-4.9 percent, 12 = 44+ percent)	29	48	—	29	48	—
Boy doll (1 = 0-3.9 percent, 12 = 44+ percent)	14	47	.05	14	58	.005
Girl doll (1 = 0-3.9 percent, 12 = 44+ percent)	0	57	.001	0	47	.001
Baby doll (1 = 0-2.9 percent, 12 = 77+ percent)	0	52	.001	0	47	.001
Child's self (1 = 0-6.9 percent, 12 = 77+ percent)	86	52	.05	86	43	.005
Proportion of total aggressive acts (1 = 0-4.9 percent, 12 = 41+ percent)	57	45	—	57	52	—

as a sequel to punishment (Table 35). Thus punishment for aggression is probably more effective with the U.S. children; and when we compare the differential superego development of the three groups and bear in mind the greater inconsistency in administering punishment by Vallecañese mothers, we would expect this kind of behavior reaction on the part of their youngsters.

Dependence and Independence

There are several scales which help us to obtain measures in the areas of dependent-independent behavior, our assumption being that each is a component of the child's adjustment and ego-development, though we do not assume that one is necessarily the converse of the other. That is, high dependence does not necessarily imply low independence, and vice-versa, though presumably a given child who seems heavily dependent in many areas of life would have a more difficult time asserting his independence than one who seems heavily independent in many areas. Dependence also does not imply submission, since we know from Levy's (1943) study that dependent children of overprotective mothers may turn out either to be submissive to, or dominant over, such mothers.

As a group Vallecañese children were very "clingy" as infants, significantly more so than either continental class group, who scarcely differ from each other in this respect. As they grew to be a few years old the same trend continues with the Puerto Rican children, while children in both U.S. groups seem to increase only slightly the frequency of such behavior. All these differences are significant, some to a very high degree. But as infants there is a somewhat greater difference between the island children and the upper-middle class children, while, at the older age grade, the difference is greater between the islanders and the upper-lower children. While differences do not go beyond the chance level, Vallecañese children tend to demand attention more often. And, as we might anticipate, since they are more clingy and demand much attention from their mothers, they offer strong objections when the mother must leave the house, even for short absences, significantly more so than either mainland group. All of the above findings are confirmed by field observations.

There are no differences between the groups with respect to the degree of sociability of the child, all of them tending to manifest relatively high sociability. However, in the case of the Puerto Rican data I may say that these children did not seem to me or my field assistant to be nearly as sociable as their mothers seemed to feel they were. And this sociability must also be seen within the very circumscribed limits of physical and social mobility described by these same mothers, which I confirmed through observation. While we do not know the U.S. data intimately, having utilized the judgments and not the original interviews, it would be our guess that their social environment would not be as limited, especially with respect to their behavior vis-à-vis older children, adults, and class superordinates.

While both upper-lower and upper-middle class children in Massachusetts show only a moderate degree of total dependency, Valle Caña children show a higher degree of dependency, falling just short of the .05 level of significance in both comparisons.

Unfortunately, we do not have scales designed to measure directly the degree of independence or self-assertiveness of these children. The one exception is a scale which attempts to measure the extent to which the child demands preschool teaching. In only four of our eighteen families did the interview elicit sufficient information for making a judgment. In the two U.S. groups, slightly more than half the mothers provided sufficient information. There was no significant difference between upper-lower and upper-middle children, both groups tending toward somewhat higher than moderate demands for preschool teaching. I would predict that Vallecañese children would not scale nearly so high if we had had enough data to make a judgment on the group.

Sex-Role Typing and Identification

In Valle Caña boys in doll play use the father, mother, and girl dolls less than girls, and the boy doll, baby doll, and self as agents of

TABLE 37

Proportionate Use of Dolls and Child's Self as Agents in Doll Play by Culture, Social Class, and Sex of Child
(percent above median)

	P. R. Rural-Lower			U. S. Urban-Lower			U. S. Urban-Middle		
	Boys	Girls	p	Boys	Girls	p	Boys	Girls	p
Father doll (1 = 0-3.9 percent, 12 = 44+ percent)	28	43	—	60	44	.05	66	31	.001
Mother doll (1 = 0-3.9 percent, 12 = 44+ percent)	14	71	—	28	66	.001	35	64	.001
Boy doll (1 = 0-3.9 percent, 12 = 44+ percent)	57	14	—	66	50	.02	72	72	—
Girl doll (1 = 0-2.9 percent, 12 = 33+ percent)	14	0	—	28	58	.001	35	64	.001
Baby doll (1 = 0-2.9 percent, 12 = 33+ percent)	57	0	.035	58	53	—	49	55	—
Child's self (1 = 0-3.9 percent, 12 = 44+ percent)	86	57	—	62	40	.005	56	44	.05

action proportionately more (Table 37). From this we could infer that girls in Valle Caña identify more strongly with the parent and same-sex dolls, while the boys identify with the same-sex doll, but much more weakly type their behavior by the standards of the principal identificants in the family constellation. This lends comfortable support to our assumptions in the earlier chapters regarding the differential identification, or sex-role typing, of the sexes. It also strengthens our data and observational findings of the greater dependency of the boy to the extent that he uses the baby doll significantly more as agent in fantasy play than the girl, indicating a possible closer emulation of regressive behavior.

By contrast let us look at the mainland children in Table 37. In both classes boys use the father doll significantly more, and girls use the mother doll significantly more, thus manifesting proportionately stronger identification of each with the same-sex parent figure. Furthermore, boys in both classes use the boy doll significantly more and girls use the girl doll significantly more, thus strengthening the picture of strong sex identification in the New England children. Since the differences are small, it seems reasonable to assume that there is a close similarity in the use of the baby doll by both sexes, thereby indicating a possible similar moderate proportion of dependency behavior in each, at least insofar as this factor provides such an index.

The much greater use of the self as agent by the boy in all groups may demonstrate that he is less willing or less capable of using the doll agents to the same extent as himself and therefore probably—relative to the situation in each class and culture—not proportionately as well identified as the girl. We know that in Valle Caña boys' doll play was not nearly as original or free from routine behavior as the girls'. However, what is even more likely is that this is an indication of the lesser experience of the boy in all the groups in playing with dolls and using them as a means of projection, as I have suggested elsewhere (Landy 1959a).

Now instead of analyzing the data by sex, let us look at the use of the doll agents by each group as a whole (Table 38). It is apparent that the Vallecañese children use the father doll somewhat more, the mother doll very slightly less than the stateside youngsters. Conversely, they use the children dolls much less than the continentals. This seems to reflect the higher status of the father in Valle Caña and the relatively more equal status of the adult sexes in the United States. It is likewise apparent that the island children use the girl doll significantly least of all, indicating again the lesser status of the female in Vallecañese society. Furthermore, the differential proportions of adult doll–child doll use in the two cultures seem to reflect the relatively greater status of children in the U.S. This is not to say that children are not valued in rural Puerto Rico, but that their social status is secondary to that of adults, while in the U.S. children are more apt to be seen and heard. Certainly much evidence exists to demonstrate that in the U.S. the statuses of female and child are not greatly subordinate.

TABLE 38

Proportionate Use of Dolls and Child's Self as Agents in Doll Play by Culture and Social Class
(percent above median)

	P. R. Rural-Lower	U. S. Urban-Lower	p	P. R. Rural-Lower	U. S. Urban-Middle	p
Father doll ($1 = 0$-3.9 percent, $12 = 44+$ percent)	64	52	—	64	53	—
Mother doll ($1 = 0$-3.9 percent, $12 = 44+$ percent)	43	47	—	43	47	—
Boy doll ($1 = 0$-3.9 percent, $12 = 44+$ percent)	36	57	—	36	70	.02
Girl doll ($1 = 0$-2.9 percent, $12 = 33+$ percent)	7	43	.05	8	48	.01
Baby doll ($1 = 0$-2.9 percent, $12 = 33+$ percent)	29	56	—	29	52	—
Child's self ($1 = 0$-3.9 percent, $12 = 44+$ percent)	71	51	—	71	51	—

While the continental children used the doll agents and themselves as agent in about equal proportions, Vallecañese children used themselves as agent very much more than the dolls, indicating not only a possible weaker identification, but much less experience in the use of dolls and other toys (see Landy 1959a). It would be fair to say, however, that the above is only proportional and relative information. In general we could safely conclude that in children within this age-grade we would not find as strong sex-typing behavior or emulation as we would expect to find in older children. Certainly the picture of relatively undeveloped identification by either sex is further substantiated by the scale on which the degree of the child's behavior resembles that of his parents as shown in Table 35. Here it is evident that in all three groups the child's behavior does not in this early stage of development clearly resemble that of either parent. Within the

Valle Caña group, when we break down the scale according to sex, we find that the mean for boys is 3.1 and for girls 3.0, which, like the group as a whole, lies in about the middle of the scale. Unfortunately we do not have the divisions by sex for this particular variable for the U.S. groups.

Perhaps one of the most difficult differences in our data to reconcile is that while we have quantities of evidence to show that the Puerto Rican society is very strongly sex-oriented and sex-segregated in nearly every aspect of life, in contrast to the more sex-equalitarian society in the U.S., it is the latter society which presents the clearest picture of identification and which would tend more closely to approximate the kind of handling of sex-typed behavior as a stage in identification that we might expect, given the psychoanalytic hypothesis. It occurs to the writer that one possible explanation is that since the child is not expected to grow up as fast on the island (we have seen that weaning, bowel control, and other learning comes much later for Vallecañese than for U.S. children), the Oedipal situation itself may be slower in coming about and in reaching its resolution.[1] One might be led to expect from the data in Table 38 that the five- and six-year-old children in both New England groups are having an easier time resolving their uncertainties about which role to play and whom to imitate than the island children. And this seems to harmonize with all the earlier evidence in this study about growing up in Valle Caña.

Superego

The superego, we have seen in Chapter 8, depends to a large extent, at least in psychoanalytic theory, on the process of identification—or, perhaps more accurately, the two processes, superego formation and identification, are interdependent, though genetically the child presumably internalizes cultural values before developing a superego. The latter is supposed to be the censoring agent of such values.

But while the picture of identification is not a clear one, if we use the indices of superego which we have selected, we find clear and

1. In fact, one might say that an Oedipal situation as postulated by Freud does not quite come about in Valle Caña. And even if we could overlook our contrary evidence and assume that it does, mechanisms for its resolution are not adequately provided by Vallecañese society. A recent discussion of this problem in the light of cross-cultural research will be found in Opler 1956. See also Fromm 1944.

highly significant differences between Valle Caña and the two mainland groups with respect to the indices of superego development which we have used (see Table 35). When we scale the extent to which the child voluntarily reports violations of familial-cultural standards to his parents, we find that while the mode of all groups is 1 on a 9-point scale, the distributions are such that Vallecañese children report deviations significantly less than either U.S. group, especially so by comparison with the upper-middle class children. The island children also tend to deny such transgressions when asked about them by parents significantly more than the upper-lower children, and nearly significantly so when compared with the upper-middle group.

Using a summary scale of evidence from throughout the interview with respect to superego development, we see that Vallecañese children show much less evidence of a strong superego than either U.S. group, at a high level of significance in each case. The two mainland groups seem to differ between themselves very little on this, the upper-lower indicating slightly higher evidence of superego.

Given the evidence on identification in the preceding section, the account of superego development among the three groups given here seems logically to be expected. When the Vallecañese group is analyzed by sex, we find a slight difference in their means, the boys having a mean of 1.5 and the girls of 1.7. While this difference points in the direction of a slightly more developed superego for the girls, as we would expect from the foregoing discussions, it is not statistically significant. Thus evidence from doll play, mother interviews, and the writer's field observations tends to substantiate each other with regard to the low level of superego development in the children of Valle Caña.

These findings lead us to suggest that perhaps the development of a superego in the child is dependent upon something other than formal inculcation of parental, that is, cultural, values. There are at least two other possibilities. One is the warmth and consistency of the relationship between parent and child, which, as we have seen in Valle Caña, is fraught with inconsistencies, discontinuities, and ambivalence on the part of the parents. Another is that the enforcement of cultural sanctions, while strongly demanded, is, as we have seen, inconsistent in these rural families. A further cause for confusion in identification is that there is a possibility that the child will want to identify with the aggressor. But while the father is the aggressor in the culture by reputation, we have seen that the lower-class caneworker is likely to curb his social aggression, despite a strong drive for it, because it is socially punishing. On the other hand it is the mother who is more often the aggressor against the child, since punishment is left largely in her hands. This could create a further source of uncertainty and confusion in the sex-typing and role-typing process.

Finally, it is possible that superego development, like much of the child's cultural indoctrination, comes later in life for these Vallecañese children, and that what we observed and recorded was not so much low level as the incipient stage of its development.

CHAPTER 11

The Summing Up

Introduction

IN THIS study we desired to explore and describe the process of
socialization or cultural transmission through generations within
the cultural and social context of a rural Puerto Rican village and to
compare child training and child behavior in its predominant lower
class with that of two New England groups characterized as upper-
lower and upper-middle class, for which comparable data were available. The purpose of this chapter is to summarize our findings.

Culture and Society

For ethnographic context we chose a cane-dependent community
in the eastern rainbelt, since cane is the most pervasive industry on the
island. In Valle Caña life revolves around the seasonal dichotomy: a
few months of work and idleness the rest of the year. Families are
large, averaging 5.7 children surviving to at least five years. A few
persons go to urban centers and to the U.S., but as a group Vallecañeses are not geographically or socially mobile. Living conditions
are crude and overcrowding is common. Diet is substandard in quality
and quantity (Perloff 1950, Roberts and Stefani 1949). Intermarriage
of European, African, and Arawak Indian strains has produced genetically "mixed" families. While racial discrimination is uncommon,
everyone is conscious of phenotypical characteristics like skin color
and hair form, though direct influences on child training were not
readily apparent.

Folk and modern medical values and practices mingle. Some modern health facilities are available in nearby towns, but the advice of the pharmacist or Spiritist medium is accepted as often as that of the doctor. Malnutrition is crucial to the problem of health and may be endemic to the whole lower class (Seijo de Zayas 1955).

Luck governs actions more than hard work, which is considered necessary for existence but is contemptuously viewed by all classes. Class obligations are feudally structured and many workers still feel deep obligations to the landowners, though this does not work usually in reverse. At early stages in child training class duties are inculcated. Traditional extended family ties and ritual kinship ties still exist but are becoming progressively attenuated.

Except as a set of cultural, rather than purely religious, values and practices, Catholicism has a loose grip on the hearts and minds of most Vallecañeses. People are inclined to tolerate all sorts of religious differences but are conversely narrow about political variation.

Teaching and school facilities are sparse, though much improved over former educational operations. Education has a somewhat dubious value with these parents; if their child is needed at home, they feel free frequently to keep him from school, temporarily or permanently. Teachers maintain to some degree the traditionally authoritarian approach, but corporal and other humiliating punishments are not as frequent as in the "old days."

Family

While most Vallecañeses eventually settle into some form of marriage, opportunities for premarital relations between the sexes are sharply limited. The female is cloistered from birth and most of her activities as she grows older are confined within a vale of segregation with members of her own sex. The male is permitted more freedom, but while driven to perform with sexual and social prowess to achieve *machismo*, or maleness, finds few pathways to this goal in the restricted atmosphere of the rural culture. Perhaps as a compensating mechanism the lower-class community accepts consensual marriage, which for many is often the first of two or more and from one point of view may be seen as a trial marriage.

Nearly a third of Vallecañese couples are consensually married, less than a fourth are united by religious ceremony (including a few Protestant marriages), and the rest had civil sanction. The latter is deemed increasingly desirable nowadays by the woman since her husband is then legally responsible for the children. It is usually the husband who walks away from a consensual marriage. But most consensual marriages endure and neither spouses nor children lose status with the lower-class community. Men and women agree that the woman's place is in the home, but these women also reveal certain hidden desires to escape their fate. Nevertheless, nearly all women in fact fulfill the customary role and remain around hearth and children. The wife does nearly all housework and child rearing, while her husband works seasonally in the cane or in the tiny patch if there is one but is otherwise free to roam about. The balance of authority is heavily weighted in the direction of the father.

Most wives express ambivalence or displeasure about their pregnancies, and while prenatal rejection does not necessarily carry over, there is much evidence of postnatal rejection. Fathers are less concerned about pregnancies as such except as they are an added debit in the family budget. But each mate displays ignorance as to the other's reaction to pregnancy. While this may be due in part to pregnancies being considered a natural event and family life becoming highly routinized, still the marital communication gap indicates that segregation of the sexes continues through marriage.

It is considered a good time to have a child if the birth occurs during the harvest season, bad if during the dead season. The median ideal number of children for wives is 2.3, and husbands 3.3, but more mates in small than in large families express desires for additional offspring. Besides the burden of work and responsibility of child rearing, pregnancy and childbirth hold many fears for the Vallecañese woman, yet most express a feeling of *conforme*, of resignation to their fate.

These men and women have departed from the traditional value of large families. But many factors prevent wide or effective use of birth control: men feel birth control devices are unsafe anyway, unmanly, and unpleasurable, and their wives will not dare their displeasure; devices are not always easily available; embarrassment attends the wives' having to request them from health units and husbands refuse to do so; in crowded quarters, the use of diaphragms and jellies is embarrassing and inconvenient; birth-control education is scant and unsystematic; and so on. While no one gives his religion as a reason, several men hold contraception as "interfering with God's will." But both mates favor sterilization of the woman, which frequently can be obtained gratis at government hospitals, and large numbers of wives have already been sterilized or would like to be.

Wives tend to be more critical of their husbands than vice-versa, probably because few men have social and economic opportunities for confirming their masculinity. There is also, however, a good deal of wifely "respect" compounded of fear and clinging to the traditional value of how a wife should feel about her husband. Wives tend to rate themselves highly as wives and mothers and attribute shortcomings in family relationships to alleged inherited behavior characteristics of the child. Self-blame and guilt as parents on the part of either mate are seldom apparent, and in part this may be attributed to their probable low superego development as children, as we shall see.

Child Training and Child Behavior

Mothers seldom work outside the home and their children are seldom separated from them. Fathers, however, are rarely home throughout the day and in general do little to take care of infants; in later childhood their domestic participation decreases even more. Infancy brings a combination from both parents of warm nurturance and casualness. The child is viewed as *sin capacidad*, which connotes not merely lack of physical capacity but of the faculty to reason, and parents seldom use reasoning with a child. The child is a *tabula rasa* on which society, through the parents, etches proper behavior systems.

Most infants are initially breast-fed and scheduling is rare. In nearly all cases the bottle is introduced but change to a non-sucking mode is fortuitous. Weaning age is from a few months to more than seven years. This tendency to prolong the sucking period is countered by a more or less equally pervasive tendency to terminate the sucking mode abruptly. There is thus no clearcut weaning pattern, either as to age or severity, though the general tendency is toward late weaning and rather pronounced harshness.

While table manners in the European-American sense are nonexistent, these parents have certain high expectations regarding eating habits. However, these are mildly enforced, except for interrupting adult conversation, which is taboo in any situation, and horseplay, which is not usually countenanced since eating is held to be a "solemn" occasion. There are few eating problems, and the child is allowed to eat as much or as little as he likes and to move about. Obesity is valued, and a *gordito* (little fat one) is considered a handsome child.

Sphincter-control training begins early for girls and later for boys but there is much variation in modes and consistency. However, a generally harsh and restrictive tone seems to pervade most toilet-training, more so for girls than for boys. Bedwetting, though punished, and perhaps because of it, continues late in some cases. The products of excretion are permitted to remain in relatively close range of living quarters. The important thing is to keep one's body clean. Neatness and cleanliness are desirable and demanded, but boys are given much more leeway than girls. Generally Vallecañeses make valiant attempts to dress their children neatly and to display the appearance of cleanliness though it is a losing battle against scarce water, few clothes, and primitive housing. High restrictions are placed on the child's handling of adult possessions, though children usually are taught to share their rewards with siblings, particularly younger ones. But there are no restrictions on bedtime.

For the lower-class individual, aggression is heavily punished in Vallecañese society and so is discountenanced strongly by parents. Mothers tend to tolerate the boy's aggression a bit more than the girl's; fathers tend in the opposite direction. But in general, interpersonal aggression of any kind—against siblings, other children, parents, or other adults—is discouraged and usually severely punished. The child is generally forbidden to fight back when attacked but must come to his parents, who will try to negotiate with the parents of the other child. There are rare cases of older boys or men who have a reputation as *guapos* (tough guys), but while most Vallecañeses have a distant admiration for them, they are not held up as models. People approve when the policeman, for whom they otherwise have little use, deals effectively with the *guapos'* antisocial activities. Public bad behavior is especially outlawed by parents, since there is a high regard for "what people will think."

Unquestioning obedience is expected and demanded of children by parents and other elders. Punishment for disobedience is severe, though not consistently administered partly because of preoccupation with domestic chores by the mother, who is chief punitive agent. The reputation of the father as supreme authoritarian is held by the mother and passed on to the children and is enough to secure obedience when he is present without frequent resort to punishment. In general, the severe external suppression produces high repression and few small children present difficult obedience problems to these parents, though they often complain that as boys grow older they become more troublesome. On the other hand there are scant rewards for good behavior. Praise is almost never utilized since, like direct rewards, it is felt to be bad in principle, to "spoil" the child, and to encourage disrespect.

"Bad" models for behavior are seldom utilized, but "good" models are used fairly frequently and include primarily parent figures, siblings, and relatives, in that order.

Deprivation of privileges and isolation of the child are infrequently used, but ridicule is fairly common and helps to produce an obedient and humble child and to reinforce the picture of the child as *sin capacidad*. Threats of dangers from a menacing environment are frequent and include supernatural and social disapproval, death, castration, desertion, kidnapping, isolation, illness, and injury. The child thus learns to trust few people or situations outside the family circle.

Only a moderate use of withdrawal of love is made by either parent, but physical punishment and scoldings are deemed indispensable in child training and are used more than any other techniques. Threats of punishment by both parents are also common, but since punishment administration is inconsistent, the child is uncertain as to when or for what things he will most likely be punished and tends, in this atmosphere of inconsistency, to get away with whatever he can.

The children's living space is restricted, especially the girls', and mothers constantly check on them, to protect them against moral contamination from the outside world. Demands for sociability in children are low, the mother preferring the child to be close to her at all times.

Wives tend ideally to prefer girls and husbands boys, though overall, as in former times, boys are evaluated more highly, especially in large families where they have been useful additions to the labor force. Despite their ideal preferences, mothers tend to be more warmly disposed, affect-wise, toward sons, and fathers toward daughters, but the small boy is handled more by both parents and feelings regarding him are apt to be more emotionally charged, in whatever direction. While he is permitted more personal freedom, the boy is nevertheless more dependent than the girl. Fathers have both the prestige and time to be more responsive to succorant behavior. Mothers, while in many respects encouraging dependency, often are annoyed with the results in their "clingy" child, but they feel this is the highest mark of love and will not be without it. As might be expected, the "clingy-ness," unsociability, attention-getting, and nurturance-seeking of these children are reinforced to a high degree. In a word, they exhibit many traits of dependent children.

It may be expected that related factors contributing to independence will not be strong. While not usually allotted to children before six years, when arduous tasks are assigned, it is with the intent not of creating independence and initiative but of fitting the boy and girl for their later roles of husband and wife. Preschool teaching by parents is infrequent and the level of parental aspiration for themselves and their children is low, for there are few incentives for success in the culture.

While the young child is regarded as a blank tablet with respect to his intellectual and manual capabilities, he is supposed to be born with a sexual potential. Extremely sharp distinctions are made at birth between male and female. In every phase of family and community life, separation of the sexes is mandatory for child and adult. The female is considered mentally inferior, innately weak and defenseless from potential male assault. The male is believed to be born with *malicias*—needs for antisocial and sexual aggression. Cultural values regarding sex establish the male as the aggressor, ever to be satisfied in marital or other relations, and the woman as submissive, to endure sex for the male's pleasure rather than her own.

While the girl is thus desexualized, the boy's sex is vigorously symbolized in his exposed genitalia, to which older boys and men call much attention, with frequent humorous castration threats. Though mothers report they do not like nudity, it is only the girl's exposure that causes them anxiety. Mingled with their sexual anxiety is a fear of incest between family males and daughters.

While autistic and group sex play by children is denied and tabooed by parents and heavily punished, it still occurs. All sorts of "realistic" and "unrealistic" reasons are given for prohibiting masturbation. And most parents report that they would lie, distort the truth, or punish their child if he asked about sexual intercourse and reproduction.

Allusions to sex are usually censored in mixed company, especially in the presence of children. Girls often remain ignorant of its operations, sometimes to the day of marriage. Boys pick up their information from the stories and jokes of older boys and men. Both sexes may observe the sexual behavior of farm animals, of course, but this adds to the general conception of sex as an aggressive act, primarily for the sport of the male.

Parents of both sexes often caress the infant boy, but both maintain a kind of reserve toward the infant girl, even where there seems to be the deepest sort of affective attachment. If a mother takes time out during the day to relax on her hammock or bed, she may take up an infant of either sex; but she always handles the girl more "delicately," the boy more roughly, but with more warmth.

Somewhere between the ages of three and six the child is given up as an object to be manipulated. He is relinquished even sooner if a succeeding sibling arrives, when parents quickly reject him in favor of the neonate. Now the dependency relationship continues, but more energy is directed toward the more "delicate" girl, while the boy's needs are largely ignored. In this post-infancy period neither is shown a great deal of warmth and affection, nor do the parents compensate with an increased interest in, say, their intellectual development, as seems to occur in the middle-class American family. During this period both sexes, but most significantly the boy, may revert to a kind of infantile negativism. Their only way to get back at a frustrating world is to refuse to do what is asked of them, to cry much (for this upsets the parents, especially the mother), and to withdraw within themselves and seek refuge in a shy, timid demeanor which they apparently hope will relieve them of the responsibilities of transacting with other persons.[1]

This stage, when the child *pierde la falda* (loses the skirt), marks a type of withdrawal of love according to the whim of the parent and/or advent of a new child. Unlike the withdrawal of love as a disciplinary method, this does not make the giving of love contingent on proper behavioral responses by the child. Affect-wise his needs are not met because of other foci of the mother's attention, and little the child can do will alter the process. Thus the groundwork for a strong superego, based on the performance of desirable behavior (first actually to receive love and finally autonomically in the parents' absence because

1. This timidity may be due also to social inexperience, which derives from relative isolation, especially in the case of open-country families, from most other children and from all adults except their parents and near kin and friends. They are taught "humility" and "respect" as paramount qualifiers in the approach to transactions with adults, to initiate no actions, and to react only when asked or ordered.

the parental values have been internalized in the process), is largely missing in Valle Caña. And the result is a relatively low development of superego at this age. Social and cultural factors like the lack of economic opportunities, which stifles motivation for achievement, lack of strong sense of communal responsibility, lack of a strong religious sense or a demanding substitute belief system, reliance on luck, a present-time orientation, dependence on external sanctions for wrong-doing, etc., form a mutually reinforcing system with the low Valle-cañese superego.

It is not until they are beyond six or seven years, when utilitarian roles have been found for them in the family division of labor, that children begin to find a place for themselves. Now boys are given increased freedom, and girls, while no freer in their physical mobility, are now considered more companionable by the mother. The boy continues to be dependent on the mother, but he can no longer seek nurturant responses from her by offering his own affection. Now he must work as he is told and bide his time. When he is in his teens, the boy begins to come into his own. At this point, all female members of the household, led by the boy's mother, and all younger male members are subservient to him. On this basis, the son's dependence on his mother continues into adulthood, and even after marriage mother and son often refuse to forego each other completely. The mother can no longer demonstrate her love for the son with bodily contact, as in infancy, but she can do things for him, a course she often pursues. As may be anticipated, conflicts between wives and mothers-in-law are frequent.

Adjustment for the girl has been not easier but more susceptible of fulfillment. If she will but be *de la casa* (a homebody) and otherwise act "lady-like" then she can easily fulfill her role. She need not constantly prove herself, as the boy is expected to assert his manliness.[2] If the restraints of the girl's role are hard to take, they do not last forever. In her middle teens she enters the marriageable stage, and while she well knows what lies in store for her as housewife and mother, she will achieve some satisfactions in managing a household and children of her own.

2. But the boy finds few ways of demonstrating this, since employment opportunities are drastically restricted, aggression is condemned unless he is willing to play the lonely role of *guapo*, sexual contacts are severely limited, etc.

Socialization in Puerto Rico and the United States

In Valle Caña mothers breast-feed oftener and longer and begin change-of-mode weaning later than in the U.S. The time needed for weaning does not differ much between the two cultures and three social groups, though upper-middle class mainland mothers tend to take longest of all. The groups also do not differ much in degree of severity of weaning, all tending to be somewhat more than moderately severe. Island mothers generally feed as the infant demands, while there is a significantly greater tendency on the part of continental mothers to schedule-feed.

As with weaning, Vallecañese mothers tend to sphincter train later than mainland mothers and to take somewhat longer. But they are significantly harsher trainers than either New England group. They are also more restrictive and severe in handling modesty and sex behavior, begin this training earlier, and show more sex anxiety than upper-lower or upper-middle class mothers on the continent.

The island mothers are more restrictive about aggressive behavior of their children within the family and in the community than either mainland group. They are also more restrictive than continental mothers regarding eating behavior, particularly as it involves the interruption of adults. Upper-middle class mothers tend to have somewhat fewer household restrictions than either of the two lower-class groups. They also have significantly less pressure for neatness and orderliness, while the rural Puerto Rican mothers have more than either U.S. group. On the other hand, Puerto Rican mothers are significantly more permissive about bedtime but slightly less permissive about noise than either U.S. group.

In line with their high sex anxiety the island mothers show a significantly higher differentiation of the child's sex than either class group in the U.S. They are more restrictive of the physical mobility of their children, keeping track of their children significantly more than either U.S. group. They allot fewer tasks to very young children but later the task pressure on the child increases. Obedience is highly valued on the island and mothers have significantly higher demands for obedience and try to enforce these demands more than either continental group. With fewer opportunities on the island they have reliably lower expectations for their child's academic achievement, though they do feel significantly more than the continentals that their children should do well in school. However, "doing well" implies getting along with others and "being good" more than it refers to intellectual attainments.

Vallecañese mothers utilize praise as a technique of discipline less than either of the U.S. groups, significantly so when compared with upper-lower mothers. They use reward less than either group also, and there is so little use of reasoning that the significant level between them and the U.S. mothers is very high. They utilize ridicule less than the mainland mothers, especially when compared with upper-lower mothers, and are significantly less depriving of privileges than mainland mothers, but, as earlier remarked, this scale may not be valid. As might be expected, however, they depend strongly on physical punishment, significantly more so than U.S. mothers. While no comparative data were used, island mothers also lean heavily on threats of dangers from the environment and supernatural beings. Consistency of following through with punishment, on the other hand, is significantly lower than that of the continental mothers, upper-middle mothers being the most consistent of all. Nevertheless, consistency of following through with demands for obedience is significantly greater than in either of the New England groups.

In infancy there are significantly more caretakers of the child in Valle Caña than in the upper-lower class and almost significantly more than in the upper-middle class. At the same time, the mother also plays a larger caretaking role than in either mainland group, but the father plays a somewhat more minor role, both in infancy and in later childhood. There is some tendency for the wife more than the husband to be chief disciplinarian when both are present, but he is probably home less than in the U.S. He is to a slight extent theoretically (though not in practice) more responsible for policy regarding the rearing of children, but it is definitely the mother who is very much stricter with the child. Just the opposite situation obtains in these respects in the New England families.

Vallecañese mothers value the mother role more highly than either continental group, though the latter also show general acceptance of the role. At the same time island mothers are more anxious about child rearing than the U.S. mothers. But they find fault not with their training methods but the child's supposed inherent tendencies. As we saw earlier, their anxiety is particularly evident in the sexual sphere but is also undoubtedly due to the conflicts that arise over the changing ways which culture change is bringing about. The mothers on the island were also significantly more ambivalent or unhappy about bringing this particular child into the world and so were their husbands when compared with New England husbands.

The low-status caneworker husband is less admired by his wife (though she "respects" him), but at the same time he retains, at least symbolically, the balance of authority within his family. He tends to think, along with the American fathers in upper-lower and upper-middle class families, that his wife is not quite strict enough, while wives in all three groups have a consensus of opinion on the over-strictness of their husbands. In spite of this disagreement, however, there is a significantly smaller area of disagreement between the spouses in Valle Caña than in the United States regarding general child-rearing practices and values, undoubtedly due largely to the father's very minor family role and the tendency of both parents to be guided by tradition. This is indicated by the significantly greater tendency on the part of the island mothers, when compared with continental mothers, consciously to attempt to pattern their child-training practices and values after those traditionally held by their own parents.

The children in all three groups manifested relatively mild reactions to weaning, upper-middle mainland children the mildest of all. Puerto Rican rural lower-class children cried slightly more than the mainland children as infants and stopped wetting their beds much sooner than the latter, significantly so when compared with upper-middle class children, though the medians for all groups are about three years. However their reactions to bowel training were much more severe than either of the other groups, falling just short of significance.

The island children display somewhat less aggression than either continental group against siblings or against parents. And they display fewer outward signs of having feelings hurt by punishment, tending more toward covering their feelings and making a show of "better" behavior. On the other hand, as might be expected, we find proportionately more aggression in doll play than the continental children though the differences are not significant. But for aggressive fantasy acts they use doll agents as a whole significantly less and themselves directly as agents significantly more. Perhaps here the Vallecañese children, who are more heavily punished, wish to vent their aggressive acts in doll play, but finding the use of parental agents even in this symbolic way too fraught with punitive possibilities, prefer to utilize themselves or occasionally supernatural or natural agents like the Puerto Rican bogey-man or the wind.

Both as infants and as larger children Vallecañese youngsters tend to demand somewhat more attention than continentals, especially with respect to the upper-lower class. They also tend at both stages to cling to their mothers significantly more, again the differences being greater between themselves and the upper-lower children. The degree of sociability of the three groups is about the same, yet the island children display significantly stronger objections to even brief separations from the mother. In general they fall just short of statistical reliability in being more dependent than the mainland children.

The interview measures of the identification of the child with parents yielded unclear results for island and continental children, which may be an indication that this age is too young in which to expect a clear identification syndrome. In fact this is just what psycho-analytic theory would lead us to expect, since identification cannot be consummated until the Oedipal conflicts have been resolved. In seeking possible measures of identification in doll play, we found more use of the father as agent, slightly less use of the mother doll, significantly less use of the children dolls, and a definite (just below significance at .05) use of the baby doll. On the other hand, as in aggression (though not significantly), the Puerto Rican youngsters tend to use the self as agent more. We have earlier offered a suggestion that the island children, to the extent that they do identify, may imitate the father most, then the mother, boy, baby, and girl. The bottom position of the girl may be explained by the inferior status of the female. On the other hand, a somewhat more equated use of all dolls by mainland children may indicate a more equal or equalitarian status for different age and sex groups. They may tend to imitate real people more while the island children may shun such emulation since it is actually discouraged and children who do so are considered "ill-bred."

Insofar as superego development may be an index of identification —or perhaps more accurately, vice-versa—we find significantly fewer guilt reactions and lower superego in Valle Caña children, especially by comparison with the upper-middle class in the mainland community.

CHAPTER 12

Culture, Childhood, and Acculturation

W E HAVE been concerned with some of the cultural determinants of behavior in a rural Puerto Rican community and the ways in which the culture is passed on to new generations, the primary cultural process. We have journeyed through a brief ethnographic sketch of culture and social structure in the village of Valle Caña, paying especial attention to the major cultural agency of socialization, the family, and the modes and means by which its members attempt to inculcate socially desirable behaviors and values in the child. These antecedents and consequents of the primary cultural process in this Hispanicized West Indian village have been compared with similar behaviors and values in two class groups in a New England community. In this final chapter we wish to bring out some possible inter-relationships between the elements of socialization and the culture of the village and to speculate on the probable impact upon the process under the current conditions of acculturation and industrialization.

Vallecañese child training is governed to a large extent by traditional values and practices, but in the present period of rapid cultural transitions and urgent demographic and economic pressures, there is some deviance from tradition and uncertainty about which courses to follow. It is not a coincidence that Vallecañese mothers are significantly higher in child-rearing anxiety than their New England contemporaries, in spite of their tendency to blame behavior problems on the child's biological heredity and their complacent satisfaction with their own roles as mothers and wives. Their bonds with tradition have been loosened but they do not as yet have another anchorage in the many sources of new information available to continental mothers (though these are more available to Puerto Ricans of greater means, particularly in the cities).

The procedures seen in this study as underlying the socialization process in Valle Caña seem to provide a weak foundation upon which the child can erect his ego structure. We have seen how the keystone of the child's ego—the mechanisms for building and maintaining his independence, self-assurance, and ultimate emancipation from dependence on parental nurturance and control—is incompletely developed, especially in the case of the boy. Patterns of training and indoctrination which sustained the kind of ego that could adjust satisfactorily in the "stable" era of Spanish hegemony may not be sufficient to cope with present-day pressures, tensions, and insecurities. In Valle Caña, for example, a quasi-feudal relationship is maintained between worker and landowner, but the latter has relinquished most responsibilities of the *hacendado* role. Responsibility for the welfare of the caneworker falls no longer primarily on the landowner's shoulders but on those of the government, which is neither wealthy nor powerful enough as yet to fulfill the broad requirements of its proclaimed role as a welfare state (see the Puerto Rican Commonwealth Constitution, *Annals:* 1953).

Nevertheless, *responsibilidad* is a much sought commodity in Vallecañese males by the parents of prospective brides. Indeed its rarity makes it the more deeply desired. But it is difficult to root out practices which, as the reader has discovered, are indoctrinated and nourished in childhood. It is the Puerto Rican girl whose socialization leads toward a greater sense of responsibility for others. It is the Puerto Rican boy whose socialization leads away from a sense of responsibility. As our earlier descriptions of Vallecañese married life have shown, male social irresponsibility often coexists with female responsibility, not only for her siblings and parents but ultimately for her children and her husband. Cloistering of the Vallecañese female insures more than a subservient woman; it makes certain that, given the carefree wandering and loose-spending of the man, at least his wife will remain at home to impart continuity and relative stability to the family group.[1] In this sense what appears at first to be a dysfunctional practice

---

1. This emphasizes our use of the concept of "opinion-directed" to describe the orientation of Vallecañese values and behavior in preference to "other-directed" as it is used by Riesman (1950). Both male and female cast their actions within the frame of reference of "what others will think"; but what others will think differs for each sex. The female is directed toward helping relevant others, the male toward helping mainly himself. The former acts from herself outward toward others, the latter acts from the

may, given the present shape of Vallecañese society, be "functional" indeed.

Sharp sexual segregation and the imbalance of privileges in favor of the male child and adult are closely related in the family to the ambivalence which so often seems to characterize the effective ties between marriage partners. To the husband the wife is the symbol of his unwanted burdens as a married man and the formal (though not always effective) block to his accustomed male freedom. To the wife the husband is the symbol of her unwanted burdens as a married woman. Far beyond her normal desire for children and a home, she has been made by Vallecañese society to bear the brunt of the labors and troubles which seem essential to the maintenance of the family unit. Her husband may behave socially and sexually with almost as much freedom as he had as a bachelor, while her own freedom, restricted from the time she is a child in every aspect of her coming of age, often becomes even more narrowly limited. Ambivalence of marriage mates is further increased by the very strong ties which the husband often maintains with his mother and his family of orientation. It is the man-child who in the earliest days of socialization is the object of the strongest family sentiments, whether affectional or hostile. It is the woman-child around whom strong affective behaviors are minimal.

An ever-recurrent theme in Vallecañese socialization is dependency, which begins at birth and is nurtured and enhanced deliberately by adults toward children and especially by women toward boys and men and which seems to continue to mark Vallecañese behavior throughout life. It is further encouraged by the objective conditions of life in Valle Caña—the lack of economic opportunities, the sharp class distinctions with disesteeming of the lower-class male, the prolongation of the weighting of privileges in favor of the male but the allocating of responsibility to the female. Since the latter frequently takes up the social slack in the family structure left by the inattention and minimal participation of the male, the dependency which began in infancy is supported through the prime of life. It would be interesting for political scientists and historians to test the hypothesis that such cul-

---

viewpoint of others toward himself. Both are in a sense other-directed, but from different points of view, and with different objectives. What others will think, however, directs the differentially aimed activity of either. What others do, which is the basis for the conforming behavior of other-directed societies, is of less importance than the opinion others have of what one does.

tural fostering of dependency has historic roots in the first instance in the traditional subordinate position of the Puerto Rican worker and peasant and in the second instance, perhaps, in the island's dependent status for over four and a half centuries as a colony of Spain and a territory of the United States.

One effect of the urgent need of the Vallecañese male to depend upon the support of others, combined with the rigidly divided life-spheres of male and female, is that the male is impelled by tradition and conditioned by child training to seek only the company of other males —except for almost purely sexual relationships. The male spends most of his life in the company of other males, but since each is dependent in his own way, and few have learned during early socialization to cater to the dependent needs of others, hardly any one is able to fulfill the dependency requirements of any other one. The more he seeks a close relationship with other males, the less the young man is apt to find it. When relationships are established they are brittle and easily frag-mented. Thus the male's poignant desires find little permanent grati-fication, and repeated short-lived relationships lead to a distrust of others. At the same time, however, he longs for nothing so much as to be able to trust the relationships of other men. And so he looks con-tinually for trust, or *confianza*, relationships. But he looks within a lonely crowd in which *confianza* relationships are rare because while demand is great, supply is short.

As he grows into adulthood the male becomes a carefree though gentle sort. He early has been taught to suppress his feelings of aggres-sion toward others, especially outside the family, though he may vent them with some impunity within the family. As a boy he had certain minimal responsibilities, but while the cost of growing up has been dear, the rewards seem to make it worthwhile. For he has the freedom which comes with occupancy of the privileged sanctuary of adult male. But the stresses upon him to comply with socially acceptable values do not extend to a deep sense of either personal or social obliga-tion. The pillars of his superego, on which little work was done in childhood, have been built on sand and easily crumble when the inner wind, which Western Europeans and Americans call conscience, whispers the needs of community, church, or family. He has learned in his growing up that to achieve full Vallecañese status he must first of all embellish his *machismo* with acts of maleness. Many of his actions can be understood within the framework of his struggle against the external cultural compulsives to increase the trappings of *machismo* and appear strong, virile, and self-sufficient, even as he is pushed from within to gratify his cravings for a strong figure with which to identify and to whom he may attach his dependency needs.

This loosely structured superego is the key to many facets of Vallecañese socialization and culture. It is both antecedent and consequent of the unrequited search for *confianza*, for *responsibilidad*, for security. It is related to the tenuous sense of community and of familism (not withstanding ubiquitous nepotism in economics and politics, a practical function of familism which will probably yield before the universalistic requirements of the future industrial society) and to unfulfilled dependency and identification needs. It fails to act as censor of the weakly supported ego and receives little reinforcement from community or church, nor from the opinion-directed values of Vallecañese society.

The process of bringing up children and of being brought up in this village is marked by many inconsistencies, or what Benedict and others have termed "discontinuities," and it is difficult, often impossible, to trace consistent and direct relationships between all of the antecedents and consequents of socialization covered herein. One by-product of the study is the finding that in spite of such inconsistencies —perhaps because of them—we find uniformities in the behavior of the child. Thus, for example, we find that weaning and toilet training, so crucial in psychoanalytic theory to character formation, are not consistently patterned, even within the small, relatively representative, and homogeneous sample we have used. Some mothers cluster in one half of the weaning and sphincter control scales, some in the other. It would take a good deal of license and data-nudging to describe Vallecañese behavior—adult or child—as "anal" or "oral." Vallecañeses do not care about the presence of excreta, but they worry over personal cleanliness and neatness. Vallecañeses are concerned about food, but this is because it is so scarce. Vallecañeses are loose-spenders and unthrifty by continental standards, but a mother will hoard her children's clothes and playthings (these, too, are scarce!).

There are other discontinuities that we have noted: high demands and many threats of punishment but inconsistent administration of punishment; high sexual anxiety but the boy's genitals are exposed and played with; demands that the child remain around home and threats of what may happen to him in a hostile world but ridicule of the child's social timidity and withdrawal. But there are many uniformities or generally pervasive characteristics in the behavior of youngsters: high dependency, low guilt feelings, low superego, shyness, low interpersonal aggression, and much displaced aggression.

We have seen some of the relationships and lack of relationships within Vallecañese socialization and between it and that of upper-lower and upper-middle class families in New England. This absence of a one-to-one correspondence between specific antecedents and specific consequents should not be surprising, however. There is no doubt that with systematic, quantifiable data such relationships or lack of them will appear in the socialization procedures of any society, as the Laboratory of Human Development at Harvard University has found, even though utilizing much larger numbers of parents and children. In this study some such associations or nonassociations are of course due in part to the size of the sample. Some are probably inherent in the socialization process itself. Some may be linked to the fact that these very inconsistencies may result in a certain patterning of behavior for the child, negative and confused though it may be. Thus, though punishment is often threatened, the child is uncertain as to where, when, or for what it will be carried out and so conforms with a general practice of "getting away" with whatever he can.

It is highly dubious that any culture will be so tightly integrated that some inconsistencies do not occur in cultural transmission. And it is arguable whether such "perfect" integration, even if it were possible, would be desirable. Person, culture, society, and "natural" environment are open systems transacting with each other. It has been shown (Bertalanffy 1950) that disequilibrium rather than equilibrium is the precondition for the life and growth of open systems. Within the framework of open system transactional theory, equilibrium is equivalent to stagnation. The very uncertainties and anxieties attendant on Vallecañese socialization are reflections not alone of traditional cultural-personal tensions but also of the changes taking place within and without the society.

This is not to say that these changes are "necessary" or "adaptive." Some are probably unadaptive, though the conditions which gave rise to them may not have been. Heavy and constant cultural pressures for the male to demonstrate his masculinity with sexual and social conquest would not be unadaptive in a situation which provided opportunities for fulfilling the *macho* role, but under current conditions of

Vallecañese life, at least for the lower class, they certainly seem un-adaptive. It is obvious that either opportunities or substitutes must be provided or values regarding masculinity must be changed. On the other hand, changes now occurring in the direction of a "small family mentality" will be highly adaptive if they can in fact materialize with a concurrent change in values regarding sex, reproduction, and, inci-dentally, *machismo*.

One should not, of course, expect simple relationships in a complex process like socialization. Perhaps future researchers would be well advised to utilize a technique like factor analysis in the search for re-liable components of antecedent-consequent associations. But the simple relationships which have been uncovered here and in related studies are preliminary steps in the search for the discovery and testing of more complex and perhaps more meaningful hypotheses (Nowlis 1952).

It is presumptuous to label this complex, ongoing process, but we might call Vallecañese training more restrictive than permissive but also more casual than premeditated, provided the reader will accept the notion that both sets of conditions attend the process of cultural transmission in all cultures. However, perhaps more crucial than simply the extent of restriction or permission is the nature of the con-stellation of values and practices which comprise child rearing. A re-striction may be less damaging to the child's body and psyche than a permission if the child understands the rationale behind it and can rest secure in the knowledge that the conditions for its presence or absence are clear and inevitable.

Baldwin (1949) has shown that indulgence may be less conducive to spontaneous behavior than warmth of feelings toward the child. For a child to behave spontaneously—notably infrequent among Valle-cañese children—there must be routinized and mutually understood patterns of social interaction between parents and children and be-tween the latter and others. As we noted, the ratio of interactive to noninteractive acts in doll play was about two to three, and this is a reflection of the kind of noninteractive social environment for the child which in earlier chapters was described in the Vallecañese home. Baldwin (1948:135) in another study sums up the point well:

These findings suggest that the predominant effect of parental behavior upon the socialization of the preschool child is to raise or lower his will-ingness and ability to behave actively toward his environment. Freedom and permissiveness in the home, by not punishing his active explorations and his aggressive reactions to frustrations, permit the child to become active, outgoing and spontaneous. Freedom alone, however, does not actively encourage the development of spontaneity; a high level of interaction between the parent and child is required to push the child into activity, particularly of the interpersonal variety. The child's expressiveness must be elicited by the parent's spontaneous expression of warmth and emotionality, and the child's attempts to establish emotional contacts with other people must be greeted with warmth and reciprocation, if he is to develop the pattern of habitual expressiveness.

Unfortunately the present study did not take enough account of variables relating to emotionality and love. By love is meant more than affectional attachment as we have used it, though that is certainly part of it. It means the kind of attachment in which, for example, the mother does things with and for the child because of her feelings of affection, nurturance, protection, and responsiveness rather than because of a conscious acting-out of a mother role as it is prescribed for her, either by old people or current practices. It is not an easy term to define. But aspects of it have become increasingly of interest to social scientists. Perhaps as we succeed in placing boundaries of knowledge and ignorance around the currently popular variables like aggression, dependency, and sex, increased attention will be paid to the more positive and possibly more integrative factors.

There are other ways, too, in which this study falls short of completing the picture of Vallecañese socialization. To the extent that we have failed to obtain or use data on the impact of internal and external social and cultural pressures on the process, the study is not complete. We would like to know more systematically of the extent of malnutrition, how Puerto Rico compares nutritionally with other societies, and what effects this has directly or indirectly on rearing and growing in a village like Valle Caña. Studies can and should be designed to obtain more systematic, scalable data on the consequences of rigid sex differentiation and anxiety, of subordinate class status, of the insecurity of living in a small cabin on land which by a whim or need of the landowner may suddenly be claimed. (This happened to one family while we were in Valle Caña and the cabin had to be dismantled, transported, and set up again in another location, by hand labor.) How do children come to moral decisions regarding actual, as opposed to hypothetical, choices (as on some tests)? What is the self-image of the child and adult and, in Hallowell's (1954) terms, how does the society teach self-awareness to the child? What are the relationships between the self as culturally conceived, as personally perceived, and various behaviors of the child?

Some of these we have touched upon, but the need for broader and deeper knowledge is apparent. The hypotheses suggested herein should be tested in comparable Puerto Rican communities as well as cross-culturally, with larger samples so that more sensitive statistical techniques may be employed.

Two other limitations of the study must be stressed. (1) We are under no illusions that we have delineated the total process of cultural transmission in Valle Caña. Insufficient data have been collected concerning those parts of the process which are not deliberately inculcated by parents and other cultural surrogates but which the individual learns through imitation and role-modeling of others, particularly, as he increases in age, of his peers and of the practices and values of their groups. Nor have we had the time sufficiently to explore other media of cultural transmission: schoolbooks, traditional poems, plays and folklore (except our minor analysis of songs sung to infants in Chapter 6). (2) It is likely that some of the differences between Vallecañeses and New Englanders are due to conditions which characterize rural as opposed to urban life, rather than differences characteristic of particular cultures or social classes.

We have shown that along some dimensions, for example, sexual values and practices, aggression training, and sphincter control, Vallecañese mothers are more anxious and restrictive than either upper-lower or upper-middle class New England parents. On others, like restrictions on eating behavior, they seem closer to the upper-middle class mothers. And in still others, like trying to pattern their training after their mothers' ways, they are closer to the upper-lower class mothers.

Thus any attempt to place Vallecañese mothers in perspective with continental mothers would have to reckon with such class similarities and differences. Vallecañese mothers are not just more or less permissive than mainland mothers, but more or less so with respect to the particular area of behavior and the class position of the mainland mothers, among other factors. All of the differences in our comparison may be "cultural" if we consider each class group as a separate culture or subculture. But assuredly there are certain possible uniformities of class position, like attitudes toward educational achievement, which cut across cultural and national borders. As Inkeles (1953) has suggested, the search for class or subclass (e.g., occupational) uniformities has barely begun. Naturally what we have said applies to measures of child behavior also.

Much has been written about the present-time orientation of Puerto Ricans and other Hispanic peoples. The *mañana* values of Vallecañeses are reflected in their reliance on the smiles of Fate, in their almost fatalistic acceptance of life as it comes, in their minimal aspirations. In socialization this outlook is not only transmitted through example by the indifference with which Vallecañeses view danger, or ill luck, but it can be seen in the modest achievement demands which Vallecañese mothers and fathers make upon their children. It may also be perceived in the comparative inability of the adult Vallecañese to postpone gratifications in terms of anticipated future rewards. As the child is not asked to endure contemporary discomforts in order to achieve future rewards of money and prestige, so the father spends his meagre earnings almost as fast as they come in. In part there is the "reality factor" of immediate and pressing need. But even for the relatively better-off lower-class families in Valle Caña, savings are almost unknown and many middle-class families share this impatience with the future. Still, as Maccoby and Fielder (1953) have found, this outlook is being changed on the island as the middle class, especially, becomes more acculturated to the values of middle-class mainland Americans.

Poverty and a present-time orientation seem to this observer to reinforce each other. We have shown that by objective standards as well as their self-perception ("We are *los pobres*"), the people are poor. If in addition they feel that there are few chances for social and economic mobility, then it can be understood why so few achievement standards (as they are structured, at least, in middle-class United States society) are accepted or enforced by Vallecañese parents. There are certain outlets for a few who migrate to the city or even to the continent. But since, with scant formal education, one can save less than a hundred dollars and make the fantastic jump from Valle Caña to New York or to San Juan for considerably less, then incentives for achievement are likely to remain minimal. However, the influences from the mainland are taking a stronger hold each year on the child and adult, encouraged by the Puerto Rican government itself. Slowly the values and practices associated with education are changing, not only in Valle Caña and San Juan, but in the Puerto Rican enclaves in the United States as well (see Annual Report of the Commissioner of Education 1951-1952). Furthermore the stepped-up "Operation Bootstrap" by which the government and quasi-government agencies are encouraging industrialization on the island (see, e.g., Johansson 1956; Annals 1953; Perloff 1950; Hansen 1955) has already begun to change the values of Vallecañeses, though at the time of the study the effects of these acculturative influences from city and continent were emergent rather than full-blown.

As these changes come, certain probabilities may be hypothesized. We have seen how the seeds for the relatively well-integrated ego of the female and the relatively poorly-integrated ego of the male are laid in the soil of childhood and fertilized with the values of traditional Vallecañese culture, as well as the lack of social and economic opportunities. The new industries seem to be requiring the labor of the female as much as or more than that of the male. One may envision not only further debilitation of the male ego but likewise further strengthening of the woman's, with some probably drastic alterations in the shape of Vallecañese culture. It seems likely that the male-dominated visage of Vallecañese life may change to one in which the woman is given greater equality, perhaps even dominance, unless opportunities for males begin to overtake and surpass those of females.

Acculturation changes plus male dominance plus paucity of opportunity have made for relative disorganization of traditional family structure. However, it should be clear here that by "disorganization" we imply nothing invidious about the present state of the family. We mean simply that deep fissures are taking place in the family organization but that these herald not necessarily "disintegration" of the family as a social unity but probably the breakup of old patterns and the substitution of new ones. It is entirely possible that as the male loses status he will come to accept a more equal status for the female, and eventually the Vallecañese family may be more "integrated" than ever. We have already seen a striking example in the decrease of consensual marriage and the substitution of the civil ceremony not only in Valle Caña but throughout the island. This frequently is done at the insistence of the woman, or her family, and thus the legal basis of the family may in the future lend it increased stability.

Apparent already are other changes in the family outlook of Vallecañeses. Both this study and that of Stycos (1955) have shown how Puerto Ricans in all sections of the island are beginning to take on a "small-family mentality." Their desire for small families is not yet matched by their ardor in taking measures to control family size. But as family size decreases, we can expect corresponding and reverberating modifications throughout the family system. For example, the now diffused complex of emotions which attend the socialization of the child will probably become refocussed, as it has in smaller nuclear families in the United States, producing more intense emotional ties within a more limited range of cathectable objects. The very existence of the ego-destructive preschool security gap, by which the child is cast unceremoniously out of the warm circle of parental love to make way for the upcoming younger sibling, will probably be lessened as fewer children are born on which to focus affection as well as care.

The anxieties which attend child training in the areas of toileting, cleanliness, and sex may also undergo changes as the lower-class Vallecañese family approaches a way of life that, while still a uniquely Puerto Rican synthesis, approximates the configuration of the middle-class continental family. Related as well to these intertwined areas of socialization and behavior will be the probably enhanced status of the woman and the ideas surrounding her position and roles.

These hypothesized cultural and psychological modifications in Vallecañese culture, family, and childhood are not necessarily inevitable. In any case, they would not obviate, without substantial economic change, the keen desires felt by Vallecañeses, who are not only faced with traditional problems of economic deprivation but are beginning to feel the waves of acculturation and urbanization approaching their community. Their living standards are still low, and the pangs are made sharper as knowledge of the better material life of continental America comes to them, through formal media, from the lips of their children (who are even more directly affected through the educational system), and from friends and relatives who move to the mainland.

Puerto Rico is in the midst of an island-wide transformation, as one recent observer (Hansen 1955) has phrased it. For present and future more systematic knowledge of cultural transmission is crucial. Changes brought about from without or within, above or below, will succeed to the extent that they are consonant with the practices, values, and needs of the parents and children of this Caribbean island.

APPENDIX A

Census and Community Questionnaire[1]

1. Wife _____ Age _____
2. Husband _____ Age _____
3. Address, if any _____
4. Place of origin _____
5. Other places lived _____
6. Other adults in household (Include relationship) _____
   _____
   _____

7. Children (Include living, dead, stillbirths, abortions, others; if dead, give cause of death) _____

Name	Sex	Age	Paternity

8. Godparents _____

EDUCATION

(If literate, but no formal education, state. State if past or present. State for each if school is public, private, parochial. State grades completed.)

9. Mother _____
   _____
   _____

1. The mother and father interviews as well as all other techniques were of course translated and administered in Spanish and pretested on several families not included in our sample.

10. Father _____

_____

_____

11. Children _____

_____

_____

OCCUPATION

12. Wife, in addition to domestic duties _____

13. Husband _____

14. Children, for income only (State which ones work and at what occupation) _____

15. Has husband or wife worked at any other occupation? If so, when, where and for how long? _____

_____

16. Why were changes made in occupation? _____

_____

INCOME

17. Husband _____

18. Wife _____

19. Other _____

20. Total _____

EXPENDITURES

21. a. Rent   _____

b. Food   _____

c. Clothing   _____

d. Fuel   _____

e. Medical—doctors, *practicantes,* midwives, drugstores. _____

f. Education   _____

g. Religion   _____

h. Amusements   _____

i. Total   _____

ECONOMICS

22. Does anyone in the household own real property or land? (List proprietors and properties) _____

_____

_____

23. If not, did anyone ever own land or property? _____
    a. How acquired? (Past and present) _____

    b. How sold or otherwise disposed? (If lost state reason) _____

24. Do you own or rent this house? _____
25. Do you own livestock? _____
26. Do you own occupational equipment? _____

CONDITIONS OF HOUSEHOLD

27. Size of house (no. of rooms). Space around house. _____

28. Condition _____

29. Facilities (light, water, fuel, furniture (approx.), stove (kind), refrigerator (kind), other. If water carried, how far? How often?

30. Number of persons in each room, each bed—list. _____

MARRIAGE

31. Kind of marriage (civil, religious, consensual; if religious, state which) _____
32. Date of present marriage. Age at marriage of each. _____

33. Former marriages of husband and wife. Reasons for separation or divorce. _____

34. Cost of present marriage. _____
35. Courtship; how long? How did wife and husband meet? _____

36. If you had not married what do you think you might be doing now? _____

    (NOTE TO THE INTERVIEWER: If informant wants to volunteer more intimate marriage details, allow him or her to speak freely but without direct questioning. Note remarks as accurately and in as much detail as possible.)

RELIGION

37. Kind: Catholic, Protestant (state sect), Spiritist, other. (If Spiritist, name group or movement, if any. If household has mixed affiliations state each.) _____

38. Who in family attends services? How often? Which holidays? _____

39. Have your children been baptized? Which? Cost of each. ____ _____

40. Has church ever aided family? Explain. _____

41. Does priest or minister visit house? How often? Which occasions? _____

42. Has anyone here changed their religion? Who? When? Why? From what to what? _____ _____

MISCELLANEOUS

43. List *compadres* and *comadres* for husband and wife, other than baptismal co-parents. List also form of *compadrazgo*.
_____
_____
_____
_____
_____

(NOTE TO INTERVIEWER: Include in this space any information about this informant you feel is important which has not been included above.)

APPENDIX B

Mother Interview

1. Number children in family, sex, age. (If there are *hijos de crianza,* indicate)

   a. (If more than one child) In this interview we want to talk mostly about X,[1] since he's in the group we are working with.

2. Has X been with you all his life, or have you been separated from him at any time?

   a. (If separated) For how long? How old was he then?

3. And how about his father—has X been separated from his father at any time?

   a. (If separated) For how long? How old was X then?

4. Think back to the time when X was a baby. Who took most care of him then?

   a. How much did your husband do in taking care of X when he was a baby?

   b. Did he ever change the baby's bedclothes? Feed him? Give him his bath?

5. All babies cry, of course. Some mothers feel that if you pick up a baby every time it cries, you will spoil it. Others think you should never let a baby cry for very long. How do you feel about this?

   a. What did you do about this with X?

   b. And during the night?

6. Did you have time to be with the baby besides the time that was necessary for giving him his care? (If yes) Tell me what you did

1. X indicates child in survey group.

259

in this time? How much did you cuddle him and sing to him and things like that?

7. Do you think that you enjoy caring more for babies when they are very young, or do you find it more interesting when they are larger?

8. Tell me about his feeding when he was a baby.

    a. Did you give him the breast?

    b. (If not) Why did you decide to give him the bottle?

    c. (If yes) For how long?

    d. (If yes) And on taking away the breast, did you pass directly to a cup or a bottle?

    e. When did you begin this?

    f. How did you decide that it was time to begin this?

    g. How did you do it?

    h. How did the baby react when you stopped the bottle (or breast)?

    i. Had you been giving him liquid in a cup before?

    j. How long did it take for him to give up the bottle (breast) completely?

9. Some people say that it is better to have a regular time to feed the baby. Others say that it is better to feed them when they are hungry. What do you think about this? Why do you think so?

    a. What did you do with X?

    b. (If have hour regulated) Up to what point did you have a certain time for feeding the baby?

    c. What foods did you give X when he was a baby?

10. Have you had any problem with X as to eating sufficiently or eating the kinds of foods that he needs?

    a. What do you do about this?

11. Does X eat with the rest of the family during meals? If not, where?

12. What do you expect of X in the way of behavior while eating?

    a. Do you expect him to keep his place during the meal or do you permit him to leave his place?

    b. Is he permitted to use his fingers?

c. Do you permit him to interrupt the conversation of adults?

d. What else do you think can be expected of a child of X's years in regard to eating behavior?

13. What have you done to teach him his eating behavior?

14. What do you do about it if he does some of the things you do not allow?

15. Let us suppose that for several days he eats very well and does not give you trouble. What would you do?

16. Let's talk now about how you taught X to do his necessities.

a. When did you begin to teach him?

b. How did it go?

c. How did you teach him?

d. How long did it take until he learned well enough (pretty well)?

e. What did you do if he forgot after he had learned well enough (pretty well)?

17. Would you tell what you have done when he wet the bed or the *coy*?

a. What is his reaction when he wets the bed?

b. What do you do when you find that he has wet the bed? (Or what did you do the last time it happened?)

18. What is your attitude about letting X go around here without clothes?

a. (If opposed) What did you do to teach X about this?

b. When did you begin to teach him about this?

c. (If it has not been mentioned) And using clothes outside?

19. What have you done when you have noticed him playing with himself?

a. How much importance do you believe should be attached to prohibiting this in a child?

b. Why do you think so?

20. And this kind of play with other children, has it occurred yet?

a. What happened and what did you do about it?

b. And the children who want to see each other, or who "do their necessities" together, or who hide when they play—what do you think when you notice this kind of thing happening among the children?

   c. (If never noticed it) Would you permit this or would you intervene?

21. What do you expect of X with regard to keeping himself neat and clean?

   a. What do you do in order that he will do this?

22. How much importance do you attach to his caring for and not abusing the furniture and other things of the house?

   a. What do you do if he does these things?

   b. Do you teach the children to respect the things that belong to other members of the family? What do you do about this with X?

23. We would like to have an idea of the ways of behaving himself that you prefer for X in general—that is, the kinds of things that he is permitted to do, and the kinds of things that he is not permitted to do. What are some of these ways of behaving?

   a. And the time for going to bed?

   b. And in regard to making noise in the house—up to what point do you permit this?

   c. Up to what distance from the house is he permitted to go alone?

   d. Some other ways of behaving?

24. Do you think a child of X's age ought to be given some jobs to do around the house regularly?

   a. Does X have any regular jobs that he is supposed to do?

   b. (If yes) What do you do to get him to do this?

25. How much do you have to keep after X to get him to do the things he is supposed to do, like tasks around the house, or complying with his ways of behavior, or any other thing that you believe he ought to do?

26. Some parents expect that their children should immediately obey them when they tell them to be quiet, to pick up something, and things like that. Others do not feel that it is very important that the child obey at once. How do you feel about this?

   a. What does your husband think about strict obedience?

27. If you ask X to do something and he does it right away, what is your reaction? (Do you say anything to him?)

28. If he does not do what you ask, do you simply forget the matter, or do you always see that he does it?

29. Do you always concern yourself with where X is and what he is doing most of the time, or can you let him take care of himself very often?

    a. How frequently do you check?

30. How much attention does it seem to you that X wants on your part?

    a. And what about following you around and holding on to your skirt?

    b. (If not much) Did he ever pass through a stage of doing this?

    c. What do you think (did you think) of this when he hangs on to your dress and follows you around?

    d. Generally, how do you react when he demands your attention (or that you do something) when you are busy?

    e. And if X asks your help in something that you think he could probably do by himself?

31. How does X react generally when you leave the house and have to leave him with another person?

32. Have you ever felt that X was growing up too fast in any way?

    a. On his starting to go to school, how did it affect you?

    b. (If in school) Have things been easier and pleasanter for you in any way since he has been in school?

33. What kind of things do you enjoy in X?

    a. In what ways do you bother each other?

    b. Do you show your affection toward one another often, or not?

    c. Do you find time to play with X solely for your own pleasure?

34. Did you teach him anything, like reading words, or writing the alphabet, or drawing, or telling time—and things like that?

    a. What other things have you taught him?

    b. How was it that you came to teach these things to him?

35. How much importance does it have for you that X do well in school?

a. Up to where would you like that he go in school?

36. Now we want to talk about whether you believe that there is a difference in bringing up boys and bringing up girls. How much importance does it have for you that a boy of X's age act like a real boy (that a girl act like a real girl)?

    a. (For boys) And if he plays with dolls and things like that?

    b. (For girls) And what about playing rough games and things like that?

    c. Do you think that there are some differences in the way in which boys and girls of X's age ought to act?

    d. What have you taught him (her) in regard to how you want him (her) to act with little girls (boys)?

37. (If X has siblings) Tell me something about how X gets along with his siblings.

    a. What do you think when they fight, that is, when they quarrel but not up to the point of hitting each other?

    b. Up to what point do you permit this kind of quarrel to reach before you intervene?

    c. What do you do when the children quarrel? Give me an example.

    d. Now, and when things go well between the children, do you do anything to indicate that you have noticed it?

    e. (If yes) What is it that you do?

38. In general terms, how does X get along with the neighborhood children?

39. Have you ever encouraged him to go out and play with other children instead of playing alone?

    a. (If yes) Tell me about this—how did the subject arise?

    b. And what about other children coming to play here?

    c. Does he (she) play mostly with boys or girls? What do you think about this?

40. And when X is playing with one of the children of the neighborhood and there is a quarrel or fight—what do you do?

41. Some persons believe that it is very important that a child not learn to fight with other children, other people think that there are times when the child must learn to fight. What do you believe about this?

a. Have you ever encouraged X to defend himself (herself) when they fight with him (her)?

42. Sometimes a child will get angry with his parents and hit them or kick them or shout angry things at them. How much of this do you think parents ought to permit in a child of X's age?

a. What do you do when X acts this way? Give me an example.

b. (If it has not happened) How did you teach your child not to do this?

43. What is it that you do when X is naughty or disobeys you deliberately?

44. We should like to have some idea of how X acts when he does bad things. When he does something deliberately that he knows that you do not want him to do when you are not looking, how does X act?

a. Does X come and tell you about it without your having to ask him?

b. When you ask him about something that he has done that he knows he ought not to do, in general, does he admit it or deny it?

c. What do you do if he denies something that you are pretty sure that he has done?

We have been talking about what you have done with X in various different situations, such as cleanliness, eating manners, and things like that. Now we would like to know what you do when you want to correct X and want him to behave as you wish, regardless of the kind of behavior it might be.

45. Do you have any system of rewarding him for good behavior?

a. Do you have some ways in which he could earn money and other things?

46. Some parents praise their children often when they are good, and others believe that one ought to take their good behavior for granted and it is not worthwhile to praise a child for this. What do you think about this?

47. In training X, do you mention other persons as examples or models?

a. For example, "Your mother and father do it like this." Do you say this? Under what circumstances?

b. Whom else do you put up as examples—his older brother (sister), grandparents? other relatives? playmates? godparents?

c. Is there anyone you mention as an example of what he ought not to do? For example—"You are acting like so and so—you would not want to be like him, would you?"

48. How often do you spank him? For what reasons?

a. And your husband—how often does he spank X?

b. For example, how often has X been spanked in the last two weeks?

49. When he was young—say two or three years, how often did you spank him then?

50. How does he act when you spank him—does it hurt his feelings, or make him angry, or what?

51. How much good do you think it does to spank X?

52. How many times do you deprive X of something that he wants as a form of discipline?

53. Now imagine that you are scolding X for something that he has done that you do not want him to do. What would you say?

a. What other thing would you say?

b. Do you warn him what could happen if he does not behave well? (If yes) What kind of warning?

c. Here is a list of certain things which a mother might say sometimes to her children when they do something she does not like. Of course, there are some things they say more often than others. Which of these do you say to your child often? Which do you say once in a while? We do not have the exact words you would use, but select the closest one to what you would say. Each is checked as "never," "sometimes," or "often.")

1. That was not a very smart thing to do.
2. Are you not ashamed of yourself for acting like that?
3. You are acting like a baby.
4. Mama will think you do not love her if you do those things.
5. You are hurting *mami*'s feelings. (You are going to make mamí cry.)
6. I am not going to talk (or listen to you) until you can behave well.
7. Go away—I don't want to see you until you smile (be good).
8. I am going to tell this to your papa when he arrives.
9. What would your father think if he saw you acting like that?

10. You are not my child, surely. A child of mine would not act like that.
11. Mama does not like children who act like that.
12. The other children will not play with you if you do not treat them well.
13. Other people will not like you if you behave like that.
14. The *cuco* will get you if you don't stop that.
15. The policeman will come to catch you (will put you in jail).
16. I am going to have to send you to another place if you keep on acting like that.

54. Is there any other kind of remark you make to X often? List.

55. How often do you tell X that you are going to punish him and then for one reason or another don't do it?

    a. What kinds of things would keep you from punishing him?

56. Let us talk now of X and his father. Would you tell me something of how they act with each other?

    a. For example, when your husband comes home from work and X is there, what happens?

    b. And after dinner?

    c. What other kinds of things do they do together?

57. How many things does your husband do on those days when he helps you to take care of X? What kinds of things does he do?

    a. How much does he help in dressing him?

    b. Does he remain with the child some time when you go out?

58. What do you think is the attitude of your husband toward the child?

    a. Does he often demonstrate his affection (hugging and kissing and things like that) or is he somewhat reserved with him?

59. When X has to be disciplined, who does it, you or your husband (assuming that you are both together)?

    a. How strict is your husband with X?

    b. Does your husband discipline in any way that you would prefer he did not do?

60. In general terms, how well would you say that you and your husband agree as to the best way to treat X?

    a. Could you give me an example of some case in which you were not in complete agreement?

61. In some families the parents think that the raising of the children is principally the occupation of the mother and leave all decisions regarding the children up to her. In other families, the father is the one who decides what the children ought to be permitted to do, what they ought not to be permitted to do, how they are going to be disciplined, and things like that. How does this work in your family? Would you give me an example?

62. And in other things in addition to those which affect the children: Who usually makes the decisions in your family?

    a. And in questions of money?

    b. Who manages the money, pays the bills, and things like that?

    c. Who has the larger part in deciding what you are going to do with your free time?

    d. If you were going to move—who would take the major part in deciding this?

63. In some families the work is divided more or less between what the wife does and what the husband does. For example, the work of the wife would be to take care of the house and work of the husband would be to plant, repair the house, and work outside. In other families everyone helps with everything. How is it in your family?

64. Do you think that X takes after you more or his father? In what ways?

    a. Does he imitate your manner of speaking or walking or your other mannerisms?

    b. Does he imitate these things in his father?

65. Do you think that X behaves better with you or with his father?

    a. Why do you think this occurs?

66. How much would you say that you and your husband resemble each other? That is, in terms of his temperament, and in those things which you feel are important in life, and things of that sort?

    a. In what ways are you different? And in what insignificant little things?

    b. (In regard to the ways in which they are different) Would you prefer that X would be like you or like your husband in this respect?

   c. (If there are no differences) In what ways would you like the child to resemble both of you and in what ways different?

We are nearly finished with our discussion. There is something more we would like to consider and that is how you felt about being a mother.

67. Think back to when you discovered you were pregnant with X. How did you feel about it?
   a. And your husband, how did he feel?

68. From the point of view of the economic situation, the ages of the other children, and the rest, do you think that it was an opportune time to have a child?

69. Considering it now, do you think that it would have been better if you had waited longer to have X? Tell me about this.

70. Did you have any kind of work before beginning to have a family?
   a. (If yes) How did you feel on having to leave your work?

71. Some mothers think that it is their principal duty to remain in their homes and take care of their children. At the same time, other mothers feel that they ought to do some outside work or at least maintain some interest in the outside world. What is your point of view about this?

   a. Up to what point do you think that you have been able to solve this problem in your own case?

   b. Have you thought at any time that you would prefer to be doing something other than what you are doing now?

72. Now, thinking of your own childhood: How would you compare the manner of your mother's raising you and the manner in which you are bringing up your own children?

   a. (If there are differences) What do you think of these changes?

APPENDIX C

Some Problems of Interviewing in Valle Caña

ADDITIONS TO THE STANDARDIZED INTERVIEW

One omission should be cited first. None of the panel families owned a radio or phonograph and television had not yet reached the island, so this question (time spent listening to radio or watching TV) was eliminated.

While still in the village, it was felt necessary to ask the mothers the following questions regarding their use of songs, stories, and poems with their children:

1. Were you told stories, sung songs, or were poems recited to you by your parents or others when you were a child? By whom?
2. Can you recall any of these stories, songs, or poems? I would appreciate your telling them to me as well as you can remember them, or at least an example of each.
3. Do you tell X stories now? sing songs? recite poems?
4. Could you give me some examples of these?
5. Are they the same as you experienced as a child?

We also felt during this time the need to raise the following questions ancillary to the standard interview:

1. Do you prefer boys or girls for your children? Why?
2. How many children do you feel a family ideally ought to have? Why?

After leaving the field, Señorita Diaz returned to ask the mothers in the sample these questions:

1. Has X asked you questions about making love, sexual relations between men and women, how babies are made, and things like that?

2. How much do you think he knows about these things?
3. How do you think he has learned about them (if she feels he knows)?
4. What have you done about such questions?
5. (If questions have not come up yet) This is not always an easy thing to discuss with children. Do you think you would have answered (or will be able to answer) his questions frankly, or would you have felt embarrassed (or think you would have felt embarrassed) and ill at ease?

PROBLEMS OF ADMINISTRATION

Most questions were asked fairly directly, but the mother was encouraged to elaborate freely, and there was a good deal of probing. We knew each mother over a period of several months prior to the first session, but nevertheless began it with a discussion of why we were in the village, what the interview would be about, what we hoped to do with the material, and how we hoped the results might ultimately benefit the Puerto Rican people. These materialistically oriented women were most· impressed, I believe, with this last statement, and this was, of course, a stated aim of the project.

The mothers would seldom take time off from their long round of daily tasks, so most interviewing was done while they worked in or around the house. If children were present they were not always asked to leave, but their presence sometimes made the mothers hesitant to speak frankly on sensitive points, and once in a while Señorita Diaz, at my prior suggestion, would indicate that perhaps the mother did not wish the child to be listening to this "grownup" subject and might be happier outdoors; since she knew the mothers very well and had a high level of rapport with them, this advice was usually followed.

Visitors came and went and listened, frequently adding their own opinions. Only occasionally, if a mother felt her visitor had a *lengua larga* (literally, long tongue; a gossip) would she restrain herself until the visitor finally grew impatient and left. This caused some delay, as did a mother's sometimes forgetting she had agreed to be interviewed at a certain hour and date, then going to a neighbor's house for a visit at that time. There were frequent misunderstandings on our part regarding time in this *mañana* culture, until we finally learned the hard way, to "make haste slowly."

It was felt best to interview the mothers when their husbands were not present, which was usually during the day, especially for those who worked. The same rule also applied to fathers, who were interviewed evenings at my house, or on a Sunday (they were loathe to give up their

Saturday jaunt to the store or to town, or casual loafing about) at their houses, usually outdoors in a shaded spot so as to obtain some privacy.

A sound recorder was not used, but the interviewer took notes on a mimeographed copy of the interview with large blank spaces between questions for note-taking. As remarked in Chapter 1, they were translated and transcribed the same evening the session occurred. In addition the interviewer would record incidental field observations made before, during, and after the interview, like other field notes. All notes were usually of a suggestive nature, with an occasional phrase or sentence quoted verbatim, and were elaborated in the transcribing.

PROBLEMS OF MEANING AND COMMUNICATION

In the question regarding the father's caretaking of the infant, "changing diapers" did not have much meaning for these parents. They knew what diapers were but could not afford them. Usually the baby's hammock is lined with old papers and rags which are rearranged after a soiling and exchanged for clean ones every several days. So the wording of the question was changed to "changing bedclothes."

Occasionally there was ambiguity in the responses concerning change-of-mode weaning and these had to be clarified at a later session. Also, and this was evident to some degree in most questions involving time, precise time of weaning, sphincter control, etc., was difficult to recall. Even the age of the child was frequently uncertain. All these points were repeated for clarification.

The concept of "table manners" was difficult to convey. We could not substitute etiquette, as this is only part of the connotation of the concept in English. A literal translation, *manera de comer*, proved ineffective during the pretests; it was taken to mean "way of eating." We finally settled on *comportamiento mientras comer*, literally, "behavior while eating," which seemed to communicate most closely what we were trying to say.

Regarding sphincter control, "toilet training" had little meaning, since either the ground or an outhouse is used by Vallecañeses, although infants were usually trained on a pot of some sort. The most acceptable phrase seemed to be "how did you teach X to do his necessities?" Thus, also, when we were talking about mutual sex play, the question was changed from "going to the toilet together" to "doing their necessities together."

Surprisingly to us, the term "playing with himself" seemed as suitable in Valle Caña as in the United States as a euphemism for masturbation.

The term "jumping up and down on the furniture" held little meaning since furniture was scant and crude. But we substituted "abusing the furniture" and this seemed to get the idea across.

To communicate the idea of "acting like a real boy" we used the term *machito de verdad* instead of literally saying *niño de verdad*, since the meaning of masculinity seemed best expressed in the local term for "little he-man." Likewise, "acting like a real girl" was best expressed as *mujercita de verdad*, "true little woman." And in other contexts similar terms like *varoncito* (little male) and *hembracita* (little female) seemed preferable to little boy and little girl.

In the same way, the collective term for children in Spanish is *niños*, the same as the plural for boy, which was sometimes confused and had to be clarified in context. And the term for siblings is *hermanos*, which is also plural for brothers. Such linguistic differences will frequently lead to unintended stresses and are difficult to translate into the highly sex-oriented idiom of Spanish.

The area of identification was particularly troublesome to communicate in a way to elicit the kinds of information desired. The question, "Does X take after you or after his father more?" was almost invariably interpreted as referring to phenotypical resemblances and had to be qualified with examples of what was intended. Furnishing such examples, while indispensable, may have had an undeterminable effect on responses.

These should suggest some of the problems centering on the translation and communication of the interview in order to achieve cross-cultural comparability of data. Since problems of this order occurred in translating an interview from English to a kindred language, the order of complexity confronting the ethnologist who would attempt to translate a standard interview into a non-Indo-European tongue must be regarded with a good deal of awe and humility. Just leaving it in the hands of a bilingual native, even one with ethnological training, will not prove a safe procedure.

APPENDIX D

Materials and Administration of Doll Play

EQUIPMENT AND PROCEDURE

Four sessions of free doll play, using materials and procedures similar to those used by the Laboratory of Human Development at Harvard and the Iowa Child Welfare Research Station, were administered to one child from each of the eighteen sample families, each child being between four and seven years of age. The group comprised ten boys and eight girls.

The materials were constructed by the ethnologist and his wife and the research assistant after we felt sufficiently familiar with the conditions of life in Valle Caña. The set consisted of a "house" formed of several movable partitions about three inches high to represent the floor plan of a "typical" Vallecañese lower-class dwelling. The rooms were the *sala* (living room), *cocina* (kitchen), and *dormitorio* (bedroom). All rooms opened into each other. A wooden *letrina* (outhouse) with a hinged door and open top was placed a few inches beyond the rear of the house. A large *hamaca* was swung across the living room and there was a small *hamaca* or *coy* (baby's hammock) in the bedroom. The living room also contained a crude table, two benches, and a trunk with a hinged top. The bedroom also contained a double bed. The kitchen contained the *fogón* (peasant stove consisting of a slab on wooden legs with an open hole and a pot over it).

The doll family consisted of a father (scoring symbol F), mother (M), boy (B), girl (G), and baby (bb), designed proportionately to the size of the set and "typically" dressed. The dolls' skin, hair, and features were medium light to dark, and their bodies were so constructed of pipecleaners, cotton, and cloth that they could easily be manipulated into almost any position by the child.

Children were brought into the doll play situation only singly. Present were the experimenter (Señorita Diaz), who "played" along with the child, mostly in the role of initiating play when the child was reticent, or during a lull, and the scorer (myself), who was sitting in a corner presumably "working" with a pad and pencil and apparently paying no attention to the proceedings. (In the laboratory situation in the United States only the experimenter is present and the scorer operates from behind a one-way mirror. However, Pintler [1945] has tried the dual role of experimenter and scorer with apparent success in attempting to assess the influence of experimenter-child interaction and the organization or lack of organization of the materials.)

Since it was discovered in pretests and first sessions that these children were often negativistic and reluctant to play in our presence, we let it be known that a reward, usually candy or a small toy, would be presented at the end of each session. This had to be changed soon to presenting at least a partial reward at the beginning of the session. There seemed to be no way out of making such an inducement.

The sessions for the mountain children took place in a rented cabin about half-way between the families involved. The others for the road children were held at the ethnologist's house. It was found necessary sometimes to bring the children in groups of two or three, though others would gather outside the experimental room unsolicited. It was also found helpful to play games and sing with them to set them at ease before entering the doll play room. There was no strict time limit to the first session, but a twenty-minute maximum was set for the second through fourth sessions.

SCORING

The "act" was the unit of measurement. An act was any completed action, whether verbal or physical. Each of the dolls, as well as the child and any imaginary beings he might mention, were considered both as agents and objects, depending upon whether they were the actor or receiver of the act. Categories of acts were: aggression, dependence, identification, nurturance, neutral-positive (all positive interactive acts not covered by the other categories), and noninteractive (where an agent acted completely alone).

Content was analyzed into five principal categories: toileting, cleanliness, sleeping, sex, and eating-feeding. Acts which took place in the midst of a theme, or a scheme of acts, but bore no relation to the main theme were called tangential acts and were divided into three types: those related to equipment, to dolls, and to the self.

Percentages and mean percentages of acts are used in a variety of ratios to get at some of the variables of interest to the study. Other variables conceivably could be studied by further use of combinations or ratios, or by varying the procedure and/or equipment. This has actually been done in the so-called problem situations of the Laboratory of Human Development, but not in the present study.

Further discussion of methodological problems of using doll play in Valle Caña as an ethnographic field technique will be found in Landy 1959a.

Reference Bibiliography

Alegría, R., H. Nicholson, and G. R. Willey
  1955 "The Archaic Tradition in Puerto Rico." *American Antiquity*
        21:113-121.
Analysis Schedule for Mother Interviews
  n.d. Laboratory of Human Development, Harvard University (Un-
        published memo).
Annals, American Academy of Political and Social Science
  1953 Constitution of the Commonwealth of Puerto Rico. In *Puerto
        Rico, a Study in Democratic Development* 285:153-166.
Annual Report of the Commissioner of Education
  1950-51 Department of Education, San Juan, Puerto Rico.
Annuario Estadistico
  1951-52 Administración de Fomento Económico. Oficina de Investi-
           gaciones Económicas, San Juan.
Baldwin, A. L.
  1948 "Socialization and the parent-child relationship." *Child Develop-
        ment* 20:127-136.
  1949 "The effect of home environment on nursery school behavior."
        Child Development 20:49-61.
Benedek, T.
  1949 "The psychosomatic implications of the primary unit: mother-
        child." *American Journal of Orthopsychiatry* 19:642-654.
Benedict, R.
  1934 *Patterns of Culture*. Boston (Houghton, Mifflin).
  1949 "Continuities and discontinuities in cultural conditionings." In
        Personality in Nature, Society, and Culture, ed. C. Kluckhohn
        and H. A. Murray. New York (A. A. Knopf), pp. 414-423.
Bertalanffy, L.
  1950 "The theory of open systems in physics and biology." *Science*
        111:23-29.
Blum, S.
  1953 *Psychoanalytic Theories of Personality*. New York (McGraw-
        Hill).

Bossard, J. H. S.

1945 "The law of family interaction." *American Journal of Sociology* 50:292-294.

Bureau of the Census

1950 1950 Census of population, preliminary reports. U. S. Department of Commerce, Bureau of Census, Washington.

Cantril, H., A. Ames, Jr., A. Hastorf, and W. H. Ittelson

1949 "Psychology and scientific research. I, II, III." *Science* 110:461-464, 491-497, 517-522.

Cofresi, E.

1951 *Realidad Poblacionál de Puerto Rico.* San Juan (Imprenta Venezuela).

Cohen, Y. A.

1956 "Structure and function: family organization and socialization in a Jamaican community." *American Anthropologist* 58:664-686.

Collins, J.

1952 "An interpretation of Skagit intragroup conflict during acculturation." *American Anthropologist* 54:347-355.

Cottrell, L. C.

1948 "The present status and future orientation of research in the family." *American Sociological Review* 13:123-136.

Davis, A.

1947 "Socialization and adolescent personality." In *Readings in Social Psychology*, ed. E. Hartley and T. Newcomb. New York (Henry Holt), pp. 520-531. (Rev. ed. 1952.)

Dewey, J., and A. F. Bentley

1949 *Knowing and the Known.* Boston (Beacon Press).

Dollard, J., and others

1939 *Frustration and Aggression.* New Haven (Yale University Press).

Dollard, J., and N. E. Miller

1950 *Personality and Psychotherapy.* New York (McGraw-Hill).

Dubois, C.

1955 "The dominant value profile of American culture." *American Anthropologist* 57:1232-1239.

Eggan, D.

1949 "The general problem of Hopi adjustment." In *Personality in Nature, Society, and Culture*, ed. C. Kluckhohn and H. A. Murray. New York (A. A. Knopf), pp. 220-235.

Federal Reserve Bulletin

1951 Bureau of Labor Statistics. Washington. August.

Frank, L. K.
  1951 "Genetic psychology and its prospects." *American Journal of Orthopsychiatry* 21:506-522.

Frazier, E. F.
  1934 "Traditions and patterns of Negro life in the United States." In *Race and Culture Contacts*, ed. E. B. Reuter. New York (McGraw-Hill).
  1942 "The Negro family in Brazil." *American Sociological Review* 7:465-478.

Fromm, E.
  1944 "Individual and social origins of neurosis." *American Sociological Review* 9:380-384.

Gillin, J.
  1947 "Modern Latin American culture." *Social Forces* 25:243-248.
  1948a *The Ways of Men*. New York (Appleton-Century-Crofts).
  1948b "Magical fright." *Psychiatry* 11:387-400.
  1949 "Meztizo America." In *Most of the World*, ed. Ralph Linton. New York (Columbia University Press), pp. 156-211.

Gordon, M. W.
  1950 "Cultural aspects of Puerto Rico's race problem." *American Sociological Review* 15:382-392.

Grinker, R. R.
  1953 *Psychosomatic Research*. New York (W. W. Norton).

Guilford, J. P.
  1942 *Fundamental Statistics in Psychology and Education*. New York (McGraw-Hill).

Hallowell, A. I.
  1954 "The self and its behavioural environment." *Explorations II*: 106-165.

Hansen, E.
  1955 *Transformation: The Story of Puerto Rico*. New York (Harper).

Hansen, M.
  1952 "The family in Puerto Rico research project." In *Approaches to Problems of High Fertility in Agrarian Societies*. New York (Milbank Memorial Fund), pp. 50-61.

Hatt, P. K.
  1952 *Backgrounds of Human Fertility in Puerto Rico*. Princeton (Princeton University Press).

Healy, W., A. F. Bronner, and A. M. Bowers
  1930 *The Structure and Meaning of Psychoanalysis*. New York (A. A. Knopf).

Henriques, F.

1949 "West Indian family organization." *American Journal of Sociology* 55:30-37.

Herbst, P. G.

1952 "The measurement of family relationships." *Human Relations* 5:3-35.

Hill, R., J. M. Stycos, and K. W. Back

1959 *The Family and Population Control: A Puerto Rican Experiment in Social Change.* Chapel Hill (University of North Carolina Press).

Hollenberg, E., and M. Sperry

1951 "Some antecedents of aggression and effects of frustration in doll play." *Journal of Personality* 1:32-43.

Holmberg, A. R.

1950 "Nomads of the long bow." *Social Anthropology Series No. 10.* Washington (Smithsonian Institution).

Hsu, F. L. K.

1952 "Anthropology or psychiatry: a definition of objectives and their implications." *Southwestern Journal of Anthropology* 3:227-250.

Inkeles, A.

1953 "Some sociological observations on culture and personality studies." In *Personality in Nature, Society, and Culture,* ed. C. Kluckhohn, H. A. Murray, and D. M. Schneider, New York (A. A. Knopf).

Johansson, B. B.

1956 "Puerto Rico: An agrarian society industrializes." *Christian Science Monitor,* Boston, May 19, 1956.

King, C. E.

1945 "The Negro maternal family: a product of an economic and a cultural system." *Social Forces* 24:100-104.

King, M.

1948 "Cultural aspects of birth control in Puerto Rico." *Human Biology* 20:21-35.

Kluckhohn, C.

1944a "The influence of psychiatry on anthropology in America during the past one hundred years." In *One Hundred Years of American Psychiatry,* ed. J. K. Hall and others. New York (Columbia University Press), pp. 589-617.

1944b "Navaho witchcraft." *Papers of the Peabody Museum of Archaeology and Ethnology,* Harvard University 22.

1951 "Values and value-orientations in the theory of action." In

Toward a General Theory of Action, ed. T. Parsons and E. A. Shils. Cambridge (Harvard University Press), pp. 388-433.

Komarovsky, M., and W. Waller

1945 "Studies of the family." *American Journal of Sociology* 50:443-451.

Landy, D.

1959a "Some methodological problems of free doll play as an ethnographic field technique." In *Selected Papers of the Fifth International Congress of Anthropological and Ethnological Sciences,* ed. A. F. C. Wallace. Philadelphia (University of Pennsylvania Press).

1959b Puerto Rico: an ethnohistorical review. *Revista de Historia de America* (in press).

1959c Culture and class in child training: Puerto Rico and New England (ms.).

1957 The primary cultural process: a transactional approach to the study of human socialization. (ms.).

Levy, D.

1943 *Maternal Overprotection.* New York (Columbia University Press).

Lewis, O.

1950 "An anthropological approach to family studies." *American Journal of Sociology* 55:468-475.

1951 *Life in a Mexican Village: Tepotzlán Revisited.* Urbana (University of Illinois Press).

Lindesmith, A. R., and A. L. Strauss

1950 "A critique of culture-personality writings." *American Sociological Review* 15:587-600.

Linton, R.

1936 *The Study of Man.* New York (Appleton-Century-Crofts).

Maccoby, E., and F. Fielder

1953 *Saving among Upper-Income Families in Puerto Rico.* University of Puerto Rico Press (San Juan).

Maccoby, E., P. K. Gibbs, and others

1954 "Methods of child rearing in two social classes." In *Readings in Child Development,* ed. W. E. Martin and C. B. Stendler. New York (Harcourt, Brace), pp. 380-396.

Manners, R. A.

1950 Culture and Agriculture in an Eastern Highland Community of Puerto Rico. Ph. D. thesis, Columbia University.

Manners, R. A., and J. H. Steward
  1953 "The cultural study of contemporary societies: Puerto Rico." *American Journal of Sociology* 59:123-130.

Mead, M.
  1946 "Research on primitive children." In *Manual of Child Psychology*, ed. L. Carmichael. New York (John Wiley), pp. 735-780.
  1949 "Social change and cultural surrogates." In *Personality in Nature, Society, and Culture*, ed. C. Kluckhohn and H. A. Murray. New York (A. A. Knopf), pp. 511-522.

Mellado, R. A.
  1948 Culture and Education in Puerto Rico. Educational Monograph 1, Bureau of Publications, Puerto Rico Teachers Association.

Mensh, I. N., and J. Henry
  1953 "Direct observation and psychological tests in anthropological field work." *American Anthropologist* 55:461-480.

Merton, R. K.
  1957 *Social Theory and Social Structure* (Rev. ed.). Glencoe, Ill. (Free Press).

Miller, N. E., and J. Dollard
  1941 *Social Learning and Imitation*. New Haven (Yale University Press).

Mills, C. W., C. Senior, and R. Goldsen
  1950 *The Puerto Rican Journey*. New York (Harper).

Mintz, S. W.
  1951 The Contemporary Culture of a Rural Puerto Rican Proletariat. Ph. D. thesis, Columbia University.

Mintz, S. W., and E. R. Wolf
  1950 "An analysis of ritual coparenthood: compadrazgo." *Southwestern Journal of Anthropology* 6:341-368.

Moore, W. C., and M. Tumin
  1949 "Some functions of ignorance." *American Sociological Review* 14:787-795.

Moses, L.
  1952 "Nonparametric statistics for psychological research." *Psychological Bulletin* 49:122-143.

Mosteller, F., and R. Bush
  1954 "Selected quantitative techniques." In *Handbook of Social Psychology*, ed. G. Lindzey. Cambridge (Addison-Wesley), pp. 284-334.

Mowrer, O. H., and C. Kluckhohn
  1944 "Dynamic theory of personality." In *Personality and the Behavior*

Disorders, ed. J. McV. Hunt. New York (Ronald Press), pp. 69-135.

Mullahy, P.
1955 *Oedipus, Myth and Complex* (orig. edit. 1948). New York (Grove Press).

Murphy, G.
1947 *Personality: A Biosocial Approach to Origins and Structure.* New York (Harper).

Newcomb, T. M., and E. L. Hartley (eds.)
1947 *Readings in Social Psychology.* New York (Henry Holt).

Nowlis, V.
1952 "The search for significant concepts in a study of parent-child relationships." *American Journal of Orthopsychiatry* 22:286-299.

Opler, M. K.
1956 *Culture, Psychiatry, and Human Values.* Springfield, Ill. (Charles C Thomas).

Orlansky, H.
1949 "Infant care and personality." *Psychological Bulletin* 46:1-48.

Padilla, E.
1951 Nocora: An Agrarian Reform Sugar Community in Puerto Rico. Ph. D. thesis, Columbia University.

Parsons, T.
1942 "Age and sex in the social structure of the United States." *American Sociological Review* 7:604-616.
1951 *The Social System.* Glencoe, Ill. (Free Press).
1952 "The superego and the theory of social systems." *Psychiatry* 15:15-25.

Perloff, H.
1950 *Puerto Rico's Economic Future.* Chicago (University of Chicago Press).

Pintler, M. H.
1945 "Doll play as a function of experimenter-child interaction and initial organization of materials." *Child Development* 16:145-166.

Reuter, E. B.
1946 "Culture contacts in Puerto Rico." *American Journal of Sociology* 52:91-101.

Ribeiro, R.
1945 "On the amaziado relationship and other aspects of family life in Recife" (Brazil). *American Sociological Review* 10:44-51.

Riesman, D.
1950 *The Lonely Crowd.* New Haven (Yale University Press).

Roberts, L. J., and R. L. Stefani

1949 *Patterns of Living in Puerto Rican Families.* Río Piedras (University of Puerto Rico Press).

Rogler, C. G.

1944 "The role of semantics in the study of race distance in Puerto Rico." *Social Forces* 22:448-453.

1946 "The morality of race mixing in Puerto Rico." *Social Forces* 25:77-81.

Rouse, I.

1948a "The Arawak." In *Handbook of South American Indians,* ed. J. H. Steward. Bureau of American Ethnology, Bulletin 143, Vol. 4:507-539. Washington (Smithsonian Institution).

1949b "The Carib." In *Handbook of South American Indians,* ed. J. H. Steward. Bureau of American Ethnology, Bulletin 143, Vol. 4:547-566.

1952a "Porto Rican prehistory: introduction, excavations in the west and north." *Scientific Survey of Puerto Rico and the Virgin Islands,* XVIII, Pt. 3:305-460. New York Academy of Sciences.

1952b "Porto Rican prehistory: excavations in the interior, south and east, chronological implications." *Ibid.:* Pt. 4:461-578.

1953 "The Circum-Caribbean theory, an archeological test." *American Anthropologist* 55:188-200.

Sapir, E.

1934 "The emergence of the concept of personality in a study of cultures." In *Selected Writings of Edward Sapir,* ed. D. G. Mandlebaum (1949). Berkeley (University of California Press), pp. 590-597.

Sears, R. R.

1943 "Survey of objective studies of psychoanalytic concepts." *Social Science Research Bulletin 51,* New York.

1950a Antecedents of aggression and dependency in young children. Laboratory of Human Development, Harvard University (Unpublished memo).

1950b Effects of frustration and anxiety on fantasy aggression. Speech delivered at Clark University's Sixtieth Anniversary Celebration (Unpublished mimeo.).

1951a "Social behavior and personality." In *Toward a General Theory of Action,* ed. T. Parsons and E. A. Shils. Cambridge (Harvard University Press), pp. 465-478.

1951b Memorandum on identification. Laboratory of Human Development, Harvard University (Unpublished memo).

Sears, R. R., J. W. M. Whiting, V. Nowlis, and P. S. Sears
  1953 "Some child-rearing antecedents of aggression and dependency in young children." *Genetic Psychology Monographs* 47:135-234.

Seijo de Zayas, E.
  1955 "Better nutrition for Puerto Ricans." *Children* 2:63-68.

Sereno, R.
  1948 "Cryptomelanism: a study of color relations and personal insecurity in Puerto Rico." *Psychiatry* 10:261-269.

Siegel, M.
  1948 A Puerto Rican Town. Social Science Research Center, University of Puerto Rico. (ms.).

Siegel, S.
  1956 *Nonparametric Methods in the Behavioral Sciences.* New York (Macmillan).

Spiro, M. E.
  1951 "Culture and personality: the natural history of a false dichotomy." *Psychiatry* 14:19-46.

Steward, J. H.
  1948 "The Circum-Caribbean tribes: an introduction." In *Handbook of South American Indians,* ed. J. H. Steward. Bureau of American Ethnology, Bulletin 143, Vol. 4:1-42. Washington (Smithsonian Institution).

Steward, J. H., *et al.*
  1956 *The People of Puerto Rico.* Urbana (University of Illinois Press).

Stoke, S. M.
  1950 "An inquiry into the concept of identification." *Journal of Genetic Psychology* 76:163-189.

Stycos, J. M.
  1952a Family and Fertility in Puerto Rico. Social Science Research Center, University of Puerto Rico. (ms.).
  1952b The Dynamics of Birth Control in Lower Class Puerto Rico. Social Science Research Center, University of Puerto Rico. (ms.).
  1955 *Family and Fertility in Puerto Rico.* New York (Columbia University Press).

Stycos, J. M., and R. Hill
  1953 "The prospects of birth control in Puerto Rico." *Annals of the American Academy of Political and Social Science* 285:137-144.

Thieme, F. P.
  1952 "The geographic and racial distribution of ABO and Rh blood types and tasters of PTC in Puerto Rico." *American Journal of Human Genetics* 4:94-112.

Walker, H. M., and J. Lev

1953 *Statistical Inference*. New York (Henry Holt).

Wallace, A. F. C.

1952 "The modal personality of the Tuscarora Indians." Bureau of American Ethnology, Bulletin 150. Washington (Smithsonian Institution).

Waller, W., and R. Hill

1951 *The Family*. New York (Dryden Press).

Warner, W. L., M. Meeker, and K. Eells

1949 *Social Class in America*. Chicago (Science Research Associates).

Wegrocki, H. J.

1949 "A critique of cultural and statistical concepts of abnormality." In *Personality in Nature, Society, and Culture*, ed. C. Kluckhohn and H. A. Murray. New York (A. A. Knopf), pp. 551-561.

White, L.

1948 *The Science of Culture*. New York (Farrar, Straus).

Whiting, J. W. M.

1941 *Becoming a Kwoma*. New Haven (Yale University Press).

1954 "The cross-cultural method." In *Handbook of Social Psychology*, I:523-531. Ed. Gardner Lindzey. Cambridge (Addison-Wesley).

Whiting, J. W. M., and I. S. Child

1953 *Child Training and Personality*. New Haven (Yale University Press).

Whiting, J. W. M., and O. H. Mowrer

1949 "Habit progression and retrogression." In *Personality in Nature, Society, and Culture*, ed. C. Kluckhohn and H. A. Murray. New York (A. A. Knopf), pp. 315-324.

Whiting, J. W. M., and others

1953 *Field Manual for the Cross Cultural Study of Child Rearing*. New York (Social Science Research Council).

Williams, E.

1945 "Race relations in Puerto Rico and the Virgin Islands." *Foreign Affairs* 23:308-319.

Wolf, E. R.

1951 Culture change and culture stability in a Puerto Rico coffee growing community. Ph.D. thesis, Columbia University.

Wolf, K. L.

1952 "Growing up and its price in three Puerto Rican subcultures." *Psychiatry* 15:401-433.

Index

Abbad y Lasierra, I., 32
Acculturation, summarized, 243-54; mentioned, 4, 5, 57n, 153, 195
Achievement standards, in child rearing, 149-51; cross-cultural comparison of, 205-7, 240; mentioned, 128, 251
Action, 168-69, 177, 188n. *See also* Interaction
Affect hunger, 181, 184, 192
Affection, in child rearing, 83, 101-2, 128, 133, 137-40, 147, 151, 181, 187, 191-92, 245, 254; and sex preferences, 94; marital, 94; of child, 165-66; cross-cultural comparison of, 212-15; summarized, 235, 237, 238, 249-50. *See also* Love, Nurturance
Age-grade, 49, 53, 180, 226
Aggression, causes of, 11; as behavior pattern, 12-13, 148n, 160, 248, 250; adult, 57, 67, 78n, 93, 149, 168, 176, 228-29, 246; control of, 114-17, 128; child, 121-22, 139, 159, 161-65, 171, 172, 173, 174, 175, 177, 181, 183, 184-87, 190, 191, 251; cross-cultural comparison of, 202-3, 212, 219, 221-22, 239, 241-42; summarized, 234, 236-37, 238n
Andean cultures, 5
Anthropology, 3, 4, 5, 6-7, 9, 10-13, 16, 17, 18, 29n, 33, 132, 176n, 185, 195, 196n
Arawak Indians, 5, 33, 53, 230

Back, K., 90n
Baldwin, A. L. 249
Baptism, 52-53, 180
Bateson, G., 7, 13
Bedtime restrictions, 120, 128, 190, 205, 234, 239
Behavior, child. *See* Child behavior
Behavior traits, desirable, 144-47
Benedict, R., 176n, 180, 247
Birth control, 90-92, 232-33
Birth rate, 3-4, 59n

Blum, S., 13
Bossard J. H. S., 86
Bowers, A. M., 13
Brau, S., 32
Bronner, A. F., 13

Caguas, 22
Cañaveral, 25, 34, 36, 67, 78, 95
Candelaria, La, 64-65
Caretaking agents, 100-1, 128, 163, 164, 210-11, 240
Caribbean society, 27, 71n, 195
Carib Indians, 5, 53
Carroll, U.S. Commissioner to Puerto Rico, 32
Catholicism, 15, 41-44, 47, 52, 71-72, 91, 119, 231
Child, I. C., 11, 13
Child bearing, 27, 82-84, 88
Child behavior, cross-cultural comparison of, 4, 17, 218-19, 230; measures of, 12, 20, 252; in village, 120, 136, 175, 183, 191; summarized, 233-38
Child development, 4, 7, 15, 133, 155-94, 207
Civil marriage, 15, 71-72, 253
Class. *See* Social class
Cleanliness, 117-18, 125, 170, 205, 234, 239, 247, 254
Climate, Puerto Rican, 24, 29, 127, 170
Cofresi, E., 90n
Coll y Toste, C., 32
Color consciousness. *See* Racial consciousness
Communciation between marriage partners, 84-86, 89, 214, 232
Consensual marriage, 15, 26, 57, 64, 65, 71-73, 81, 231-32, 253
Coroso Indians, 5
Cottrell, L. C., 5
Courtship, 45, 62-69
Cruz Monclova, L., 32

287